THE
TIME
OF MY
LIFE

AN AMERICAN'S JOURNEY

by

JOHN PAUL LEWIS

Cover Photo: John Paul Lewis in 1944 in a US Army colonel's
uniform. The uniform was a gift from Tex, a copy of his own
uniform.

ISBN: 149102786X
ISBN 13: 9781491027868
Library of Congress Control Number: 2013915365
CreateSpace Independent Publishing Platform
North Charleston, South California

ENDORSEMENTS

John, besides being a really good guy, has always been innovative and hard-working and his wide variety of experiences over the years has given him a great prospective on life.

—Jim Erwin, Managing Partner, Erwin, Graves & Associates, LP

John is a great friend who has leveraged his intellectual capacity, integrity, and experience, into a fascinating career in global business and finance. He's had many business and personal successes and continues to have close business and personal acquaintances that span the globe. A very keen and insightful businessman.

—Jerry McElhatton, investor and director of several companies and former President of Global Technology and Operations, MasterCard

INTRODUCTION

One piece of advice I can give you is to never offer to pay for drinks when you are with a billionaire before you have seen the bill. That is a lesson I learned in Rio de Janeiro in the Spring of 1968.

It was summer in South America and I was in Brazil on business. I was in the international banking business and was working for a bank headquartered in Los Angeles.

During a meeting with the President of the Banco do Estado di Guanabara (this is the state bank of the state of Guanabara, where Rio is located; it's a substantial financial institution, which was good customer of mine), he asked what my schedule was for the coming week. I told him I would be busy in Rio for several more days and then I had meetings scheduled in Sao Paulo. He told me that would be a waste of time, as the Carnival celebration started in the next few days and all businesses would be closed. He invited me to remain in Rio, and offered to get me into some of the most interesting Carnival balls. All of Rio's hotels were completely booked, but he happened to own the Lama Palace Hotel, so he picked up the phone and reserved the penthouse suite for me.

The Lama Palace Hotel was located on Copacabana Beach, very central to the balls and parties that took place during Carnival. The biggest and most prestigious event was held at the Copacabana Palace Hotel ballroom, which was only a block away. Suddenly I found myself with a terrific opportunity to remain in Rio for the upcoming festivities and I couldn't resist the temptation to see one of the best parties in the world. The Carnival Festival is the start of celebration and revelry which leads to Lent in the Catholic world.

What a treat! Carnival time in Rio is madness – everyone takes off from work to drink and play. After settling into the hotel I needed to call and reschedule my appointments in Sao Paulo, which is the largest city in Brazil and is several hundred miles west of Rio. The gentlemen I had scheduled to meet were more than willing to postpone the meetings one week, as neither of us had realized the meetings would fall during the Carnival parties when we originally set them several months before. Brazil is a very religious country and most everyone takes Lent and Easter very serious.

That night, I dined at Antonino's, an excellent restaurant in Rio. After my meal, I was enjoying an aperitif when a man came over and asked me if I was an American. I told him I was and he asked if I was eating alone. When I said I was, he asked if I would care to join his table. I thanked him and did so. He handled the situation very cordially and when we arrived at his table he introduced me to Walter and Elizinha Morera Salles, whose names I recognized, as they were known as one of the wealthiest family in Brazil. He next introduced me to a couple from the Bahamas, who were sitting with them, and then to his own wife, Cristina, and finally introduced himself; he said he was Henry Ford. I was completely surprised. I did not recognize the man until he told me who he was. He was so personable and easygoing; it was easy to forget about his wealth and business position.

I joined his table for a drink; everyone was extremely friendly. They were all incredibly beautiful people. The Morera Salleses were in their fifties but Elizinha looked much younger. She was a slim, shapely blonde woman who always dressed immaculately. The couple from the Bahamas looked to be in their forties and were equally attractive. Cristina looked like a model. She was blonde, blue eyed, Italian, sexy and elegant in her dress and mannerisms. She was born into a wealthy family and had been married to a very rich Italian husband before she met Henry Ford. She loved parties and traveled around the world attending the most coveted events. Before long, Ford suggested that we move the party to a nearby nightclub. The Morera Salleses decided to forgo the trip to the nightclub. Arrangements were made to meet them at their home later in the evening.

The remaining five of us then proceeded to our next destination, where we all enjoyed drinks. Flush with fondness for my new friends, I asked the waiter to bring me the bill. What I hadn't realized is that the restaurant had taken one look at Ford and added a hefty pad to the bill... The waiter slipped me the bill. What an unpleasant surprise I got when I turned it over. I unobtrusively counted my money under the table and realized to my horror that I was short! How would I finesse this? But before I could panic, I felt a light tap on my knee. Ford, sitting across from me, was quietly handing me a fat wad of money under the table. (And when I say a wad of money, I mean it! The exchange rate was 8000 Cruzeiros to $1, so a drink could cost 100,000 Cruzeiros!) He never even looked at me. Relieved, I covertly peeled several bills off the roll and handed the rest back under the table. Ford winked at me. I placed the money on the table and a waiter whisked it away with our check. Ford was sensitive – and discreet – enough that when he sensed that I did not have enough cash to cover the bill, he quietly helped me out without anyone being the wiser. My pride remained intact, and my appreciation and esteem for Ford went up another notch. He was a true gentleman, and it was the beginning of a delightful friendship.

The rest of the week was a whirlwind, and included a tour of a most impressive mansion, a tackle and takedown of an attempted robber during the riotous Carnival parade, being insulted by a Baron, and wound up with my picture in Time magazine – all of which I will recount in greater detail – but the week served as a wonderful reminder of something I had found in the past, and would experience repeatedly in the future: some of life's most interesting surprises occur when plans change or opportunity arises and you are open to the new possibilities that surface.

I have worked hard my entire life, and traveled over five million miles. But somehow, along the way, in the course of work, life happened. My work has allowed me to see so many interesting places, and meet so many remarkable people, each of whom has had an impact on me. At some points, the details of the journey may have grown hazy, but the substance of the encounters remains. I hope you will enjoy reading about my experiences as much as I have in re-living them.

It's a long way from dinner with Henry Ford in Rio to the flat, wide open plains of west Texas, where my life began. While this is not a story about Texas, there's no escaping the fact that the state has played a central part in my life; it is a unique way of life and in many ways a state of mind. I have lived in Texas a total of fifty out of my seventy-six years, and even when I lived in other parts of the country, I was always proud of my Texas heritage. Some people in the rest of the United States stereotype Texas as a land of unsophisticated, uneducated natives. They don't realize that Texas is a land of big-hearted, hard-working people. Sometimes the slow-talking Texan may be good bit smarter than others realize, and it is never safe to underestimate him!

The expansive spaces of this great state seem to encourage its natives to dream big, and to dare to pursue those dreams. There are many opportunities in the state to build a life and a career. There were times in my youth when I looked forward to leaving home and venturing out into the world, but it was always wonderful to return to my home state.

About a quarter of Texas is forestland from the eastern border to the beginning of the rolling hill country of central Texas. The hill country is beautiful and it continues to the plains of west Texas. Each region has a distinctive beauty of its own.

I grew up in west Texas, where the plains are so flat that a drive down the long, straight highways gives you a panoramic view for miles around. It is too hot in the summer and too cold in the winter. It has sand storms and hail storms. Travelers who pass through the state find it a long monotonous drive.

To most of the people who live on the plains, however, it is a fine place to reside. With bluebonnets and wildflowers in the spring and flourishing farms in the fall, west Texas has a majestic splendor. It has also been known as the buckle of the Bible Belt. When I grew up, there was a saying that 'there were churches on almost every street corner'. Our family was conservative and God fearing. We were deeply religious and believed in hard work and charity toward others. Those beliefs formed the basis for my upbringing and my life.

In fact the story of my life and history began in Texas, well before my birth in 1936...

PART ONE

ORIGINS

CHAPTER 1

My father's parents, Allen Crocket Lewis and May Irene Lewis traveled from Tennessee to Texas in a covered wagon in the 1800's. The trek west started about Christmas time in 1867 when they crafted a boat, hauled it by oxen to the Little Pigeon River and floated down to the French Broad River. They followed that river until they arrived at the Tennessee River then to the Ohio and on to the Mississippi. They then barged up the Red River to Jefferson, Texas. They then came overland to Collins County. They acquired a farm near McKinney, in the north central part of the state, and started raising a family.

Allen Crocket Lewis and May Irene Lewis (my grandparents)

My father, Allen Jefferson Lewis, was born on the farm on August 25, 1884. He was the fourth of seven children – five sons and two daughters. Large families were not unusual at the time; the need for help on the farm almost demanded it. Every child was put to work on the farm as soon as they were able; there was never a shortage of things to be done. Collin County, where McKinney is located, has black clay soil that made for hard work; it was difficult to plow but rich for growing things.

Lewis boys, circa 1910

The family worked in the fields from early in the morning until dusk. In the spring, they planted the seeds for the cotton, alfalfa and corn crops that would appear in the summer, when the plants began to grow they would continually hoe the weeds that would grow up between the furrows. It was hard work but not nearly as hard as harvesting the cotton crop in the fall. Without refrigeration, there was work to do to preserve food for the winter. Fruit, such as peaches and apricots, would be pitted and dried on top of a smokehouse. All kinds of hams, beef and pork were cured in the smokehouse, saved for winter or made into jerky that could be taken on the trail without spoiling.

Somehow, between schoolwork and farm work, my father and his brothers found time to stir up all kinds of mischief. Dad loved to tell a story about the trouble they once got into in a cornfield shortly after harvest. They started to smoke corn silk wrapped inside dried corn husks. The dry field caught fire almost immediately and they ran – but not before the fire singed off all of their eyebrows and part of their hair. None were injured, but it was a rag-tag group of boys that straggled home, reeking of smoke. Pat, Dad's youngest brother, lost his pocket knife as they ran from the spreading fire.

At home, their father lined them up and asked if they knew who set the fire that was now raging across several farms. Scared to death, they swore they didn't know a thing about it. Dad would just laugh and laugh when he described the scene – six sooty, eyebrow-less boys denying any involvement in the fire. Their denials were completely unbelievable, but for some reason, my grandfather didn't punish them and never brought up the subject again. I suppose he thought they had already been punished enough.

The next day, the boys found Pat's knife. Unfortunately, someone else had found it first – it was sitting in the window display case at the general store with a note asking if anyone could identify it. The boys stood around looking at the knife, but were too afraid to claim it. Everyone in town must have known they were guilty.

With four older brothers, my Uncle Pat was bound to be the target of some fun. One time, the boys all talked Pat into putting his tongue on a metal wagon wheel when the weather was freezing cold. Of course, Pat's tongue stuck to the wheel, and they left him there, stuck out in the cold. After fruitlessly yelling for help for some time, Pat finally jerked his head back and left a portion of his tongue on the wheel. He never forgave his brothers, and probably learned a lesson about blindly following their orders!

In Dad's youth, nothing was easy. They didn't have toothbrushes and so would clean their teeth by chewing on cut-off tree branches. There were no cars, no TVs, no radios, no airplanes, no refrigerators and no indoor plumbing. They lost their teeth early and if they got sick, even from the flu, it was often fatal. There were no wonder drugs and medical treatment, if available, was not very advanced. The average person only lived until about fifty.

Unfortunately, I never met my father's parents because they had passed away before I was born, but I heard a great deal from my father about what life was like in Texas at this time.

One of the highlights of life on the farm came in the late summer, after the crops had been gathered – the whole family would attend a Christian camp meeting held in a nearby county. People came from miles around to thank the Lord for the bountiful crops, hear preachers warn about the wages of sin and sing songs from hymnals. They lived in makeshift tent-like shelters, and meals were served under the stars. The food was always good because there were fresh vegetables from the harvest. There would also be fresh milk, eggs and lots of beef cooked over an open fire. A hog would be slaughtered to provide bacon, ham, ribs and flavoring for the beans and black-eyed peas.

While the grownups listened to sermons, the children had the time of their lives, playing games, chasing crawdads in the nearby creek, and sleeping outside with their friends. I'm sure they told plenty of ghost stories to scare the fool out of each other. I'm also certain that the boys put some effort into sparking the girls. The people they met would often become friends for the rest of their lives. The camp meeting would last about two weeks and was talked about for months afterwards.

Another pleasure my father described was the monthly shopping trip into town. It was a time to buy flour, sugar, salt and all the other necessities you couldn't grow on the farm. Once in a while they would buy new shoes, a frock, a tool or school supplies, but mostly they window-shopped, toured the general store, and caught up on the latest gossip. Going to church was also an important social outlet, but it was much more serious and not as much fun as going to town.

School was taken seriously. I recently saw an eighth grade exam from 1895 (see Appendix II) and I could not have passed it. Reading, writing and arithmetic were just one part of their studies – they also learned Latin, geography, history and a number of other subjects that are no longer found in present-day curricula. For some reason, every person from this era claims to have walked to school three miles in each direction – uphill both ways – and my father was no exception. How every house wound up exactly three miles from school, I'll never know...

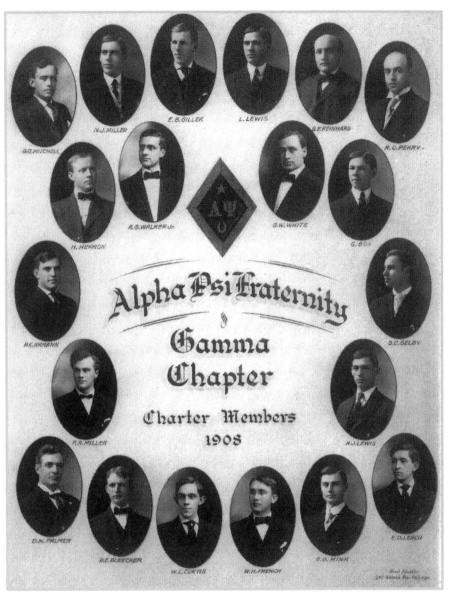

Dad's college fraternity

My father was ambitious, and after graduating from the local high school, decided to study veterinary medicine. The only veterinary school in 1907 was the Chicago Veterinary College. It was a long way to Chicago and it must have been quite a change for a young man from a farm in a sparsely populated area of north Texas, but he seemed to thrive there, playing on the college baseball team and participating in a number of student activities.

He was one of around forty seniors in the graduating class of 1910. I still have the class picture and they were a fine looking group, decked out in suits, white shirts and ties. They look ready to conquer the world. College was a civilized, serious endeavor in those days, and was considered a special opportunity since most people did not have the resources to attend college. Particularly in an agrarian society, most people saw no reason to acquire a more formal education.

Allen Jefferson Lewis (Dad) at college graduation

The newly designated Dr. Lewis came back home after graduation and hung out his shingle in Haskell, Texas. Between 1910 and 1931, he built a thriving practice. When the United States got involved in the First World

War in 1917, Dad was already 33 years of age, considered too old to enlist, so he concentrated on work. He was good at his job and he became respected in west Texas as someone who could usually find a way to cure the ills of the indispensable farm animals that provided families with food, milk – and in some cases their entire family income. During that period, Dad sometimes made up to $1000 a month, a handsome living at that time.

He bought his first car in 1915, one of the first in that part of Texas. It was a Hupmobile, which was considered pretty snappy in that era. Dad and an older brother, Turner, traveled all the way to Fort Worth, probably by train, to buy it. The 150-mile drive back to Haskell took several days. There were no paved roads yet and the existing dirt roads had been built to accommodate wagons and buggies with wheels much wider apart than those of cars. As a result, the car rode with one wheel several inches higher than the other because one side was always in a wagon rut.

The car sometimes got stuck in the mud, and their progress was further slowed by the need to pull over to the side of the road to let each horse and buggy pass. The engine would be turned off and my father and uncle would help guide the frightened horse past the unfamiliar sight and sound of the car. Then the car would have to be re-cranked in order to start it again. This made the trip back to Haskell a bit of an ordeal. It must have been the novelty of having the only car in town that made it appeal to my father, because it sure didn't allow him to get anywhere any faster!

The Hupmobile stuck in the mud, circa 1916

Workers in the fields would come running to the fences to see the noisy contraption pass by, most likely the first car they had ever seen. Back in Haskell, Dad's car made him the talk of the town and a hot commodity among the single women who worked as milliners, clerks and schoolteachers in the area.

Stories his family told me described Dad as quite a handsome young man, but he waited until his parents had died to marry. Children were expected to look after their parents in their old age, and because Dad was the last sibling to marry, this duty had fallen to him. His father died in 1920 and his mother in 1917. Then in 1924, at the age of forty, he asked Sarah Alice Bates to marry him.

CHAPTER 2

Sarah Alice Bates, my mother, was born in Denton County, Texas on February 21, 1894. The Bates family was Scotch-English by ancestry but left Northern England for Virginia in 1635. They were nearly all Methodist, with several ministers in the family tree. One of these early settlers was an architect, who built Monticello for Thomas Jefferson. He also secured the contract to build the state house in Richmond, but his business failed before he could finish that job.

Sarah Alice Bates (Mother)

My Great-Great-Grandfather Ruben Bates was born in Amherst County, Virginia in 1774 and moved to Barren County, Kentucky in 1820, where he settled near old Rocky Hill. My Great-Grandfather Willis Hubbard Bates was born in Kentucky in 1815 and his son, Charles Willis Bates was born there in 1849. My grandfather Charles grew up to marry Mary Elizabeth Witt, a fellow Kentuckian, born in 1852. Together, they moved to Texas shortly after the Civil War, trying to avoid the chaos of wartime and in search of more productive, affordable farm land. There was a large influx of settlers into the area in the late 1800's as the government began giving away land in an effort to cultivate the prairies. Aided by the introduction of the one-plow and the motorized tractor, settlers could farm more land than had ever been possible before, and actually make a profit.

Charles and Mary had a total of nine children. Later, Charles was elected a county commissioner of Denton County during the era when such notorious outlaws as the James brothers and Sam Bass lurked in the region. I was only eleven when Grandmother died in 1947 at the age of 95. I wish we had owned a tape recorder, because the stories she told were so exciting. She described how she and Grandfather would sometimes be held up by bandits on their way into town; her solution was to roll their money up into her hair bun, where no one would ever think to look.

She also told vivid stories about the beginnings of Civil War tensions back in Kentucky. She was eight when the war broke out, and she watched her uncles go off to fight. After her family moved to Denton County, they faced hostile Cherokee, Comanche and Shawnee tribes, and some of them were killed trying to protect their livestock from Indian raids.

Grandmother lost an eye somewhere along the way – I can't remember how – and she used to go outside every afternoon and look at the sun, believing it would make her remaining eye stronger. She was a bit irascible until she had her 'medicine' every afternoon. The 'medicine' was a big jug of red wine that she kept under her bed; after two or three glasses, her whole attitude would change. This is when I would always try to visit with her, because it put her in a better mood, and the stories she told were always better.

Mother was the seventh of eight children. She was considered quite an attractive woman, but by the age of thirty, she had several strikes against her, according to the mores of the time, for she was divorced with an eleven-year-old son, Charles Bates Thornton, who was known as Bates. After her divorce, Mother and Bates had traveled around the state, struggling to find work and a place to settle. Eventually the two arrived in Haskell, and Mother worked in a women's salon while Bates went to school and delivered papers. It was here that she met my father.

Mother and her sisters

Mother and siblings

Mother and Bates, 1920

Mother and Dad, 1957

Once she and Dad were wed, they moved into his house. After the wedding, Mom and Dad couldn't find Bates anywhere. They finally found him outside, under a big tree in the front yard, crying. Dad asked him what was wrong and Bates looked up at him and asked if he could be allowed into the house too. He hadn't known where he was expected to live. Dad took him in his arms and told him that it was a package deal and that this would be his family and home too.

I remember Bates and me flying over Fort Stockton, Texas in his private plane in 1966. He looked down on what appeared to be just a wide place in the road and told me about the time he and mother had spent there before she met my father. He said that there had been many tough times in his life but Fort Stockton was probably the worst – they arrived there with only a dime to their names, but despite their desperate situation, my mother never gave up. She soon found a job and they were able to rent a room and eat. The hardships they endured together bonded them and they had a very close relationship throughout her life.

The contrast was so great between the years before and after Mom married Dad, that Bates and my Mother called Dad "Dr. Lewis", never referring to him as Dad, Jeff or Father. They had a great deal of respect for him and that was their way of showing it. Their next few years were happy and prosperous.

CHAPTER 3

My parents began a family together in Haskell. Allan Jefferson Lewis, Jr. (who they called Jeff) was born in 1925 and Jeanetta was born in 1931, the same year Bates graduated from high school and left to go to college at Texas Tech College in Lubbock. But Dad's business began to slump as the region suffered a terrible drought and the country fell into a depression.

During most of the 1920's the United States had enjoyed a period of unbalanced prosperity: prices for agricultural commodities and wages fell at the end of the war while new industries (radio, movies, automobiles and chemicals) flourished. The optimistic financial mood encouraged more and more people to borrow on credit in order to invest in a variety of things, including the booming stock market.

But commodity prices began to fall worldwide, and with business inventories larger than they had ever been, and demand for those goods decreasing, everything began to slip downward. The whole world was caught in the same financial net, and the market crash of 1929 kicked off the Great Depression. Unemployment soared from 3% to 25% and manufacturing output collapsed by one-third. Helplessness, hopelessness, homelessness and hunger stalked the land.

Worsening matters in Texas and most of Oklahoma was a severe drought that began in 1933. Once fertile areas became a desert soon known as the "Dust Bowl". Violent dust storms blew for weeks on end, and sometimes sent dirt clouds almost two miles into the sky, literally blotting out the sun, so that noon was as dark as midnight. At its zenith, the dust bowl spread over 100 million acres. All that dust was actually rich topsoil that farmers desperately needed for the production of cotton and maize. Without crops, it was difficult for farmers to pay off equipment loans, and many farms tumbled into foreclosure. Farmers no longer had the money to pay for veterinary services and couldn't even trade their goods for Dad's help. Many of those who had lost their homes and livelihoods to the storms turned westward, migrating to California. Those that remained behind sometimes got literally buried by dust in their half-underground dugout homes. Others survived but lost everything. As the fragile agrarian economy collapsed, my father lost most of his veterinary business.

Desperate for options, Dad went to work for the State of Texas as a State Veterinarian. At first, this seemed like a blessing, but, as few people remember, the State of Texas became financially bankrupt in the 1930's. Miriam (Ma) Ferguson had become governor for the second time in 1932. She was first elected to the position in 1917 after the impeachment of her husband. I'm not sure that Ma Ferguson could be altogether held responsible for the economic failure of state finances, but her inaction caused a lot of grief.

As a result, Dad did not receive a paycheck for over six months. The family moved into a dugout home that had been abandoned near the Canadian River in north Texas, and Dad sold the tires off his car in order to buy food for the family. It was a time he would never forget and he related the story to me on many occasions. His ambitious nature was crushed, and he was no longer interested in taking risks – this would influence his job and investment decisions for the rest of his life. He and Mother would look along the highways for wild mustard greens that could be cooked with a little bit of fat for flavor. Dad would also trade his work for an occasional chicken or a piece of beef. It was slim pickings and they came close to starving several times, but they cinched in their belts and made it. The drought lasted seven long years until finally, in 1941, rain began to pour down on the region, nourishing crops and revitalizing the region's economy.

Family dugout, 1931

In 1933, the veterinary office of the State of Texas asked Dad to move to Lubbock and cover a large territory west of Fort Worth with an abundance of ranches and farms. Dad would test cattle for tuberculosis and cows for Bang's disease (which prevented them from bearing young and giving milk) – either of which would render the livestock worthless to the rancher. There were also occasional outbreaks of hoof and mouth disease, which necessitated the slaughter of all exposed cattle. Ranchers could lose their whole herd and be financially wiped out. Cholera and other diseases were also treated in hogs, horses and from time-to-time in the farmers' dogs.

Dad took this work seriously and put over 50,000 miles on his car in most years while covering the vast terrain of west Texas. He seemed to know every farmer and rancher in the entire area and was often away from home for extended periods of time. On the enormous King and 6666 ranches, with several thousand head of cattle each, tuberculosis testing alone could take up to six weeks!

Families stayed put in those days, and Dad came to know several consecutive generations in west Texas, sometimes treating their livestock over several decades. He was almost like a family doctor who made house calls all over the state. He could always be reached in an emergency and would drop everything to help. Everyone counted on and liked him. Years later, when I would meet a farmer or rancher from west Texas, they would invariably know my Dad and always had a story about a time he had helped them.

When I remember my father, I picture a lean, rugged individual whose well-tanned skin reflected the fact that he spent most of his life outdoors. I can't recall him ever getting sick. Bald-headed from middle-age on, he always wore a hat, usually a Stetson in the winter and a straw hat in the summer. Except for Sunday go-to-meeting clothes, he wore a khaki shirt and khaki pants every day. He was a loving man and I can remember seeing tears in his eyes when he sang 'Rock of Ages' at church.

PART TWO

ALONG CAME JOHN PAUL

CHAPTER 4

In my earliest memory, I am standing on top of the Empire State Building, scared to death. At that time, the Empire State was the tallest building in the world, at one hundred and four stories, and the view was breathtaking. It was 1939, and I was three years old. Bates, then twenty-six, thought it would be wonderful for the family to attend the World's Fair in New York, so Mother, Jeanetta and I rode up on the train, and Bates came up from Washington, DC, where he was working. It was a bright spot during what must have been a difficult time for my parents and the rest of the country, still enduring the Great Depression, but my memories of these early years are warm and have sustained me throughout my life.

Mother, Jeanetta, JPL, and Bates at the Empire State Building

Jeanette and John (JPL) at Arlington Cemetery

At the time of my birth, my father was fifty-two and my mother was forty-two. In retrospect, I would guess that that my conception was a mistake, although neither my mother nor my father would ever have discussed such a thing. Sex was not a subject I can ever remember being discussed in our household, and I certainly wasn't going to be the one to bring it up.

Our household was full of affection, respect and laughter. We didn't have an abundance of material things, but my parents supplied a foundation built on love. Home was a very special place, filled with comfortable, reassuring people, smells and sounds. Of course there were no televisions and no computers – we created our own fun: singing, reading, playing games, exploring and climbing trees. We were never bored.

Lubbock was a terrific place to grow up. It had great schools and life revolved around church, family, school and work. It had a population of about

45,000, and, without much oil-related industry, it was economically centered on agriculture, small manufacturing and Texas Tech College. With several hospitals and clinics specializing in a wide range of medicine, Lubbock also served as the medical center for west Texas and a large part of New Mexico.

We lived in a small white stucco house, one long block from the grade school and about a mile from the junior high. It wasn't very large but it had four bedrooms, a living room and a dining room. We only had one full bath and a half bath, and it got a little hectic in the morning trying to get ready to go to school. We had a storm cellar in the back yard that could be used during a tornado, but I can't remember ever using it. The one tornado warning I remember sent us all down to the basement. It was raining like crazy and the electricity had gone out. We sat down there with only a single candle providing light until the coast was clear. That was after several hours and we didn't know what was going on outside. It was scary and the only way to know if it was safe would require someone to go up stairs and listen for the sirens that would signal that the danger was over. My Dad finally had to chance it and we finally knew we were going to be all right.

The kitchen was the center of activity: warmed by the stove, which was on every day, year round, it served not only as the cooking and baking center, but also as our laundry room, and the best place to read and listen to stories. Food was stored in a small pantry off the kitchen.

We kept things cool in an old-fashioned icebox. Small, compared to today's refrigerators, it was about five feet high, eighteen inches wide and eighteen inches deep. The iceman would come at least once or twice a week and sometimes more frequently to deliver a new block of ice, which was placed in a top compartment, under a lid. This would keep perishables fresh for a few days. Dad bought milk in two or three two-gallon containers from a nearby dairy farm each week. One was set aside to sour and be used for butter. After churning, it would produce a portion of butter; the remaining liquid was 'old fashioned' buttermilk, which we drank and used for cooking, especially in buttermilk biscuits. Buttermilk was never my favorite, but Mom and Dad loved it. The other container would be for the family to drink and we had fresh whole milk at every meal. Milk was not pasteurized at that time.

We didn't know pasteurization at that time and we stayed healthy throughout the period in spite of our ignorance.

The basement was usually full of food that Mother had canned herself. We would buy fresh fruits and vegetables from farmers by the bushel, then take it home and snap the beans, take the black-eyed peas out of their hulls, remove the pits from the fruit and shuck the corn... It would be washed and seasoned, then put in jars, pressure cooked, and stored in the cellar until it was needed. Mother would also can meat and preserves. Even later, during wartime rationing, we were never in danger of starvation! Our canned goods would keep us alive for a long time. The depression was tough for Mom and Dad, and even after it had ended, they remained determined to prevent the family from ever going hungry.

To my memory, Mother was a terrific cook, but later in life, my sister Jeanetta remarked to me that she recalled our mother being a terrible cook! I felt that keeping us all well-fed was a worthy accomplishment, but Jeanetta lamented that almost everything Mother cooked had been fried and very fattening. This was definitely true, although in my mother's defense, many of the things we now know about nutrition and healthful eating were not yet known. We had fried chicken, fried pork chops, fried meat or chicken fried steak with mashed potatoes, gravy and biscuits or some variation almost every night. Once in a while we would have meatloaf, smothered steak, hot beef sandwiches and eggs and sausages. These would always be accompanied by fried okra, green beans, black-eyed peas, corn on the cob, carrots or a combination thereof. It spite of all that food I never gained a pound. I was always very skinny. Dad used to say that he thought I had a hollow leg, because no matter how much I ate, it never stuck to my bones – he figured I must be hiding it somewhere else. Even when we didn't have a lot to eat, Dad would come up with some real treats. He used to take sorghum molasses and mix it with butter for us to spread on bread. It was delicious and made a good dessert.

Once in a while, Dad would buy a side of beef from one of his customers and bring it to the butcher's to have it cut into steaks, hamburger meat, roasts and other cuts that could be frozen. We would then take it to a space we rented in a shared frozen food locker, where it was labeled by the type of cut and stored.

Sometimes we would take a portion of beef – or occasionally pork – home, where we would put it though a meat grinder, season it, and make sage sausages. We could only take as much as we could use immediately, as it wouldn't keep long in the icebox. There were no home freezers at that time and I don't believe they appeared in homes until the fifties.

Not only was food preparation more labor intensive in those days, but so was the production of many household items that we now take for granted. For instance, we made our own soap, from the fat of animals slaughtered for food. The fat was mixed with lye and cooked. When it was ready, we poured it into a flat pan to set and then cut it into handier pieces. Many of us had never even heard of deodorant until we were in our teens and radio jingles suggested we prevent body odor by buying Lifebuoy soap! Once a month, we washed our hair using the homemade soap (the women probably did it more frequently). There was one comb for the whole family and only when too many teeth had broken off would we buy a new one.

There was no air conditioning in homes at that time, so we just slept with the windows open and hoped to be lucky enough that a breeze would cool us off enough to fall asleep. The west Texas summers broiled with an unrelenting heat that was particularly grueling. At times, I thought I would melt, especially since we were usually so active all day in the heat. Our bodies turned as brown as toast and somehow I don't recall ever getting sunburned, although I'm sure we must have!

Later on, evaporative coolers arrived on the scene. A large metal container with straw on the back and sides was placed in the window. Water would flow down the sides, wetting the straw and a fan inside the box would pull air from the outside through the water-soaked straw and inside, where it would cool the room. We had only one of these, so we would keep the bedroom doors open to try to get some of the cool air. We later had a small round evaporative cooler without a fan that could be placed in the window of our car. The wind would blow through the cooler and cool down the interior of the car. It wasn't very efficient but it beat having nothing at all.

When I was quite young, Mother made me stay indoors from one to four in the afternoon, because a polio epidemic had struck a number of young children. Two of the boys in our neighborhood got mild cases and had to be treated. The common wisdom of the time was that staying out of the afternoon heat would give you a better chance of avoiding polio.

Even though our family would have been considered very lower-middle class, we had a black woman that helped mother around the house for a half a day, twice a week. Her name was Hattie and she became a part of our family for the twenty years she was with us. She was a kind woman and all of us thought the world of her. I'm sure she couldn't have been paid very much, but she took home lots of food and clothing for her own children. Jeff and Bates used to go see her every time they came back to Lubbock, and for the rest of her life, whenever she needed anything, someone in our family took care of it. While there was a real separation between the races in those days, with black people living only in the east part of town, I can't remember animosity between the races in our town as I was growing up, although I'm sure I wasn't aware of all that went on.

CHAPTER 5

On December 7, 1941, I was five years old. It was a Sunday morning and as a rule we would generally be getting prepared to go to church. Instead everyone was huddled around the radio. I didn't know exactly what was going on but I knew it was serious. President Franklin Delano Roosevelt was on the air and my mother was crying. Pearl Harbor had been attacked by the Japanese, and we were at war. Now I sure didn't know where Pearl Harbor was, or even who the Japanese were, but I knew that whatever had happened had made a lot of people, starting with my parents, upset and afraid. The war would influence all of our lives for the next five years.

World War II was a time of sacrifice for all Americans. Economically, things had started to get better as the country began to pull out of the Depression, but the war meant that people had to endure additional hardships "for the duration", which was as long as it would take for the war to end. The government had a catch phrase: "Use it up, wear it out, make it do, or do without".

American farm families ultimately sent more than 1.8 million men and women into the armed forces. I noticed as more and more young men from our area began to disappear, and small rectangular flags went up in the windows where they had lived. Each flag was about four by ten inches, with a red fringe, a white background and a blue star representing each son or daughter in the military. As the war continued, some of the blue stars were replaced with gold stars, denoting the loss of a son or daughter.

Every day, eight million US soldiers had to be fed, yet farmers were facing a shortage of farm workers and farm equipment. To bridge this gap, food rationing was instituted and became a regular part of everyday existence. The government issued food stamps, which could be used for essential staples such as sugar, coffee, meat, fish, butter, eggs, cheese, shoes, rubber, canned milk and other scarce items. The stamps, smaller than a postage stamp, came in several colors and in sheets of about twenty each. Every family was issued a certain number of the stamps each month, which determined how much of each product you could buy. When the stamps for a particular item were gone, you could buy no more for the month. This made everyone very aware of what they used, causing an immediate cut in consumption. It was vital that each family use the stamps wisely so they wouldn't run out of food before they received their next allowance. I still have some of the rationing stamps today. We learned to be very careful what we ate and how much.

Silk and newly-invented nylon were used for parachute production, so women around the country found it hard to obtain fashionable stockings. All hosiery at that time had a seam running up the back of the leg. When women stopped being able to get hosiery, women would sometimes draw a line up the backs of their legs so that it looked like they were wearing stockings. Styles changed to accommodate shortages of certain materials; for instance, wrap-around skirts became popular when zippers and metal snaps grew scarce. Everyone adapted to the changes and there was little complaining about the inconveniences.

Gasoline was also in short supply. People were issued rationing cards for gasoline and, unless you were in a critical business, such as a medical doctor, the amount you could buy was miniscule. As a veterinarian, Dad was considered a "critical business", which gave him certain advantages. Everyone started walking a great deal more and certainly didn't go on any driving trips. Copper was needed for war material, so the government began minting pennies from zinc-coated metal. Towns had paper drives, rubber drives and scrap metal drives. People collected old tires, tinfoil, paper, engine grease and metal of almost any kind, bringing it to collection points to be recycled for the war effort. Children went door to door in their neighborhoods, gathering further. Those drives generated a strong sense of community and a patriotic satisfaction that everyone was contributing something. Americans bought savings bonds in order to help finance the war. Even the children in school contributed. We were given an envelope with slots where we could put dimes and after the amount reached about five dollars we could trade the envelope in for a War Bond of the same amount.

Men and women from all over the country went to work in defense plants building ships, tanks, bombs, ammunition, guns and the other weapons our soldiers needed. A great many people moved to the West Coast because many new defense plants were opened in San Diego, Long Beach and Los Angeles. While the western movement started during the depression, the mass migration brought about by the war really transformed a great deal of California. Rural residents found new jobs off the farm. New military bases were also built far from the coasts, where they would be less vulnerable to attack.

The country went from being mainly a rural nation with quiet streets and close neighborhoods, to a nation where people were uprooted from their homes and scattered all over this country. Before the war started most folks did not lock their doors when they left. They were also eager to help their neighbors when they needed it. The American people were busy building and training and migrating to those locations where they were most needed, and a great many never returned to their roots. The towns, farms and cities would be forever changed, and our nation would never be as simple and naïve as it once was. Community and family closeness would never return to the way it was before. The war affected who lived and who died, who married who and where people lived. Many sons and daughters gave their lives and never returned, changing entire families forever.

There were many such losses in our neighborhood. The bad news was heralded by the olive drab sedan with military markings that would drive up to a house, where two soldiers would get out and inform the family of a loss. The whole neighborhood would be aware of what had occurred and the women would go to see if they could help out in any way.

There were three pilot training bases in the Lubbock area – Goodfellow Field and South Plains Army Air Force Base north of town, and Reese AAFB to the west. The flat terrain and accommodating weather made it an excellent training ground for fighter and bomber pilots, and there were several thousand trainees in residence at any one time. Sometimes, it felt like there were more military personnel in our town than residents. As soon as they had completed the training courses, the young pilots were shipped overseas.

Sadly, there was no way our town could handle the influx of young women who came hoping to see their loved one before they went to war. There were not nearly enough places to stay in the area, so each evening, young women would knock on our door and ask if they could stay with us. We had a small house, but mother would always prepare pallets made of blankets and quilts for four or five of these young women to sleep on the living room floor. The next morning she would feed them breakfast before they left and tried to find their husbands. The women usually stayed more than one night, but Mother never asked for any recompense. In many cases, it was the last time they would ever see their husbands. Mother received letters for years from the women who stayed with us. They described their losses and sorrows and told Mother how much they appreciated her kind gesture in their time of need.

When we recited the Pledge of Allegiance each morning in school, it took on a special meaning, and when we sang the national anthem it was with tears in our eyes. Remember, there was no assurance as to how the conflict would turn out. It was a time of fear, uncertainty, dedication and faith, and our family prayed together daily. There were rumors of an impending Japanese invasion on the West Coast, and a widespread suspicion of Asian people. Our family would gather around the radio each night to listen to the news reports from all over the world, informing us of developments on all the fronts of the war. We listened to President Roosevelt's fireside chats, which encouraged the nation throughout this uncertain time. Of course, the war did not affect me as much because I was too young to understand the significance of all that I heard and saw, but when the news grew negative, I was acutely aware of the change of tone in both my family and the community as a whole.

My oldest brother, Bates, had gone to work in Washington, D.C., around 1937, after attending Texas Tech College for a couple of years.

A good friend of his, George Mahon, had been elected to Congress, representing the new 19th Congressional District, which included Lubbock, and Bates transferred to George Washington University and began working toward his degree in accounting. George Mahon, I'm sure, helped introduce him around town.

Washington was just a small Southern town before the war started and there weren't enough workers to provide support for the growing number of people that were required to manage the war effort. Bates got a job as a secretary to Harold Ickes, who was the Secretary of the Interior in the Roosevelt cabinet. When the war began, Secretary Ickes then recommended Bates to Robert Lovett, the Assistant Secretary of War, and to several members of the Joint Chiefs of Staff to fill a need which quickly became apparent.

The army needed to create a proper logistics system in order to manage and allocate the mountains of materials under its control, so Bates was given a commission and asked to form a new unit that could achieve this goal. He was so successful that he rose from the rank of second lieutenant to full colonel in about twelve months and became the youngest colonel in the military. He was twenty-eight years old. He spent the war years in Washington, D.C., making sure our troops received the materials they needed to fight the war.

My brother, Jeff, was born in 1925, so he was not eligible for the draft until 1943. That year, he was sent to basic training and then assigned to Fort Belfor in Washington State. He had very bad asthma and was initially told that he would be limited to non-combat duties, but instead was put into the engineering corps and trained to blow up bridges and other structures. He kept waiting for an asthma attack that would have changed his assignment, but for some unknown reason he did not have a single bout until he got out of the Army in early 1946.

After VJ Day, Jeff was sent to Japan and spent about a year in that country. He was primarily involved in reconstruction programs and seemed to enjoy the experience. When he returned, he had a number of beautiful Japanese ceremonial swords that were made with gold engraving, and I have always wondered what happened not only to those items, but also to the Indian arrowheads he found in Texas and the coins he collected from all over the world. Unfortunately, I never got a chance to ask him.

Jeff, 1944

I feel I never really knew Jeff very well. He was eleven years older than me and I was only seven when he left for the army. He was a sickly child, which might explain why we did not interact much when I was young. In fact, I can hardly recall having a single conversation with him before I was in my twenties. I remember things like his being in a car accident, wrecking Dad's car and coming home all bloody, but I don't remember the details. He was a handsome fellow, about 5' 9" and slight of build. He was always a bright student and even though he often had to stay home from school with one malady or another, he always passed with flying colors. He was a talented oil painter and everyone complimented his work. When he was thirteen, after painting some of his best work and receiving accolades for it, he suddenly quit and never painted again. I gather that he was a lonely child, but didn't seem to make much effort to make friends.

Upon Jeff's return from the war, he stepped straight into some major responsibilities; he got married and he and his wife, Veida, had three children, Jeffery, Johnny and Julie. He found a way to support his growing family and pay for his education at the same time, working his way through college as an architect, drawing plans for residential housing. He was in demand,

I suppose partly because he was good and partly because he was inexpensive. I think he earned a degree in engineering and architecture and got a job with Southwestern Public Service, which was the electrical utility in that part of Texas. It was a good job and he got several promotions while he was there. He later left SPS to take a job with a private contractor named Paine. He was sent to a special school to learn how to bid contracts; when he came back, he was asked to bid on government contracts primarily dealing with converting old military properties to alternative uses by peacetime agencies. I gather he was good at it and the Paine firm made a lot of money from his activities. I never lived very close to Jeff after I had finished college, but the men who worked with him praised his efforts and his talents.

CHAPTER 6

Despite the big changes happening in the country, my childhood in Lubbock was relatively carefree, insulated as I was from world events I could barely grasp at that age. Our neighborhood was full of kids, and there were regular games every summer night, well after dark. We played "Annie Over", "Tag" and "Who's Got the Bacon?" There were easily twenty to thirty kids between the ages of seven to fourteen playing together every night – enough to make full teams for baseball, football, basketball or any kind of game we might invent on the spot.

Great rivalries sprung up between one city block and another. Competition was fierce, and lots of fun. No one worried about us being out at night. There was virtually no crime. Houses were left unlocked and strangers were not regarded with suspicion. If you were hungry you could get food from almost any house, and if you were in trouble people in the neighborhood would help. It was truly a wonderful time to grow up.

When we got a little older, we played organized baseball at the Boys Club. Those teams were made up of boys from eleven to eighteen years of age. This presented a bit of a problem for me when I first joined – I can assure you that when you are eleven you should not be playing baseball with high school boys. They were so much bigger and could throw the ball harder and hit it farther. One time, an eighteen-year-old pitcher nailed me with a glancing blow to the head, and I thought I was finished. The next thing I remember was the plate umpire telling me I could go to first base. The trouble was, I was still so dizzy I didn't know where first base was.

I was most excited about playing flag football. In grade school, we played against other schools. We would get so energized on the day of the game; we'd put on our uniforms and sprint out on to the field to the sound of wild cheering! I played end and was a good wide receiver. I scored a lot of touchdowns and it felt as exciting as if I was in the pros. No one got hurt in flag football and we had such fun.

When I got to junior high, the boys were much bigger and faster and the game changed to regular tackle football. I wanted to continue playing, but my mother had more sense than I did and refused to let me. I think she knew her little skinny boy would have gotten creamed. My sister had a boyfriend that played football at Texas Tech. He came over one night and I asked him if he would tell Mom that I wouldn't get hurt playing football. He turned toward my mother and said, "Mrs. Lewis, your son won't get hurt playing football". He then proceeded to take his teeth out, throw his shoulder out of joint, and exhibit the surgery scars on his knee and shoulder. Needless to say, mother was not convinced, and the conversation was over. It was the end of my Hall of Fame aspirations, and gave me a good dose of reality.

There were other neighborhood events too. Every Halloween, the town had a parade down Broadway with children in their costumes. Each age group was judged and awarded prizes. I remember participating in a jaunty pirate's costume one year – a great time was had by all, especially as there was candy and fruit given out to everyone, regardless of who won. We also went trick-or-treating all over the neighborhood on our own, without any worries of danger.

One of my schoolmates, Diane Smith, lived about five blocks away from me. Her father owned several movie theaters in town, and when we trick-or-treated at their house, Mr. Smith gleefully gave out free movie passes instead of candy. Preston Smith later became a two-term governor of Texas and lived to the ripe old age of ninety-one. I saw him several times over the years and we always reminisced and laughed at the Halloween memories we shared.

Needless to say, everyone knew their neighbors back then. Our next-door neighbors were named Scales. They had two sons who were much older than I was: Jim, the oldest, and Bill, several years younger. They were just terrific, and looked out for all the kids in the neighborhood. They also had a dog, a collie-shepherd mix, named Dopey, who – contrary to his name – was the smartest dog I have ever known. Dopey looked out for us kids even more devotedly than Jim and Bill.

He was a constant companion and supervisor. If we tried to cross the street when traffic was coming or against a red light, he would herd us back to the curb. Sometimes he would grab hold of our pants and restrain us until the coast was clear or the light turned green. Every year, Bill would bring him over to our house for his vaccinations. As soon as Dopey saw Dad, he would lie down and put a paw over his eyes until Dad had finished giving him the shot. Never a whine.

One time, in the middle of the night, Dopey came to the back bedroom where Dad slept and softly cried until Dad woke up. Dad came out and saw that Dopey had a broken leg; he had probably been hit by a car. He gave the dog a shot, then reset the leg and put a cast on it. When he was finished, Dopey returned to his own house and went to sleep. He knew exactly where to come when he had been hurt. When Dopey was about seventeen years old, he disappeared one day. We searched everywhere for him, and finally found him under the house where he had gone to die. It was a terrible loss for all of us. We missed him every day, but at least we were old enough to cross the street responsibly by the time he died.

CHAPTER 7

When I was growing up, television was still a thing of the future. The first television station wouldn't arrive in Lubbock until around 1951. Even then, the picture was black-and-white and tiny, the tubes were always burning out and the reception was so poor that there was "snow" on the screen much of the time. When you could manage to get a signal, there wasn't much programming to choose from – mainly older movies, weather and news. So radio was still king.

The radio was a big part of my life. I listened to programs such as "Suspense", "The FBI in Peace and War", "The Shadow", "The Green Hornet", " Gang Busters", "Sgt. Preston of the Yukon", "Sky King", "The Thin Man", "Burns and Allen", "Roy Rogers", "Fibber McGee and Molly", "Amos and Andy", "The Lone Ranger", "The Shadow Knows", "Gunsmoke", "The Jack Benny Show" and "Edgar Bergen and Charlie McCarthy". These and many other shows loomed large in our lives; I made sure to fit my homework in around them and tried to never miss an episode. In some ways radio was better than TV. Your imagination could visualize things better than they could be produced in real life.

The excitement and drama was much more real and suspenseful than in motion pictures. The sounds and scene descriptions were alive.

Dad and I used to get sandwiches prepared and gather in front of the radio in time to listen to the prize fights from Madison Square Garden in New York. Don Dunfee was the ringside announcer and we heard fighters like Joe Louis, Sugar Ray Robinson and Rocky Marciano fight world championship bouts. I remember one night we got our food all ready and sat down with great anticipation to listen to Gus Liznovich fight for the middleweight championship. It was supposed to be a very exciting bout. The ringside bell rang and Don Dunfee announced the start of the first round. The fighters came to the center of the ring. Gus hit his opponent with a series of left and right punches, and knocked him out about thirty seconds into the first round. We hadn't even gotten a single bite of our meal and the fight was over. What a disappointment!

We even had our very own prize fighter, a man who lived for a short time in our small garage apartment with his wife and baby son. His name was Lavern Roach, and he was considered a good fighter in the middleweight class. After a few victories, his manager got him a shot at the title against the middleweight champion of the world, Marcel Cerdan, but it was a disastrous mismatch. Cerdan was much more experienced, and was the better fighter. During the bout, Lavern was knocked down many times before Cerdan finally knocked him out. Lavern Roach never recovered consciousness and he died in his dressing room. We listened to the fight and aftermath on the radio. Dad was the one who went out to tell Roach's wife about the tragedy. It was very sad and I felt terrible for his family.

Another boarder who rented the garage apartment, whose name I cannot recall, was an avid baseball fan who often invited me to come to games with him. We frequently went to see our local team, which were called the "Lubbock Hubbers". The Hubbers were a farm team for the Oklahoma City 89ers and the Dallas class AA team, they were pretty good for their league. On one occasion, we went to see the Cleveland Indians and the New York Giants play an exhibition game. I got a baseball and convinced most of the players on both teams to autograph it. Among the signers were Mel Ott, Bob Feller and Hank Greenberg, all of whom became Hall of Fame members. Unfortunately, I don't know what happened to that ball... I probably gave it away at some point, because signed balls weren't worth much then. That baseball today would be worth a fortune because the players were so famous and they are all dead.

Dad loved football but never got to go see many games; he just listened on the radio. Lubbock and Amarillo High Schools had a fierce rivalry – the Lubbock Westerners against the Amarillo Sandies for the pride of the Panhandle – but in recent history, Amarillo had beaten us for nine straight years. That year's game was to be held in Amarillo, and Lubbock had its best team in years, so with my encouragement, Dad got tickets for the game. Amarillo was about 120 miles due north of Lubbock. We drove up for the game. It was a full stadium and the crowd was very pumped up.

We had no idea how strong the Lubbock team really was – and Dad had the time of his life yelling as the Westerners beat the Amarillo team by about forty-two points! We were on cloud nine all the way home. In the next few years, Lubbock High went undefeated two years in a row and won the Texas state championship twice. We never got to attend another game, but we listened and yelled at the radio during each and every one.

Other radio highlights were the World Series games, and many great collegiate football games with stars like Charlie "Choo Choo" Justice from North Carolina, Doak Walker from SMU, Doc Blanchard and Glenn Davis from Army and Leon Hart from Notre Dame. It was gripping entertainment, and we yelled and cheered just as hard as we would have if we'd been at the game. For some reason, the pictures that later came through on the television never could equal the things our imaginations could create while listening to the radio. The jokes were never as funny, the drama never more intense and the songs never more beautiful than when we heard them on the radio.

Later in my life, I had the opportunity to meet Doc Blanchard and Glenn Davis, two of the best players ever to play football. Blanchard was known as Mr. Inside and Glenn Davis as Mr. Outside when they played on the Army team. Both had won the Heisman Trophy and, during their time on the team, Army won something like forty-one games and tied one. I met them when they were in their eighties. Doc Blanchard had been a pilot in the Korean War and retired after twenty-eight years of military service. Glenn Davis was the more glamorous of the two. He was in several motion pictures and was Elizabeth Taylor's boyfriend for a time. He worked at the Los Angeles Times in public relations until his retirement, and died only recently, in 2005. Meeting them definitely took me back to the days when I sat in front of the radio with Dad, listening to Army mow down yet another rival!

In addition to sports, I listened to a lot of music on the radio. One of the things I loved the most was gospel singing, particularly the gospel quartets. There were a number of them that were well known across most of the country at that time, including the Statesmen, the Stamps, the Jordanaires, the Sunshine Boys. The best and most famous quartet, though, was the Blackwood Brothers. At that time, religious singing was very popular in many parts of this country.

The Blackwood Brothers had been formed in the early forties and when I first heard them they were comprised of James Blackwood, R.W. Blackwood, Bill Lyle and Bill Shaw. They sang such incredible harmonies, each member with a unique vocal range. They had the best voices, song arrangements, harmonies and the best pianist. They traveled around the country, appearing before large, enthusiastic crowds in churches or high school auditoriums, where they would usually appear on a bill with several other groups. I loved to see them sing, and even started taking voice lessons of my own, with aspirations of singing nearly as well as they did!

Around 1952, James Blackwood decided that they needed an airplane to better reach the three-hundred dates they played each year. Later that year, just after an acclaimed television appearance on the Ed Sullivan show, R.W. Blackwood (baritone) and Bill Lyle (bass) died in a crash while practicing landings in Mississippi. It was a real tragedy. James decided not to go forward, and what was perhaps the most talented singing group in America seemed finished.

A few years later, James reconstituted the quartet and it once again became the best around. But the era of gospel quartets soon started to wane. Years later, out of curiosity, I tracked down James Blackwood and found him living in Memphis, Tennessee. I rang him up and we had many telephone conversations over the next few years, and he was surprised to hear that I had always thought of him as a star. He told me stories of how a young Elvis Presley, who was a big fan of gospel music, had come to James to audition for a part in a junior quartet they were forming. He said that Elvis had a great voice but after the audition, James told him that he would be better off as a single performer. Elvis was crushed, but he remained friends with James though his life, and in later years told James that his assessment of his singing abilities had been right. Elvis maintained his love of gospel singing, and recorded many gospel songs. Elvis tried to copy their style in many of his songs and actually recorded an album with a quartet, the Jordanaires, which contained many of the songs that the Blackwoods made famous.

I ran across a recording of the Blackwoods in an oldie section of a record store in the 1990's. Around this time, James asked me to come to Memphis and visit him. I intended to go, but as happens with so many things, time got away from me and I didn't make the trip. I treasure my conversations with my childhood hero, who was in his eighties and still singing when he passed away in 2002. When I heard the news, I called his wife Mim, and told her what James had meant to me.

The death of James Blackwood was the end of an era. Singing in church was such fun and listening to the very best was a memory I carry with me even today. With the singing, church was such a happy place and the hours spent listening to the joyful voices and clapping remains one my happiest times.

CHAPTER 8

I liked school very much, and since most of the year was spent in the classroom, I have many happy memories of my school years. As much as I enjoyed summertime, the smell of September filled me with excited anticipation. My elementary schoolhouse was only a block from our house and I knew most of the children there. Our teachers were very dedicated and the quality of our education was superb. The focus was on the basics – reading, writing and arithmetic. Geography was taught in such a way that I still remember the capitals of most of the fifty states and of most of the countries of the world, and can find them on a map too. Today, too many children cannot tell you that information. Sadly, educational standards across our country are inconsistent, and even basic foundational skills like reading and writing are often lacking. I am glad I attended a school where everyone had to earn the grades they received and misbehavior got you nothing but a seat in the principal's office and certain punishment.

My principal in grade school was named Mrs. Trow – a stern name to match her stern expression, which scared me to death whenever it was aimed in my direction. I can distinctly recall the blouses she wore, with lace trim that went all the way up to her chin. Being sent to her office felt like a death march. While I never got spanked by Mrs. Trow, I did receive a dressing down that convinced me to do whatever was necessary to guarantee I would never make a return visit.

Even worse than the actual punishment was the note you had to bring home to your parents stating what had happened. You were expected to have it signed by your parents and return it to your teacher. When you had such a note in your pocket on your way home, it felt like you were carrying a ten-pound rock. The trip took twice as long as usual. I knew that my parents' reaction to the note would probably be a spanking, and the threat of this punishment-greater-than-the-crime was a pretty effective preventative measure. I think I was probably only seriously punished in this way about three times as a child, but the effects lasted years! I knew what the rules were and I tried very hard to never disappoint my parents.

There were some exceptions to my usual good behavior. One summer night, when I was eight or nine years old, my friends and I were running around the neighborhood and came upon a florist's warehouse that had been left open. We went in and excitedly looked through all the materials and fixtures. I guess kids are not much different than scavenger birds – like crows, we were most interested in the brightest, shiniest thing there. We swiped four big rolls of tin foil and brought it to a little cave we had dug in a vacant lot.

Now that we had all this tin foil, we needed to come up with a plan for its use. Although I knew we had done something wrong, I was terribly excited by this caper. We wadded the tin foil into balls that we could easily throw – now we needed a target. Someone proposed the idea of throwing the balls at passing cars. We all liked this plan, and decided it would be best if we waited until dark to put it into action. We spent the following day working extra hard to prepare our ammunition for the next evening. It was hard to sleep that night knowing I had helped to rob the florist. I was almost afraid to pray and ask for forgiveness. But my fear ran parallel with excitement over enacting the scheme we had cooked up.

The next night, we got together to plan our assault. We found a good spot to hide behind some bushes; when a car drove by we would jump up and pelt it with tinfoil balls. It worked tremendously, but the drivers of the cars we attacked weren't too happy with our game. Finally, one man screeched his car to a halt, jumped out and came after us! We scattered, and I must have gotten a slow start, because it was my shirt he grabbed first. While pulling my hair and slapping my face, he demanded to be told where I lived. I was scared silly and immediately led him to my house. He rang the doorbell and my mother came to the door. He explained what had happened, all the while yelling and jerking me around by my hair.

My mother simply stared at the man and told him to take his hands off of me. He hesitated a second and then, surprised, did as she ordered. He once again tried to convey my terrible deeds. Mother very calmly looked him in the eye and asked, "Do you know who Grady Harris is?" Grady Harris was not only the longtime County Sheriff, but was also, unfortunately for this man, a friend of my mother.

The man slowly said that he knew who Grady was. Mother said, "Since you have been wronged, I am going to call Mr. Harris and ask him to come over right away. I want him to know the harm my son has done. I also want him to know how you slapped him. And I want him to know that you were drinking and driving before you started abusing my boy".

The man paled, sputtering that he didn't think we needed to bring the Sheriff into the matter. Suddenly accommodating, he said he was willing to forget the whole thing, then ran back to his car and made a hasty departure.

Of course, that was not the end of it for me. Mother marched out to the willow tree right outside our back door and I was told to cut two limbs off of it, which she used to give me one of the few lashing of my life. The limbs weren't very big around but when you swung them they made a swishing sound. It hurt, but the worst part was the sound of the 'swish' just before it hit me. I made sure to try never again to do anything that would cause Mother to go back to the willow tree.

I recall Dad disciplining me once and crying as he did it. I think that these rare punishments were a good thing for me. Mother and Dad believed that discipline and hard work were as much a part of raising children as was love. I sure learned right from wrong because my parents spelled it out very clearly.

CHAPTER 9

Mother believed that all young men should have a job. I found my first one when I was nine years old. During long hot summers in Texas, I rode my bicycle all over town selling ice cream on a stick, popsicles and nibblets (fudgesicles). I was furnished with a padded insulated bag that fit in the basket of my bike and held about two dozen of each product, kept cold with dry ice. I would pedal down the streets calling out, "ice cream" as loud as I could. Kids would come out of nowhere, running after me with their money. When my wares were sold out, I would cycle back to the little back office factory and buy more ice cream to fill the bag again. I did this repeatedly from about nine in the morning to six in the evening, every day but Sunday. I would then ride home and give the profits to my mother. When I was eleven, the owner of the little company gave me a job in the factory, making the products and sweeping the floors of the ice cream store in the front part of the building. I remember that I worked every day except Sunday from about nine in the morning until seven at night. For this job, I received a fixed salary of nine dollars a week, paid to me every Saturday night. I gave this money to my mother as well, and felt very proud of what I was contributing to the family. It was tough work, and I learned a clear lesson about how hard it was to make money.

One time, my father took me to a farm where the cotton crop was being picked. I had never picked cotton before and when they offered me a quarter for each sack I filled with cotton to work with them, I was thrilled. I was given a cotton sack, about eight feet long. It was open at one end, with a strap that fit over my head and shoulder. I waded into the cotton fields, filled with stalks about two to three feet high. I slowly made my way down the row, bending and picking the cotton out of the hulls, and stuffing it into the sack I was pulling behind me. By the time I finished one row of cotton, the sack weighed about ten or fifteen pounds, but they wanted me to continue until

I had fifty pounds. When I finally accumulated that much, I dragged the sack to a scale, where it was weighed and I was paid my quarter. They asked me if I wanted to continue and I said no.

I had never been as tired as I was then, from picking those fifty pounds of cotton. My fingers were bleeding from hulls so sharp they would stick right into your fingers. My back hurt so badly from bending over that it took several days to recover. One thing became abundantly clear; I did not want to pick cotton ever again. It was a real education. I had greater respect for my parents because they had worked in the fields from sunup to sundown all of their adolescent lives and I guess they wanted me to understand more about their journey.

My next job was at the Piggly Wiggly supermarket. It entailed sacking groceries next to the cashier and then carrying the sacks to the customer's car or home, if it was within three city blocks of the store. Late in the evening, I would restock the shelves, remove the produce from the bins and carry it to the refrigerated storage unit, clean the bins and finally sweep and mop the store so it was ready to reopen the next morning. During the school year, I had to arrive at work at seven in the morning on Saturdays and I didn't leave until eleven at night. During the summer, I would work from seven in the morning until around eight at night each day except Sunday. There were no child labor laws at that time. I was paid thirty-five cents an hour and I went home exhausted every night. I remember sometimes being so tired that I would lie down and cry in a small park on the way home. I didn't want my parents to know how tired I was. On a good day, I could clear six dollars, including tips and after paying for my lunch. I would give the money to mother, keeping about a dollar a week for the movies and candy. (The movies only cost about ten cents for a double header and a hamburger cost five cents. You could actually get six hamburgers for twenty-five cents at the Doll House, which was a small burger shop not too far from our home.) I was rolling in dough but was sometimes too tired to enjoy it.

For two summers, starting in 1946, I got to attend a church-related summer camp in Salome Springs, Arkansas. A group of kids from my church rode almost four hundred miles in an old bus from Lubbock to Salome Springs, which was about fifty miles north of Fayetteville in the prettiest area of the Ozarks. It was heavily wooded and had several streams running through it. There were people from about thirteen different states and there must have been a hundred and fifty kids.

We attended fun church services at night; they involved a lot of laughter and games. During the day, there were competitions in badminton, croquet, soft ball, swimming, darts, races and horseshoes. Each contest was like being in the Olympics. Everybody wanted to win for their group and they tried as hard as they could. During the few slow times, several of us would go wading down the various creeks and streams looking for crawfish. It was a wonderland of water and wild life that is the stuff of so many boys' dreams. I made a lot of good friends that I explored with, ate with and competed against. I still think about those carefree days; I didn't know it would last such a short time!

Our whole family attended what is now referred to as a Pentecostal church. It was called the Foursquare Gospel Church, a denomination that had been formed by Aimee Semple McPherson by splitting off from the Church of God. McPherson was a dynamic and powerful speaker and the church she founded flourished and was worldwide in scope. Later, she became embroiled in controversy; she was accused of marital improprieties and of faking her own kidnapping. In 1944, I heard her speak at the tabernacle she had built in Los Angeles. I was greatly impressed by her presence. She appeared in a long, flowing white dress and robe. She was beautiful and spoke with such emotion that the audience was carried away with her message.

I had gone to Los Angeles with Reverend Westbrook and his family in their car. The Reverend was a minister in a church in the north part of Lubbock. We drove from Lubbock to the West Coast in two days. I stayed with my sister, who was already living in Los Angeles. I took the streetcar each day from her apartment in Hollywood to downtown Los Angeles and back again after the church meetings were over. At that time, you could ride the streetcar from Hollywood to Long Beach or to Santa Monica for about a dime. Incidentally, that was the first time I had seen streetcars, and I rode them all over town. This trip was also the first time I saw the ocean; the view seemed limitless and awe-inspiring.

Unfortunately those tracks were dug up and the streetcars were eliminated in the fifties. (There may have been a number of different societal and geographic reasons why Los Angeles abandoned its electric streetcars in favor of cars and buses, but the most sinister explanation involved a holding company funded by GM, Firestone and Standard Oil – all of whom were financially motivated to encourage car and bus travel – which bought out and dismantled streetcar systems in forty-five cities, including Los Angeles.) At the time, when gasoline was cheap, people did not realize the implications of this change, but in my opinion, it was a monumental mistake that I fear Los Angeles will never recover from.

Los Angeles was a beautiful city at that time. The air was clean and you had a constant, clear view of the San Gabriel Mountains, which were snow-topped much of the year. Wildflowers were growing in almost every direction you turned; the temperature was mild and the population was still of a manageable size. I loved roaming about the city and seeing things that I had only heard about. I got tickets to go and see various radio shows being made. Most all of the shows were live broadcasts, so mistakes were heard by everyone.

Back at home, my family usually went to church on Wednesday nights, sometimes on Friday nights and again on Sunday. On the Sabbath, we attended Sunday school, twelve o'clock services and then night services. In addition, Mother read me two or more chapters from the bible every night before bed until I was thirteen. I can tell you I knew the bible almost by heart. The only difference between our church and most of the others I have attended was simply a matter of noise and exuberance. We sang lots of songs accompanied by musical instruments and church was a happy place. It was one of the most positive experiences of my life and it helped me through some very low and hard periods. I don't go to church much anymore, but all the religious teachings of my life have stayed with me. I hope that I have lived my life, for the most part, in a manner so that my parents and God would be pleased.

I remember when my mother heard that Oral Roberts was going to give a sermon in Amarillo. Oral Roberts was well-known as an excellent preacher who often would pray with an individual who was sick to be healed. When the day arrived, Dad drove mother and me to Amarillo, which was about a hundred miles north of our home. The service was conducted in the biggest tent I'd ever seen. It held around five thousand people and was supported and lit by forty or fifty aluminum light standards, each of which was about four to five feet across and forty feet high.

The night we attended, the tent was full and there were people overflowing outside to hear the service. The evening had a joyful tone to it, with lots of singing and performances before Oral Roberts stood up to speak. It had started to rain outside and there was quite a bit of lightning. As he began his sermon, there was a loud swishing noise. I watched as Roberts was suddenly knocked to the ground. The tent rose and then the standards began to fall and the whole place went black. My Dad tried to hold the collapsed tent up to keep people from suffocating, but as he tired and let it rest on his head, he was pelted by marble-sized hail, which raised knots all over his head. Mother, Dad and I started crawling to the edge of the tent to try to get out from under it. There was chaos. You could hear people crying and moaning. We finally got to the edge of the tent and ran to our car. We were soaked and each of us had some bumps and bruises from the hail. We sat there for quite some time, in shock but very thankful we had escaped.

A miracle had occurred that night. Oral Roberts had been knocked down by a jolt of electricity, but it didn't kill him. The tent had been struck by a tornado and those enormous light standards, weighing hundreds of pounds, fell on a packed house. Yet, of the five-thousand people in attendance that night, not one had been seriously injured. The chairs in the tent must have collectively kept the poles from crushing the audience. My mother said that God had protected the audience that night. That sounds good enough for me.

CHAPTER 10

In 1947, Texas City had an explosion that killed about 1700 people. Two ships filled with chemicals entered the harbor and something started a chain reaction. The blast destroyed Texas City. Ten miles away, people in Galveston were dropped to their knees by the blast. Windows were shattered forty miles away in Houston. People felt the concussion two hundred fifty miles away in Louisiana. I remember listening to all the terrible details on the radio; everyone was in shock. It was one of the worst industrial disasters in our country's history. The federal government did not replace anyone's home.

JPL, 1947

It was also the year I started learning to drive. Dad took me with him on one of his trips to a farm or ranch that had a problem, and decided on the way home that it was about time for me to start my driving education. We were way out in the country and I guess he figured nothing I could do there would jeopardize other people. That was probably true, but I sure scared the devil out of Dad! He let me drive down a peaceful farm road, and told me to turn left at the next intersection. What he didn't tell me was that I was going much too fast for the turn. Dad began to scream for me to slow down, but of course it was too late. I tried to brake, but the car began to skid and I ended up about a foot from a cotton gin. Dad just sat there for a while to gather himself and regain his composure. He then came around the car and got behind the wheel. Nothing was said about me learning to drive again for several months.

I finally finished my driving education in 1949, in a '46 Studebaker, and was awarded my driver's license that year at the ripe old age of thirteen. Part of the reason I was given a drivers license at such a young age was that my mother had fallen and broken her hip and she had a hard time walking. That said, I can't remember ever driving my mother anywhere, and besides, we had only one car.

Mother had never learned to drive. Dad loved to tell the story about the time Mother wanted to learn, and asked him several times to teach her. He put her in the driver's seat of the car they had at that time; the accelerator was on a short handle on the steering shaft and the brake was on a handle in the middle of the car between the seats. Mother got behind the wheel and Dad went to crank the engine to start it. When the car started off, Mother drove off on her own and went around the block. And around the block. And around the block... Dad was up on the front porch and every time Mother came by, they would wave to each other. After a while, Mom began to shout as she passed the house, but Dad would just wave at her. Pretty soon, Mom was screaming, but still, Dad just waved. The car finally stopped when it ran out of gas. Mother never asked to learn how drive after that episode. I'm not sure I blame her.

It was also in 1947 that Dad and Mom decided that the three of us should take a driving trip together through the West. I was familiar with the various states in the US and knew the capital of each. Geography was a big subject in school; we used to draw maps of each state, putting the capital in the right location. I also had learned the primary attributes of each state, including minerals and agricultural specialty, plus any special features such as National Parks. So I was real excited about seeing some of those states.

Gasoline was only about thirteen cents a gallon and we could share a single motel room if I slept on a cot-sized blow-up pad on the floor. We bought prepared foods along the way to cut down on eating costs. First we went to

Arizona to visit my Uncle Raymond, Dad's younger brother. Raymond and his clan had settled in the little town of Sanders, which consisted of post office, a diner, a curio shop and the two houses where Uncle Raymond's family lived. Raymond owned the whole town, and they ran the diner and curio shop. Raymond traded with local Native Americans for jewelry to sell in his shop. It was a sparse living and I think his children got the heck out of there as soon as they could get away. Raymond, however, lived the rest of his life in Sanders.

Our next stop was the Grand Canyon. The Grand Canyon is awe-inspiring whether you've seen it once or many times, but it was the very first time any of us had seen that magnificent sight. It's hard to imagine the erosion of rock that took so many millions of years creating such a beautiful sight. My parents especially loved seeing a part of the country where they had never been before.

We continued across the Mojave Desert, which was a bit of a nerve-wracking adventure! The route still had remnants of the old wooden road that had been used to travel west before paved roads were built. This consisted of two 2" by 12" boards laid on top of the sand for each tire to ride on, and every quarter-mile or so there would be a pullout so one car could get past another. At that time, if you met another car on the road, one of the vehicles had to back up to the nearest pullout. Even at the time we drove across the desert, motorists had to drape bags of water all over the front of the car to be used as drinking water and as an emergency supply in case the radiator overheated from the terrible heat, which was a common occurrence.

There was no air conditioning in cars at that time, and it seemed to me as though we might melt. I just prayed we would have enough water to make it across. There were no emergency vehicles to bail you out. When we finally reached the far side of the desert, we were all soaking wet from perspiration and thankful our luck had held. As we drive across the desert today on modern highways, it is easy to forget the dread and anxiety of doing so during the first half of the last century. I wish everyone could see that old board highway and remember the courage that a great many Americans exhibited when they traveled west.

Our next leg took us up through the central valley of California. We passed through the agricultural centers that stretched from Bakersfield up through Fresno and Sacramento and then headed up into the Sierra Nevada Mountains. We went to Yosemite National Park, in the central part of the state, and then on to Mount Shasta in Northern California. The scenery was breathtaking. I recall the beauty of Yosemite Park and all the mountains, streams and wilderness associated with that mountain area. We slept in a cabin on the floor of Yosemite Valley. The smell of the wood-burning fires, the sound of the waterfalls and the aroma of the pines in the morning are unforgettable. We built our own fire to cook on and the food was extra delicious. There were no crowds and the beauty and serenity of the area was something we had never seen before. We got a sense of what John Muir must have felt as he first glimpsed the spectacular Yosemite Valley. From there, we traveled north toward Oregon, through the mountains around Dunsmuir and some of the most picturesque scenery in America.

We drove along the Oregon coastline, through beautiful small seaside villages like Coos Bay, Florence, Coquille and Bandon. The countryside was lovely and the coastal waters in Oregon have very dramatic features, with cliffs rising sharply up from the surf. Dad had always liked Langlois cheese, a blue cheese with a very strong taste and distinctive smell, somewhat similar to Limburger cheese. We made a point to go through Langlois, Oregon and visit the facility where it was made. Dad bought some for the trip and Mother and I made him eat it away from the two of us! Unfortunately, the Langlois facility burned to the ground a few months after our visit and, to my knowledge, the cheese was never produced again.

We drove through parts of Washington, southern Idaho, part of Montana and down to Yellowstone National Park in Wyoming. Each area was very special. From there, we went through Colorado and finally back home. Although we saw so many gorgeous sights – majestic mountains, shimmering streams, the endless expanse of the Pacific Ocean – by far the most meaningful memory for me is of the three of us spending such a long stretch of uninterrupted time together. We had a great time exploring parts of the country we had never seen, but the love we had between us was something I will remember and cherish the rest of my life. Before long, I would leave home, and the three of us would never spend as much time together again for the rest of my parent's lives. Of course, in retrospect, I wish I had spent more time with my parents, but when you're young there are so many things that seemingly can't wait. Everyone needs to take the time to appreciate their life and embrace the people who are an important part of it.

CHAPTER 11

My sister Jeanetta was five years older than me, which is a large gap when you are still young. I don't remember much about her from my early years. She didn't have much use for a younger brother and we didn't have a relationship until I was about thirteen years old and she was eighteen. I do remember Mother and Dad talking about her. She was a rebel and they didn't know how to deal with that. Mind you, she lived in a house that did not allow dancing, drinking or carousing! My parents, particularly my mother, considered that sort of thing sinful. When Jeanetta became a teenager, all of her friends were having a lot more fun than she was; she was chomping at the bit and Mother kept trying to rein her in.

Jeanetta was a very pretty and very bright girl. She had brown hair, brown eyes and a petite figure. She was an excellent student and was well liked by her classmates. She became involved in dramatics, and one year won the leading role in the high school play, "Smiling Through" and that increased her popularity. She was obviously a fine actress and began to compete in one-act play competition and in debating. She won all the awards a young girl could garner.

Still she seemed unhappy. I remember when our parents bought her a new bedroom suite for her room; it didn't seem to help. Dad and I went by train to Detroit where Tex was working at Ford Motor Co. and we drove back a new 1946 Ford coupe for Jeanetta. She was thrilled with the car but still felt hemmed in and she spent as much time as possible away from home. Mother didn't know what to do.

Then came the crusher. She and a high school boyfriend got married. I don't know whether she was old enough to marry, but they told Mother and Dad they were. My parents were really hurt; they felt they had tried everything they could do, to no avail. Mom and Dad borrowed some money and bought a small house so Jeanetta and her new husband would have a place to live.

The marriage was rocky from the start, with lots of fights between the newlyweds. I don't know the details because I was only about eleven years old at that time, but I do know that Jeanetta would come over to the house to describe the horrid things that were happening and just bawl. Finally after only a few weeks, she moved back home and a divorce was obtained. Of course, now she was regarded as a "scarlet woman", which was both good and bad. Her friend and classmates thought of her as more mature and experienced but their parents certainly didn't want their own darlings to follow such a terrible example.

I think she had one more year of high school after that and once she had graduated, she started thinking about escaping. She went to Texas Tech for a little while, where she participated in drama classes and performed one act plays in intercollegiate competition, which she regularly won. She was frequently told what a wonderful actress she was and that she should do something with that talent, and she decided to head to Los Angeles. She talked Tex into letting her live with his family while she went to UCLA. I really think that my parents were relieved when she left; life at the house got much quieter again!

CHAPTER 12

As religious as Mother was, she felt it was important for me to be educated in a Christian environment. She did not think the public schools were a proper place for a young man to learn, so when she read about a boarding school in Anaheim, California that was run by a minister and his wife that was inexpensive, academically ambitious and taught religious principles, she became convinced that I should go there. I thought it sounded like fun, and with my brother and sister in Los Angeles, my mother felt comfortable enough to send me across the country to California.

In 1949, at the age of thirteen, I traveled to California, was picked up at Union Station in Los Angeles and driven to Anaheim. It seemed to take forever to get there. There were no freeways and we had to take surface streets; a trip that would take less than an hour today took three hours at best. Once we arrived at the school, I was shown to the room that I would share with about ten other boys. As I became acquainted with the other students, I realized that they were either orphans, abandoned children or boys who had been in reform school. One of the other boys in the school was someone I knew from my home town. He was not a bad kid, but had come from a dysfunctional family and really just wanted some attention. The first night I was there a young boy in our room wet his bed and was summarily spanked with a round stick about four feet long. The minister's wife took care of the punishment, and she absolutely terrified me.

The school was nothing like my mother had imagined. Instead of an enlightened, academic haven, it was more like something out of a Charles Dickens novel. Yet I never told my parents anything about the times I was beaten with a rod or the verbal abuse I learned to handle. I reasoned that it would have upset my mother to hear about this, and I sure didn't want that. Instead, I internalized a lesson about how lucky I was to have a family to return to. I felt most sorry for the other kids at the school. They had no choice in their lives. Either their parents didn't want them around, or else they simply had no parents. Every night someone in our room could be heard crying. They were lonely, sad and no one seemed to care.

Classes were small, which made the studies personal and concentrated, but the schoolwork itself was pretty basic. In addition to classroom activities, I was assigned two chores. The first was to get up and go out to the barn each morning at five o'clock to milk a goat. It always seemed to be cold that early in the morning, and the goat wasn't too pleased to see me either. It's not easy to milk a goat; you have to get behind them and reach between their hind legs in order to reach the udder to start milking, hoping they don't start moving around, putting their legs in the bucket. The second chore was to cook lunch on Sundays for about thirty people. The menu was always the same. I cooked meatloaf in large square pans, mashed potatoes, carrots, green beans from a can, and for dessert, a cake in large pans with cream-colored frosting. It was a good meal and everyone liked it. I decided during this year that I would never be a chef or raise livestock if I could possibly help it.

There was a very pretty girl of about fifteen at school. As I recall, she was physically very well developed. I was only thirteen years old, with absolutely zero experience with the opposite sex. In fact, I'm pretty sure I had never even touched a girl in my whole life. For some reason, this girl decided that I was a good target for her display of affection and she started following me around, popping up in the most remote locations and attempting to kiss and hug me. If the same thing had happened to me a couple of years later, I'm sure I would have enjoyed it, but at the time, I was terrified and did everything I could to avoid her. That girl must have thought I was from Mars.

One experience I had while at the school was a very positive one for me and would come in handy later. Another boy and I began singing as a duet in church services. We were pretty good and were invited, twice, to sing on the ABC radio network during a program called, "The Old Fashioned Revival Hour" that was broadcast from Long Beach, California every Sunday morning. It was my first national broadcast, and it lit a fire inside me for performing.

I was there for one long year, and when I went home, I was more grateful than ever to have one. During my summer break, I told Mother that I wanted to continue my schooling by correspondence and I showed her some materials on a school that did just that. Thankfully, she agreed. Several years later, I read a story in the newspaper about the minister's wife from the school in Anaheim; she was convicted of burning a young boy's arm as punishment for playing with matches and was sentenced to serve several years in prison. The orphaned children in her care were placed in other facilities. I still wonder what became of their lives.

In retrospect, I wish my parents had not sent me to that school. I think it set my education back in a way that affected me for years to come. That said, however, I try not to see this episode as a negative in my life; I try to look at it as a building block. All of us are simply the result of the whole of our life experiences. We are made stronger by adversity and wiser by good times. There were many times in my life when it seemed as though everything was falling apart, but my experiences kept me focused and aware that all things eventually change.

PART THREE

HEADING WEST

CHAPTER 13

In 1950, before my fourteenth birthday and with my parents' blessings, I dropped out of school and left home. It now sounds like a tender age for a boy to venture into the world, but at that time it was a more common occurrence; people tended to leave home, get married and have children earlier than they do today. In addition, I had already been away from home for a year at school, which I'm sure made the transition easier for both my parents and me. There were no good jobs for young teens in Lubbock and I had it in my head to try my luck out West. I had been to California twice already, and the idea of plunging into the cloud of legends and myths that surrounded Hollywood appealed to my sense of adventure. Jeanetta, an aspiring actress, was already living in Los Angeles, and she would be able to keep a watchful eye on me.

Before leaving home, my mother told me that Mrs. Hardwick, a family friend who was especially close to mother, wanted to see me. I wasn't sure what she wanted to tell me, and I don't think mother did either. We arrived at Mrs. Hardwick's house and she hugged me warmly and said how much she would miss me. She then looked me in the eye and said, "John, do you know that there are men in the world who like young boys and that you must be careful to stay away from them?" Well, that surprised me, and all I could say was a polite "Yes, ma'am, I do and I will be very careful".

When mother and I returned home, she took me into her bedroom and looked at me very strangely. She gingerly asked me what Mrs. Hardwick was talking about: why would men like young boys and what exactly did they do to them? I basically knew what Mrs. Hardwick had been alluding to, but it certainly wasn't something I had ever encountered, nor expected to. At that time, when such topics were rarely discussed, let alone featured on the evening news, I was at a loss as to how to answer my mother. I hemmed and hawed and tried to avoid answering the question, but she persisted. I finally explained Mrs. Hardwick's warning in a way that was factual but not terribly descriptive. To this day, I count this as one of the more uncomfortable corners I have been in!

With much enthusiasm and few expectations, I arrived in Los Angeles. Jeanetta had been living there for a year and a half, studying and trying to find work as an actress. She was very talented and had won many accolades for her work in stage productions in high school and college. Like so many young women from all over the world, she had ended up in Hollywood, and found it a tough, competitive world. While studying her craft at UCLA and the Geller Workshop, she auditioned for parts in motion pictures, radio show and television. She also worked at CBS in Hollywood as a receptionist, distributing tickets for the public to see radio and television shows. The tickets were free because the network needed audiences for their productions, which were all broadcast live.

With Jeanetta's help, I found work as at usher at CBS. The salary wasn't much, but it allowed me to pay my expenses. I stayed with my sister for a while before moving in with her boyfriend, who had an apartment on Gower Street just off Sunset Boulevard. He was also an usher at CBS, working while attending the pre-law program at UCLA. He became fascinated with a drama class he was taking from James Whitmore and decided to change his major from pre-law to dramatic arts. Shortly after his switch to drama, he became smitten by an actress he had met in an acting class and broke up with Jeanetta. The split was a very traumatic and emotional for both of them, with a physical scuffle that got out of hand, and much drama.

Jeanetta and James Dean, 1951

Jeanetta's ex-boyfriend was named James Dean, but we had called him Jim. Jim's new flame was Pier Angeli, who eventually became a famous actress and dumped Jim to marry a singer named Vic Damone.

Jim had come from a small town in Indiana and I had liked him a great deal. Jeanetta, Jim and I had spent a lot of time together. We laughed a lot, went to movies and dreamed of things to come. When I knew him, he hadn't been in Hollywood long and didn't quite know what he wanted to do. I think he was a bit lonely, and the two of us goofed around a lot. Sometimes we would go to the park for a picnic, or simply drive around town and talk. He bought me a ukulele and I learned to play a little bit. We would sing old barbershop quartet songs while I played. Jim liked to draw and I still have two pictures that he gave to me. I thought he showed a lot of talent, enough that he probably could have been a professional artist if he had chosen to pursue it.

James Dean in high school. A photo he gave to Jeanette.

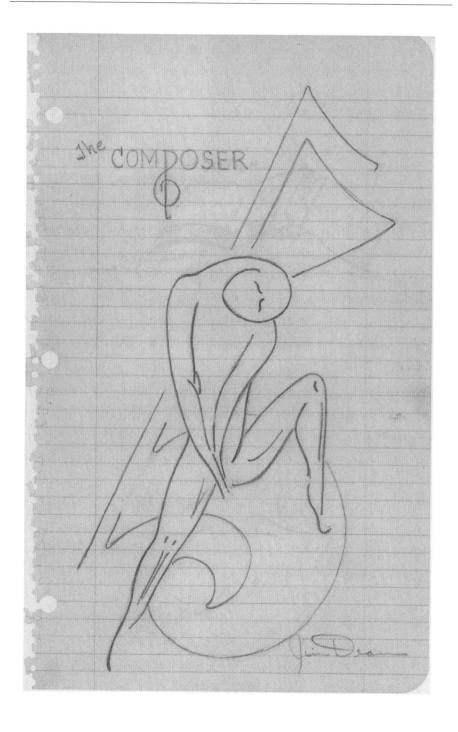

Two sketches James Dean gave to Jeanette

A recently published book contends that Jim was gay. I must put my two cents in here, because I never saw a man who liked women more than Jim. In my opinion, the author of the book is an inventor of facts. He has written a number of items about Jim Dean that I know are false. When he first decided to write a book about James Dean, he got in touch with Jeanetta and asked if he could borrow the many pictures that she had taken of him so that he could include them in his book. She unfortunately sent them to him and he subsequently refused to return them, and claimed that they were his pictures. Quite a guy! I would not give any credit to his recollection of events. Whatever Jim became I can't say, but I'm more than a little skeptical about these stories, and suspect that they are little more than sensationalism.

Not long after Jim's breakup with Jeanetta, he decided to try his luck in New York. He attended the prestigious Actor's Studio, which was run by Lee Strasberg. His first movie role was the lead in "East of Eden", for which he won the Oscar for Best Actor. Jeanetta and I only saw him one last time. We were invited to the premiere of "East of Eden". Jim sat about four rows in front of us. I told Jeanetta that we should go down and say hello to him. She looked at me with tears in her eyes and said, "No, we are in his past. We are unimportant to him now. We need to let him enjoy his fame and future. We will applaud his success and then move on". We never saw him again. He made only two more movies before he was killed in an automobile crash at the age of twenty-five.

I thoroughly enjoyed my time working as an usher at CBS. Ushers at the networks did not actually seat the audience; instead, we directed them to the seating areas after making sure they had tickets for the performance. After that, we stood near the stage, usually during and after a broadcast to discourage the audience from coming down to the stage area. At that time in Hollywood, there were very few television shows. Radio was still king, and many shows were broadcast live from Hollywood. My world consisted mainly of the area bounded by Sunset and Hollywood Boulevards and Vine and Gower Streets, where most of the shows were done. I got to spend my days in close proximity to many radio and movie stars I had only heard about, listened to on the radio or seen in films. Hollywood was a pretty small environment in those days and if you worked in some form of the business you would run into most of the current stars. I didn't have any particular ambitions in show business; I was just happy to have new experiences and meet interesting people. If I had been older, I might not have been able to meet as many people as I did. As today, well-known people are leery of those who may want something from them, but because I was only fourteen years old, I was perceived as 'safe' and my friendliness and curiosity got me a long way!

One of the first shows I went to was the Kraft Music Hall, starring Bing Crosby. I was positioned up front near the stage as the announcer introduced Bing Crosby. As I stood there waiting, a relatively short man with a bald head and prominent ears walked out. I didn't recognize him. Then he opened his mouth and began to sing Bing's theme song, "When the Blue of the Night Meets the Gold of the Day". I was floored. It was Bing! I felt like I had glimpsed a private view of the man that the general public never saw, and once he started to sing, everything changed. He had the most mellow voice and, after listening to him on the radio all those years, it was even more impressive to see firsthand how relaxed he was at the microphone. Of course, he had been a star for about fifteen years by the time I saw him.

I was privileged to have the opportunity to see Dean Martin and Jerry Lewis at the top of their popularity, making their first television shows. I also got to meet Betty Hutton, Jack Benny, Bob Hope, George Burns, Gracie Allen and many others, and it was great fun to watch them work.

I only worked on programs produced by CBS. One show I worked on was not quite as much fun for me. Gene Autry had a weekly broadcast called "Melody Ranch". He had a habit of arriving a little bit tipsy and on my first day he spotted me on the stage and went ballistic. He started cursing and yelling and demanded that I leave immediately. I disappeared from view and the producer tried to calm him down, telling him that I was an usher working for the show. Autry settled down and started rehearsal, and the next time he saw me he practically ignored me. Still, I can tell you the whole episode scared me half to death and I never got near enough to him again to risk a repeat performance.

Other shows I worked on or was present at were "Fibber McGee and Molly", "Amos and Andy", "Your Hit Parade" and "The Red Skelton Show". Red Skelton was one of the leading comedians of the '40's and '50's. From time to time he would let the word out that he was going to have a special show at (I believe) the Pantages Theater. The tickets were free, but they were a hot item; everyone wanted to attend. Skelton would take the stage with a script about six to eight inches thick. Each page had a number of jokes or a comic situation on it. He would go through each page and if the audience laughed he would keep the page; if they didn't laugh he would wad up the page and throw in at the audience. I can truthfully say that I have never laughed so much as I did during these special shows. Some of the jokes were off color and couldn't have been used on the air in any case. Skelton was primarily a character comedian, and I never saw him do standup except on those evenings when he tested his material.

One of the radio shows broadcast from CBS was "Suspense", an adventure episode that starring Joan Crawford and Jeff Chandler. Jeff was an acquaintance of mine and one night he invited me to sit in on the broadcast. "Suspense" was usually a dramatic program with lots of twists and turns. That night the script was excellent and it was incredibly entertaining to watch Jeff and Joan Crawford seated in front of the microphones, performing the script while the sound man and the orchestra simultaneously created the sounds and music that set the mood for the show. After the show, Jeff introduced me to Crawford. She was already considered one of the top dramatic actresses in Hollywood, and had a reputation of being very temperamental and difficult to work with. Funnily enough, I probably have never met a nicer, sweeter person. She gave me a big hug and we talked for quite a while. She invited me to visit her on a movie set, but unfortunately, I never took her up on the offer.

I also used to visit Jeff Chandler at another radio show he worked on, this one a comedy called "Our Miss Brooks", which also starred Eve Arden and Richard Crenna. All three actors would eventually become successful in both film and television. Eve Arden would appear in many movies over the years and was known as a great comedienne. Richard Crenna starred in several television series and became a movie star. Jeff Chandler had started out in radio and had a very deep resonant voice that attracted the attention of Hollywood. He was a handsome man of about twenty-six when I first met him. He had prematurely grey hair, a wonderful family and a winning personality. For some reason, probably because I was young and no threat to anyone, we became friends. We used to go eat together sometimes after the show and he would always give me a ride home. He was a very kind man with great ambitions, who would later star in a number of films, but his career was tragically cut short when he was thirty-six. When he complained of discomfort, his wife took him to a hospital in Santa Monica for tests. During the tests he had an aneurism and died. There was never any explanation for his death and his wife ended up suing the hospital for negligence and winning a large settlement. Of course that didn't bring Jeff back. I always felt that it was a needless loss of a fine man and a talented performer.

By and large, this period was a time of fun and excitement for me. I got to explore the world, meet interesting people, and spend time with Jeanetta. Just as Jeanetta looked out for me, we had people who sometimes looked out for us. One was Dutch Shankle, an acquaintance of my brother from the war years. Dutch had retired from the military before World War Two, but was recalled after Pearl Harbor. One of his first tasks was to open Love Field in Dallas, which functioned as an Army base throughout the war. We called him "Colonel" because that was his rank in the Army. He had pilot license number twenty-one, because he had been twenty-first in line when they handed them out. He knew all the Army Air Corp Generals during the war because most of them had reported to Dutch at various times in the past. He was a colorful character and had married three times, in each instance to a wealthy woman. One time, I told him I thought he was awfully smart to marry only rich women. He replied that it wasn't all that great, because not one of his wives ever forgot to remind him whose money it was, and always prevented him from getting his hands on any of it. Dutch was a good friend to Jeanetta and me, and used to take us to shows around Los Angeles.

One memorable night, he took us to Olympic Arena to hear a music show with Jimmy and Tommy Dorsey's orchestras and several singers, one of which was Frankie Laine. Laine was a top star with such hit songs as

"High Noon", "Jezebel" and "Mule Train", among many others. He had been a jazz singer, but crossed over to the popular genre during the late 40's and early 50's. It was a wonderful evening. About twenty-five years later, I had the opportunity the see Frankie Laine again. This time he was in his sixties, with gray hair and beard, and was much smaller than I remembered. He performed in a small room to an audience of about twenty-five people, which was a far cry from the several thousand cheering fans that had attended the Olympic Arena show. This time, his voice wasn't as strong, but he still had terrific style. After the show, I approached him and told him how I had seen him perform so may years earlier; he told me he remembered the show I had seen. Then he just smiled and said that was a long time ago. Indeed it was.

In the 1950's, as today, Hollywood was an exciting place, but for all the famous people I encountered, there were many more young attractive people on the sidelines, waiting for their big break in show business. Few succeeded and I'm sure it was hard returning back to a small hometown and admitting defeat. Jeanetta found some work as an actress, including a small part in the movie, "So Big", which starred a friend of hers from UCLA named Steve Forrest and Jane Wyman. She also won a regular part on the weekly hit radio show called "Life with Luigi", starring J. Carrol Naish, but when it became public that Naish was being investigated by the House Un-American Activities Committee, Jeanetta became a victim of the politics of the time and had to leave the show. Tex was with Hughes Aircraft and as that company was a large defense contractor, it would not have been good if it became news that she was associated with Naish. She was offered and encouraged to take a job as a receptionist at Hughes Aircraft, but it wasn't what she wanted. Unfortunately, she never found the larger success she sought as an actress, but later found a place behind the cameras, and became a successful and sought-after script supervisor. As for me, I think I was able to enjoy it all because I was not striving to get into 'the business'. What I remember most about all the entertainment personalities I met were that for the most part they came across as genuine individuals who were never snooty or unkind to me. As my Dad always said, they put their pants on one leg at a time just like everyone else. I was not star struck or in awe of the big stars. In a lot of cases, I learned, it wasn't always the talent you had that counted; sometimes it was who you knew. One thing I knew was that I wanted to get an education, and that my time in Hollywood was only temporary. Other things awaited me.

CHAPTER 14

In 1952, I went back home to Lubbock to work and study. My interest in radio had been piqued, and I found a job as a record librarian at a local radio station. It was interesting to me and I jumped into the project of devising a catalog system to organize all of the station's phonograph records. At that time, records came in two sizes and three speeds: 33 1/3 rpm (the speed used for full-sized albums), 45 rpm (for singles on a small record), and 78 rpm (for singles on a large record). It might sound like that would be fairly simple to organize, but the disk jockeys wanted to be able to pull their entire program quickly before they went on the air, so every record had to be cross indexed by artist, by size and by song. I embraced and completed that project, and along the way was given the opportunity to try my radio broadcasting skills with some limited airtime. On the weekends, I did the station breaks and introduced the upcoming programs. I was scared at first, but with some practice it became second nature, and I was able to really enjoy myself.

When the radio job ended, I got a job at a local television station as a boom operator. This entailed handling the boom microphone during live telecasts and helping change the set over in between programs. I had to make sure the boom was in the right location, close enough to clearly pick up sound and dialogue but never so close that it would be seen on camera or even cast a shadow that could be seen on camera. I worked on some great musical shows, interview programs and of course newscasts. I was there when they interviewed Dizzy Dean, a Hall of Fame pitcher and many singers, actors and other celebrities of the time.

I remember the time I heard that they would be interviewing two of my football heroes, Doak Walker and Bobby Layne, who had led the Detroit Lions to a National Football League championship. I had been following both their careers since college – Doak Walker was a great football player at

SMU, where he had been named All-American three years in a row and won the Heisman Trophy, the award given to the best college player in the country. Bobby Layne had played at the University of Texas and had also been named an All-American. It was so exciting to see and meet these two men; this was the kind of work that I would have paid to do! Years later, when I met Doak's daughter, I told her about that day and how surprised I had been to hear her father's voice. Unlike Bobby who had a deep bass voice, Doak had a very high soprano. She laughed and said that his voice always surprised everyone.

During this time, I was also taking correspondence courses from a place called the American Correspondence School. After work each day, I would come home and study course materials covering all the general topics one would take in a regular high school. I remember that the lessons were very thorough, involving a lot of reading and essay writing. Tests were taken on the honor system, which meant I couldn't look at the textbooks while taking the exams. Surprisingly, I felt I learned quite a lot. I finished the first two years of high school this way. Pursuing my high school degree in a classroom might have been better, and I did miss the contact with other students, but I needed to work, so this was the best option for me at the time.

At this point, I started looking for a school that would accept my home study and allow me to start in the junior year of high school. Although my mother only had a third-grade education and didn't put much importance in where I chose to study, she still thought it was important for me to get my diploma, and we found out about a school in Oregon that would give me credit for my correspondence work. It was called Canyonville Bible Academy; the school was not accredited by the State of Oregon but Mother thought it would be a good atmosphere for my development, so in 1953, I went off to Canyonville, Oregon, hoping it would be a better experience than the last time I went off to school! The Academy let me take a series of tests that measured my academic level, and allowed me to enter as a high school junior.

Now Canyonville was not a thriving town. Economically, it revolved around the lumber industry, with sawmills and cutting operations providing the main employment opportunities. But it was a solid community of people, many of Scandinavian heritage, and the school turned out to be a jewel.

The teaching and the level of students were above average. The hundred or so students came largely from California, Washington and Oregon, and I found most of them to be good people from very interesting backgrounds. The classes were small and the material concentrated; you had to work hard to keep up. There were several church services a week but they were fun. I worked at several chores to pay for my tuition, room and board.

I immediately made a number of friends, some of whom lasted for many years. One fellow, Duane Spellman, was a fine athlete from Borger, Texas. We both started on the varsity basketball team. Playing basketball at Canyonville was quite an experience. We had no coach and no gymnasium, so all of our games were "away" games. Duane and I played guard; Bill Seizer, from Sacramento, played forward; a great fellow from Medford played the other forward and we had a really good player who was about 6'8" that played center. Our opponents were the local high schools in Days Creek, Tiller, Riddle, Glendale, Wolf Creek, Gold Hill, Union Creek, Camas Valley and most likely others I can no longer recall. We would come up with our own plays, but they weren't very good and neither was our team. Since we only played away, the referees were always from the opposing school, and they tended to be prejudiced against us. We decided that if we were going to be called for fouls in every instance we should make them count. The games sometimes got pretty rough but we had a lot of fun. The one thing we had going for us was that most of our competition was even worse than we were! We won about half our games and with the cards stacked against us, that was a good record.

I also got very involved in the school drama program, which staged about four productions – usually two dramas and two comedies – each year. I made the happy discovery that I enjoyed and was very good at acting. I was cast as the lead in every production during the time I was at the school. Canyonville had a reputation of putting on good shows, and the school's productions played all over central Oregon. We would first open a play at the Canyonville High School auditorium, which was packed with about a thousand people each night. Then, we might take the play to Myrtle Creek, Winston, Myrtle Point, Coquille, Coos Bay, Reedsport and maybe even

Roseburg, playing one performance in each of the various towns, always to a full house. Not much entertainment came to these small- and medium-sized towns, so we were it, and the shows were very popular. We were written up in all the community papers.

In retrospect, I realize it was theater on a fairly small scale, but it felt like big stuff to me. I loved to perform and hatched dreams of becoming a successful actor. Acting on the stage is a tightrope act – it can bring either instant gratification or despair. Luckily I got the gratification. It was always thrilling to be embraced by an appreciative audience, and I loved being able to pretend. Sometimes when I had moments of sadness or loneliness later in my life, I would recall the applause and the elation I felt at those times; it helped raise me above the pain and gave me a moment of joy.

During this time, I also got to exercise my love of singing when I helped form a quartet we called "The King's Messengers". I sang baritone. A girl named Modesta sang tenor; she had a very good voice and was also an accomplished pianist. I can't recall the name of the bass singer or the lead singer, although I do recall that the lead singer had grown up in China; his father had been the minister in Kunming, the town where the Flying Tigers were based, and had been portrayed in the book and the movie entitled "God Is My Co-Pilot".

The King's Messengers at graduation

His stories of life in China during the Second World War were fascinating and scary, because the Flying Tigers had been the only line of resistance against the Japanese. In any case, he had a beautiful voice with a lot of range. My background in gospel singing came in handy and with practice we began to sing some spectacular harmonies. We appeared in churches in towns around the region and when we arrived, we were usually expected to sing on the local radio station. Often, there would be a potluck dinner beforehand, most often at the church, and then we would perform in the evening. People were so kind to us and we generally had a full house when we sang. I was even asked for my autograph by the young kids who come to hear us! It was fun and exciting and we were in demand during my time at the school. My time at Canyonville was terrific all around, and made up for – or at least balanced – my previous, ill-fated boarding school experience!

While in Oregon, I also had the opportunity to attend a number of music concerts by artists that I might not have otherwise been exposed to. The nearby town of Medford, one of the larger cities in the state, hosted a variety of acts. One time, I attended a concert featuring Stuart Hamblin. Stuart was a man of some note in the 1950's. He had run for President in the 1952 election (and lost to Dwight Eisenhower). He had written several hit songs and was also a singer. Our quartet used to sing one of his best-known songs, "It Is No Secret". He owned racehorses and was a successful businessman. After he performed in Medford, three of us were invited to go out for dinner with him, and it was a most entertaining evening. I remember a story he told us about a racehorse he owned and loved. He spent a lot of time with the horse and apparently they developed a close bond. About three-quarters of the way through a race at the Santa Anita racetrack, the horse broke a front leg, but continued to run on three legs, dragging the broken one, and ended up winning the race, even though it had to be put down afterwards. Stuart had tears in his eyes as he described the scene. It was very moving. The evening was an exotic and sophisticated treat for a bunch of school kids at a rural bible school!

Stuart Hamblin had so many talents, they seemed hard to catalog. He was a songwriter, singer, writer, actor and national politician. I was impressed.

He didn't talk down to us; instead he described events in his life that had an effect on his thinking and his career. Like all of us, he had been lonely, sad, happy, triumphant and heartbroken. I learned a lot about life in those two or three hours. I had experienced some of those same feelings but because of his age and experience, his story had greater depth and intensity.

I got a lesson in showmanship at a concert given by William Warfield. Warfield was a classical singer with the greatest bass voice I have ever heard. He had starred in "Showboat" on Broadway and went on to repeat the role in the film. During the concert, he sang many classical tunes, but by the end, even after his encore, he had not sung "Ol' Man River", the classic "Showboat" song the audience had been clamoring to hear. The crowd was about to leave when, from back stage, Warfield's magnificent voice began to sing the song a cappella. Goosebumps formed all over my body. It was an incredible moment and the crowd responded enthusiastically.

And I was truly inspired by a concert I saw by the Vienna Academy Choir. The Vienna Boys Choir is known because it performs in the US quite a lot, but the Academy Choir is made up of advanced music students from all over the world, and the audition process was very difficult. I remember noting that there were two Americans in the group at that time. The choir had a wonderful and varied program and the entire repertoire was presented without musical accompaniment. The conductor would simply sound a tuning note and the song would begin; the choir would change keys throughout the number, sometimes going from major to minor keys and back again. Their musical ability was amazing and the audience was very appreciative. I have never again heard a singing group as gifted or as good.

During the summer before my senior year, I drove up to Seattle to look for a job. My timing couldn't have been worse. Boeing, which was the largest employer in the area, had just laid off about 20,000 people and there was a lumber strike going on. I walked the streets, knocking on doors and asking everyone I saw for a job but had no luck. The minister of a local church allowed me to sleep in the church basement while I continued my search. I don't think I had money for food, but members of the church provided me with some while I was looking for work. Several days later, a man at the church offered me a job in his restaurant on Stevens Pass, which was about seventy miles east of Seattle. Of course I jumped at the chance and drove up there immediately. The restaurant was the only building for several miles, and was located at about 5,000 feet. When I arrived at the beginning of June, the snow was still up to the roof of the building! At night, the warm covers felt awfully good.

My job entailed washing dishes, setting the tables, waiting on guests and cleaning up after each meal. I also mopped the floors and cleaned the stove and grill. In exchange, I got all my meals, a sleeping bag in the attic and $125 a month. There was a good group of people that worked there and I enjoyed the company. Since there was no place to spend money, I left at the end of August with $375, which was quite a bit of money at the time. I left just in time to head to Canyonville for my last year, which was full of theater, friends and music.

Just after graduation, I heard about a group that was trying to form a quartet in Springfield, Missouri. I tried out and was chosen to sing the baritone part. We sang in churches and auditoriums in Missouri, Oklahoma, Arkansas and Kansas. We also sang quite a bit on the radio in that region. The Assembly of God Church had a national radio program on ABC on Sunday nights that originated from Springfield, and we sang on that program for several months. Two of the members of our quartet were asked to join a better known and more widely heard group and so we broke up. As it turned out, I had other obligations that I needed to attend to. For one thing, I was slated to be drafted and so I decided I would enlist in the Air Force. But I also had to take care of another, more personal situation that had developed.

During my senior year, there had been a girl that I was attracted to. Her name was Marilyn Hendrix and she was from Yakima, Washington. There wasn't a lot of formal dating at Canyonville, but there were a lot of school activities where we were all kind of thrown together and the tendency was to pair off during the picnics, after basketball games and on some of the school trips. Marilyn was a nice girl from a dysfunctional family. Her father was an itinerant miner who always felt he was just one strike away from finding uranium and thereby his fortune. Her mother had been in and out of mental hospitals for about ten years before I met Marilyn. When school let out, I drove her back to Yakima and during that trip we had an intimate relationship. That turned out to be a terrific mistake. She became pregnant and I began to get pressured to marry her. In my day, this was considered the only gentlemanly way to handle this situation. We were married in 1954, in between my graduating from high school and entering the military service. A baby girl was born in the spring of 1955, after I had finished my Air Force basic training.

My first military assignment required that the three of us move to Biloxi, Mississippi, where I was assigned to attend electronics school. Another child was born early in 1957, but the marriage was difficult and we were divorced in 1958. Obviously, there is much more to this story, but I have intentionally chosen not to elaborate. Marilyn and I were from very different worlds and the marriage was a mistake from the very beginning. On top of this rocky foundation, the strains of military life and a hand-to-mouth financial situation were too much, and the relationship crumbled. We also had different dreams and could not have achieved them if we had stayed together. I wanted to go to college and she did not want to live in the same limited circumstances for the next four years.

Marilyn soon married a military officer who she felt could better allow her to reach her goals. I had no money and no way to pay child support. I was asked to allow our two children to be adopted by her new husband; it was made clear to me that I would not be allowed to see the children in the future. They had moved to another state and I had no rights. I agreed to the adoption and only saw the children once after they were grown, at which point neither of us was interested in establishing much of a relationship. Too much time had passed and there was no impetus to rehash the past. There were no bad guys in this story – just two eighteen-year-old kids who got in over their heads. In the end, the right decision was made, and I wish everyone involved nothing but the best.

CHAPTER 15

While I was getting older and hopefully wiser, spreading my wings and seeing new parts of the country, my older half-brother Bates was busy making his own impressive mark in the world.

A businessman from the start, Bates began his career at the age of twelve. I suppose Mother gets some credit for advising him to put the money he had earned from odd jobs into real estate. He started investing in land, and by the time he was fifteen, he had accumulated forty acres and was an established businessman in Haskell. He and a friend operated a successful gas station and car dealership that he sold when he went off to Texas Technological College in Lubbock. After two years at Tech he left for Washington, D.C.

He got a degree from George Washington University in accounting. To pay for college he got a job as a secretary to Harold Ickes, who was a cabinet secretary. While working there it came to Ickes attention that the military was looking for someone who could help put together a unit that would create an inventory of all the men and equipment in the military worldwide and keep it current. If you can believe it the military had no idea where anything was or in what its condition was. Secretary Ickes recommended Bates for that job and after meeting with the powers that decided those things, he was selected.

It was there that he went to work for the government, creating and overseeing a new logistical unit that accounted for all men and materials used by the military during World War II. He had interviewed both existing military personnel and fresh blood from academia, putting together a crack team of ten, including Bates, who was now known as "Tex" Thornton. This group became known as the Whiz Kids, and several books have been written about their skills and accomplishments. He was recognized for his work and received many promotions. In the next few months, he went from being a second lieutenant to being promoted to colonel. He was 28 at the time – the youngest full colonel in the military. At one time he had 15,000 men reporting to him around the world.

Colonel Bates "Tex" Thornton receiving the Legion of Merit

Once the war ended, the country's economy picked up and there was a strong need for experienced management talent in the business community.

Tex and his group were pursued by a number of major corporations. Henry Ford II, only twenty-eight years old, had recently taken over the Ford Motor Company from his ailing grandfather. Ford Motors was in serious trouble. As its founder had slipped into senility, the company had been run by one of his old cronies, named Bennett. Under Bennett's oversight, almost all of Ford's profits had been wiped out. The automaker's market share had dropped from a high of 60% after World War I to less than 20%. It was losing a million dollars a month and Henry couldn't stop the loss. He needed a good management team to help reassert control. As the story goes, Tex fired off a telegram to Henry Ford II offering the Whiz Kids' services as a group – all ten, or nothing – to bring the money-losing company under control. After several meetings with young Henry Ford, they joined the Ford Motor Company. At thirty-one, Tex was the oldest in the group.

Under the supervision of the Whiz Kids, the company began to flourish; they were later credited with the reinvention and rejuvenation of Ford. Of the nine people who joined Ford with Tex, two eventually served as president of the company (one of whom, Robert McNamara, went on to serve as the US Secretary of Defense during the Vietnam War era). Several others became Ford division heads, and one became the Dean of the Graduate School of Business at Stanford. Tex felt that as the catalyst in Ford's reversal of fortune, he should have been made president of the company. He tried to force the issue but was opposed by one key advisor to Henry Ford II, Ernest Breech. Stymied at Ford, Tex left the company.

Tex soon accepted a position as Vice President and General Manager of Hughes Aircraft Company. Within five years, he had proved his effectiveness by reorganizing Hughes and increasing their annual sales from $1.5 million to over $200 million. During the time Tex was at the company – 1949 to 1953 – Howard Hughes was almost never present. Tex told me that there were many times they needed his authorization for some big project or another; sometimes they would attempt to reach Howard Hughes without success. Other times, he would show up in filthy clothes, but refuse to make a decision. It must have been trying. Finally in 1953, Noah Dietrich, Hughes right hand man, locked the management team out of the company, ending Tex's tenure there. Two engineers who worked for Tex at Hughes Aircraft were Dean Wooldridge and Simon Ramo; both left the company at the same time Tex did. They went on to join forces with Thompson Products and form Thompson Ramo Woolridge, later known as TRW, an aerospace and defense company that became a major competitor to Hughes Aircraft.

While Tex was at Hughes, I distinctly remember attending a dinner party at his house one evening to which Hughes also came. I must have been only about fourteen years old at the time. Aside from Hughes, Tex and me, the other guests at the small affair were Tex's wife, Flora, and General Harold George – a Vice President and General Manager at Hughes – and his wife. Hughes was a tall man and very hard of hearing. During dinner, he was unable to hear conversations conducted at normal volume, and so would get up and venture into the library next door to browse through the books. At this point, everyone would all notice he was gone, and raise their voices so that he could hear the conversation. He would then rejoin the group until we all forgot to keep the volume up, and the same sequence of events would repeat itself. His hearing loss probably at least partly explained the fact that he was extremely quiet and didn't say much, although he was cordial to me. That was the only time I ever met Howard Hughes, but it left a vivid impression.

After he left Hughes in 1953 at the age of thirty-nine, Tex approached the investment banking firm Lehman Brothers to raise money for a business plan he had devised. They put up $1.5 million as seed capital and Tex bought a company that became Litton Industries. Litton grew into a giant electronics and communications company, one of the hundred largest companies in the country. In its first decade, sales increased by 18,570% and its earnings by 10,175%. Products ranged from nuclear submarines to tiny electronic tubes that could send radio and TV signals millions of miles through space. Litton made guidance systems that fly airplanes virtually without human help, devices that generate light beams to burn holes in steel plates and gyroscopes to smooth the passage of ships. It became the third largest ship builder, first in seismic exploration, second largest maker of cash registers and the largest maker of inertial guidance systems. They developed and sold the first consumer-market microwave ovens. Litton achieved over $5 billion in sales by 1980.

Many analysts considered Tex to be the best business executive in the US during the 1960's. Tex later became a member of the prestigious Business Council, a trustee of the University of Southern California, a member of the Selection Committee of Harvard University, and a board member at Lehman Brothers, United California Bank and Union Oil, among others. Tex was asked to consult on the reorganization of MGM studios and was also invited to join the board of MCA, which then owned Universal Pictures.

Tex and Jeff, 1968

Tex appeared on the covers of Time magazine, Forbes, Fortune, Electronic Times and many other periodicals. He truly was a management genius. Twenty-two of his original employees became millionaires at a time when a million dollars was a hell of a lot of money. Those who worked for Tex and left to form other companies were called LIDOs (Litton Industry Dropouts). The companies they formed or ran were some of the largest in America and had combined revenues of over $100 billion dollars. Tex was given credit by each of them for their success. One other interesting fact is that he was one of the first political supporters of Ronald Reagan. On the night Reagan was nominated to be the Republican candidate for President of the US, he and Nancy were having dinner with Tex and Flora.

In my opinion, Tex had three main traits that led to his success. First, he was one of the world's greatest salesmen of his own abilities, and carried an aura of success. Second, he was realistic about his shortcomings and hired the brightest people he could find to fill those gaps. And finally, he was an absolutely tireless worker who remained utterly committed to the project at hand.

Tex was an incredibly successful businessman and he lived well, but was also very generous. He donated the law library at Texas Tech, where he also endowed a professorship in the names of George Mahon and Charles B. Thornton. He bequeathed the LLL Ranch in Colorado to a non-profit organization for use as a boys' home. He was awarded the Legion of Merit during the war, and in 1981, President Reagan awarded him the Presidential Medal of Freedom, the highest civilian award given by our country.

Tex, May 1979

He lived in the Holmby Hills area of Los Angeles, with such neighbors as Walter Pigeon, Walt Disney, Bing Crosby, Claudette Colbert, Jules Stein, Barbra Streisand and Irene Dunne. He bought his house from Frank Sinatra for $250,000; it was sold after his death for $19 million!

In 1963, Tex said, "in the past twenty years we have seen more technological change than in all recorded history. It took 112 years for photography to go from being discovered to a commercial product, 56 years for the telephone, 35 years for the radio, 15 years for radar and 12 years for television. But it took only six years for the atom bomb to become an operational reality and five years for transistors to find their way to the market. During the next ten years, there should be more scientific and technological advancement than in all of history – more than double that of the last 20 years". He was right on the money, but unfortunately, Tex died in 1981, before he could see the computer or communication revolutions transform the world.

When Tex died, too young, at the age of sixty-seven, it was truly a very sad day for me. I regret that I did not come to know him well until I was in my twenties, but we became fairly close after I had gone to work in California. We used to go riding on his ranch and we talked for hours on the trail. He was like a father figure to me; I could always call him when I needed advice and he never let me down. He was so busy that it was hard for him to have time for his own children, much less me, but he always found the time. When I worked at United California Bank, he would come to see me after bank board meetings and we would have great conversations. He wanted to help me with my career but at the time, I was a little stubborn and determined to do it on my own.

His funeral service was held at a local church and afterwards we all were invited back to his residence for a quiet reception. I arrived at the same time as Jimmy Stewart and his wife, Gloria. We walked in together and Gloria asked if I knew that she had lived in what was now Tex's house before she married Jimmy. I told her I was not aware of that. She said when she and Jimmy wed they decided to live in his house, so she had sold the house to Frank Sinatra, who later sold it to the Thorntons.

Henry Singleton, the Chairman of Textron was there, as were Roy Ash, Harry Gray, Frank King and a great many other captains of industry. Jules Stein and Lew Wasserman, major powers at MCA, attended, having become personal friends during Tex's tenure on their board.

Tex lived such an incredible life and I will never forget him. I think he respected me and felt I had done very well despite my poor education. I am proud to say that I think I may have changed his mind a little bit from his original opinion that only Harvard MBA's had a chance in business. Tex did not include me in his will, and his lawyer, Clarence Price, told me that Tex had said that I didn't need any help, that I would be just fine on my own. In retrospect, it would have been fine if he had given me just a little head start!

PART FOUR

INTO THE WILD BLUE YONDER

CHAPTER 16

Sandwiched in between World War II and Vietnam, the Korean War has been called "The Forgotten War". It began in the early hours of June 25, 1950, when North Korea, advised and armed by the Soviet Union, invaded South Korea. Within three days, they had captured Seoul, the capital of South Korea, and Truman was convinced that World War III had begun. In the early days of the war, the inexperienced US soldiers found themselves in retreat, but the US military soon staged a highly successful landing behind enemy lines at Inchon. The Chinese then entered the conflict and ensnared the First Marine Division. Only intense fighting by the Marines allowed them to escape the trap. It was a brutal war, with much savage hill fighting and hand-to-hand combat, often in freezing weather. Some of the soldiers I knew who fought on the front lines said that their battles were especially terrifying because they fought thousands of Chinese up close, with bayonets. The war resulted in more than two-and-a-half million deaths, over 54,000 of which were American.

During the Korean War, young men over eighteen years of age were subject to the draft. This was before people no longer cared about their government or the price of freedom. We were all going to war. In December of 1954, I had enlisted in the US Air Force. At the time, I was told that my choice was signing up for four years in the Air Force versus being drafted into the Army and, after training, being sent into combat – to me, the Air Force was definitely preferable. As it turned out, though, the war ended before I was even out of basic training. However, I feel that my time in the military was very worthwhile. It gave me a chance to mature, to prove myself to others, to excel in competition and to lead my contemporaries. I believe every young man should serve at least two years of military service.

When I first reported for duty, I was put on a train and shipped to Parks Air Force Base in Pleasanton, California. I remember a young man who was boarding my train being told by his mother that if he didn't enjoy it or if they treated him badly, he should just come right home. I can tell you he was in for a surprise – and so was I! I had been of the belief that Air Force training would be somehow less grueling than basic Army training. But when we arrived in San Francisco and were driven on buses into the training camp, I was greeted by the sight of men marching and doing calisthenics. I was sure that I was either at the wrong place or that army recruit training was being done at the same place. Boy, was I ever wrong.

Approximately 30,000 young men were going through the thirteen-week basic training program in this location. It was thirteen very long weeks. We were woken up at five a.m. with shouting and yelling and bright lights. I, and the fifty-five others in my unit, then had about thirty minutes to shower, shave, dress and fall out for inspection. We were then marched to the mess hall and given thirty minutes to go through the line, get our food, eat it and be in formation in front of the mess hall. I learned to eat very fast. It may not be healthy but it was better than being punished, or not eating at all. Then we marched back to the barracks to prepare for a hard day's work. During any given day we might spend hours repeating certain marching maneuvers over and over; we might take firing practice at the rifle ranges; we might have to do up to two hours of group calisthenics; or we might be sent to classes to memorize military rules, regulations, ranks and a seemingly infinite catalog of organizational details.

It was hell, but we were so busy that at least the time seemed to pass quickly. The discipline I had learned at home made the adjustment to the military system less difficult. I didn't have any trouble saying "yes sir" and "yes ma'am". I had done that all my life and still do it from time to time. Unfortunately, not everyone adjusted easily, and when one person screwed up, we often were all penalized as a group, given extra duties, marching or calisthenics. But the person who had been responsible for causing the punishment was often subjected to individual punishment later, from some especially tough characters within our own unit. We had several convicted felons, mainly from the Chicago area, who had been given the choice of either going to jail or joining the military. I can tell you they were a mean bunch and no one wanted to make them angry. But inevitably someone would, and they would be on the receiving end of what was called a 'blanket party'. After lights out, the tough guys would come to see the person who had screwed up, put a blanket over him and proceed to beat the heck out of him. The blanket would keep scars from forming and usually prevented any bleeding.

Whether it was because of my upbringing, or through sheer fear, I became an exemplary trainee. I did the best on tests and was appointed the right guard of my unit. That meant that, as the best marcher, I got to march at the head of the unit, positioned on the right side, one place ahead of the rest of the flight. Man, talk about proud! I thought I was really something. In addition, at the end of the thirteen weeks, I was recognized as the outstanding trainee on base and given a ribbon and a letter of commendation.

Toward the end of basic training, we were asked which schools or special training we would like to do. We had undergone a series of tests, including I.Q. and skills testing, that determined what we could qualify for. I applied for Electronics School, specifically radio and radar fundamentals. The orders came down that I had been accepted, and I was to report to Kessler Air Force Base in Biloxi, Mississippi.

On the way to Biloxi, I drove through Los Angeles to see Jeanetta and we went to a musical variety revue at CBS. Joni James appeared and sang her hit "The Wayward Wind", which was one of my favorites. Debbie Reynolds was another guest, and she came down to talk to us after the show. I remember she was very excited because she had just become engaged to marry Eddie Fisher, who was then at his peak as a singer. Of course, later, Fisher famously left Debbie Reynolds for Elizabeth Taylor, but at that moment in time, she seemed very sweet and happy.

It was a brief moment of fun before heading back into the jaws of the military. I arrived in Biloxi to find the biggest mosquitoes and the hottest, most humid climate I had ever experienced. The town had about 13,000 residents and about 40,000 military personnel. The townspeople didn't like the troops and treated them with total distain, although they didn't mind the millions of dollars that poured into Biloxi each month because of the base.

They raised the prices on everything from rent to food in order to gouge the young soldiers. It got so bad that the Base Commander met with the town leaders and asked them to roll back the prices, but they refused. In response, the Commander placed the town off limits to military personnel. That meant no one from the base could set foot in Biloxi, let alone spend as much as a dime there. This lasted about four days before the contrite town leaders agreed to lower prices and forever mend their ways, as long as the town was declared once again on limits. For once, greed lost the fight.

My electronics course at Kessler was an intensive thirty-six week-long program. We would gather at our squadron headquarters at seven each morning to march in formation past the Commander's platform, just like all the other troops. Several thousand troops had to pass in review, and though it seemed like the ranks went on forever, the march was completed rapidly. We would be at school by eight for eight hours of class, and at the end of the day we'd line up again to march in review.

We were taught – in great detail – electronic fundamentals. At the same time, we dismantled complex radar and radio equipment and learned how to repair many types of malfunctions. The class work and practical lab applications were very interesting and I enjoyed them. As a result, I did well, which provided an important boost to my self confidence. I wound up scoring higher than anyone else on the series of tests we took at the end of the nine months. A high score usually guaranteed your choice of geographic assignments. I say "usually" for a reason... The second place student got his choice of Landsburg, Germany, and spent the next three years there. As I recall, my first choice of assignment had been Hamilton AFB, located just north of San Francisco; however, my "reward" for doing well was to be assigned to stay at Kessler as an instructor of the same electronic fundamentals course that I had just finished studying.

I spent the next few months teaching in Biloxi before applying for a transfer. I found teaching the same material over and over became a little boring, although by the time I had finished my tour of duty in Biloxi, I knew the subject by heart, which did help me during the rest of my time in the Air Force. While I probably would have chosen the same destination, the powers that be wanted me to go to Carswell Air Force Base in Fort Worth, Texas. It was one of the largest and most active bases in the US Air Force. From Carswell, Air Force planes anywhere in the world could get a weather report on atmospheric conditions anywhere they were or would be heading.

Carswell was a Strategic Air Command base which served as a center for B-36 Squadrons. The B-36, a bomber with ten engines, was the largest warplane in the world. The tail section was nearly fifty feet tall; it had a wing span of 236 feet, and carried a crew of fifteen people. It had a 10,000 mile range, which gave it the capability to fly from US bases to Russia and back without refueling. It could carry two atomic bombs or one hydrogen bomb on combat missions. It was the main US deterrent during that period of the Cold War, and was never used in a combat situation during the entire period of its service.

When I was first assigned to Carswell, I was part of a special radio and radar specialty unit that kept the various radio, radar and navigation sites in our region of responsibility in good working order. In addition, I sometimes flew on B-36 – and later, B-52 – bomber missions. On those occasions, the planes would head far off-shore, perhaps south toward Venezuela or out over the Atlantic or Canada. The plane would then come back, trying to penetrate US air space without being detected. If they succeeded without an alarm going up, all hell would break out. I would be immediately dispatched to any base, station or facility in the southern portion of the US that had failed to detect the bomber, where I was responsible for determining who or what was at fault. As you might expect, my arrival was not usually a cause for celebration, but I had the power of the commanding general behind me. I would help to correct the problem and be on my way. The equipment I worked on was very complex and expensive. Some of the equipment was so large you would literally walk inside of it to make repairs.

In addition to that responsibility I was also placed on a high priority team for overseas deployment. We had to keep a complete wardrobe on the base at all times and in an emergency would be called to report there. Our personal effects would be loaded onto a plane that would then take off as soon as possible, flying us to a trouble spot that could be located anywhere in the world.

The team was charged with setting up an airfield with control tower, radar and radio facilities in a potential war zone. Three times during my tenure on this team, we were awakened, put on board and whisked off, although we never had to set up the facilities. One time, we were flown to Lebanon when the marines went ashore, but our mission was aborted before our plane could land. We simply turned around and flew, very tired, back to Carswell. The second time, we were flown to Taiwan because of the Chinese threat to Quimoy and Matsu, and the third time, I don't know where we flew, because they did not tell us the destination, even after our return.

There was one incident during my service at Carswell that I will never forget. I had been sent to Matagorda Island, which was located just south of Galveston, Texas, to check on some equipment problems. On my way back, I caught a ride back north on a C-47 that was headed first to Tinker AFB in Oklahoma City, where another problem had developed that they wanted me to repair. As we flew close to Carswell, we received word that I was needed there more urgently, and that they should land and let me off. When we arrived, a young colleague came out to the plane and said he had been ordered to replace me on the flight to Tinker. We hurriedly changed places and the plane took off for Oklahoma City. By the time I got to the control center, the plane had crashed two miles north of the base and all aboard were lost. I went to the crash site, where I found my flight jacket, which I had forgotten, in the wreckage. How easily I could have died in that crash.

Flying was a big part of my job. I don't know exactly how many miles I traveled, but there were many thousands of them – our missions on the B-36 were about twenty-four hours in duration, entailing long trips over the Atlantic and Pacific oceans. We never landed; the round-trips were intended to show our enemies our capabilities. When the B-52 came along, the flights were about twelve hours long and usually involved airborne refueling. The B-52 flights were always pretty rough, as the plane's wings had quite a bit of flexibility and a tendency to bounce us around a lot.

While my tour of duty in the Air Force did not pass quickly, I did enjoy most of it. I learned a great deal about life and how to get along with all kinds of individuals. I'm glad that I didn't have to serve in a war zone, but my experiences gave me enormous respect and admiration for anyone who has. I've had many friends who served in combat and the experience will be something that stays with them the rest of their lives. I've never had to worry about someone killing me or me killing them, and I hope to God I never will.

As an enlisted man, the officer corps always controls your future. You must impress the officers above you in order to advance and succeed. While business is a little like that, military authority is more absolute, and in many cases there is no second chance. I was always a little nervous around senior officers and tended to keep my mouth shut and leave those meetings as quickly as possible. Later in my life, I would end up spending a great deal of time around generals and admirals. In Washington, I walked up to the first four-star general I saw after my time in the service, introducing myself and shaking his hand. I told him I had always wanted to shake a general's hand, but had been too afraid. He just laughed.

I did suffer one personal loss while I was in Fort Worth. It had been raining for about three weeks and the dams on the three lakes northwest of the city started to overflow; the pressure kept building until finally the levee burst, causing the worst flood in the history of that area. When I left the base that day and returned to the small house I was living in, I found about four feet of water inside. Everything I owned was floating around, ruined, and all of my photos and memorabilia from my youth were destroyed. To this day, I miss those photos of the people I knew, the only physical representations I had of memories that remain dear to me.

When the time came, I requested an early release from the Air Force in order to attend college; I was given a release from active duty, effective September 1, 1958. While working at Carswell during the day, I had taken some night classes at Texas Christian University and had earned twelve hours of credit in some basic courses. I had taken the SAT test and scored sufficiently high to be admitted to Texas Tech in Lubbock. When my release was granted, I was told that it was because I had been chosen the number one-rated enlisted airman in the Air Force twice during my service. I had done pretty well in my time away from Lubbock – but now it was time for me to return.

PART FIVE

OFF TO COLLEGE

CHAPTER 17

When I interviewed with the head of admissions at Texas Tech, he looked at my educational background and said that there was no way I would be able to make it through college. If I were he, I probably would have reached the same conclusion. I had not even finished two years of traditional high school, choosing instead to work and take classes by correspondence. Then I had attended an unaccredited school in Oregon to obtain my high school diploma. What wasn't written in the papers in his hand was that I had studied very hard and I was highly determined to succeed. Thankfully, I got the opportunity to prove myself.

I jumped straight into academia, determined to major in a dual program that would give me degrees in both Electrical Engineering and Physics. That program indicates a person who is ambitious, eager to please and out of his mind. I soon discovered that I was not terribly strong in mathematics and that engineering principles caused my eyes to glaze over. I decided to change my major after the first semester, switching to a degree in Economics. I was really impressed by the caliber of the economics professors at Texas Tech; every class was an interesting challenge and I learned a great deal.

Of the nine thousand students enrolled at that time, probably half were military veterans who were much older than the students coming straight from high school. This broke the student body into two distinct and very different groups. The veterans were not interested in the fraternities and social activities that were central to campus life for the younger students.

I remember one year when we were going through the line to register for classes. At the end of the line, the various fraternities and campus organizations were soliciting interest from students as they passed by; they weren't getting much attention from the veterans. The last booth was an organization for independents. As we passed it, the representative asked the veteran just ahead of me if he would be interested in joining. The vet looked at the fellow and said, "If I were to join the independents then I wouldn't be very independent, would I?" Absolute silence ensued.

Lubbock was a dry town, which meant that there were no liquor stores and you couldn't buy alcohol in the restaurants. This posed a dilemma for college students; the solution was to either make your own or drive ninety miles to a little town in New Mexico where alcohol was sold. I went to a party at the ATO fraternity house one time when they had concocted a brew and put it into glass bottles, which they arranged in rows around the various rooms on a ledge of molding about eighteen inches below the ceiling. It was snowing that night and they had a fire going in the fireplace and the heat turned up in the furnace. It got pretty hot in there and around eleven p.m., we heard an explosion, and then another and another, as one-by-one the bottles started blowing up. Beer and glass were flying everywhere, so I hid under a coffee table!

At another event – a Lil' Abner party, to which everyone wore crazy costumes – they put Everclear in the Kickapoo joy juice. Now, Everclear is one hundred eighty proof and has very little taste. I had a date with a young coed. After one glass of that punch, I decided that the young lady and I should get out of there. My date was not happy about leaving and she decided to stay with some friends. The next morning, the newspaper reported that the attendees had torn up the hardwood floor, pulled down the ceiling and knocked holes in the wall. The damage was estimated at about $300,000. I don't know if it was good sense or good luck, but I'm glad I made the decision to leave!

Although I was a veteran, I relished the opportunity to enjoy campus life, and pursued several extracurricular activities, in addition to my studies. I began writing about sports for the campus newspaper. We had good teams and it was great fun going to the games and interviewing players and coaches on both sides. We had a terrific All-American football player, E.J. Holub, who was a very nice young man and fun to be around. He was drafted by the Kansas City Chiefs and was All-Pro in the NFL for ten years. Tech also had a good basketball program that was very competitive in the Southwest Conference. I knew the players and enjoyed the games. Our biggest rival was

Southern Methodist University, whose star player was Max Williams, a great shooter who somehow always seemed to find a way to beat Tech. Ironically, Max is now a good friend of mine and loves to kid me about those days.

I also got to rekindle my interest in music during this time. There was a very active group of musicians in Lubbock, and I struck up a friendship with Jim Wilson, a disk jockey for a local radio station, who introduced me to a group called the Crickets. They were the back-up singers for Buddy Holly. I never met Holly, but one of the Crickets was Waylon Jennings, who went on to great solo fame as a country singer.

John Deutschendorf, who later became better-known as John Denver, attended Texas Tech for at little while before hitting the big time. Mac Davis, who was a little younger than me, grew up just a few blocks from my home. Mac had his own television show and was a talented songwriter. He wrote "In the Ghetto", which became a big hit for Elvis Presley. He also wrote "Lubbock In My Rearview Mirror", which seems to indicate that he was happy to leave.

While I was at Tech, I met a young singer named Tommy Sands through an acquaintance of mine, Otis Echols. Otis was the head of a gospel quartet that sang in churches and on the radio in Lubbock, and when I was younger, I had taken voice lessons from him. He later moved to Clovis, New Mexico, where he bought a radio station. Otis wrote a number of songs, one of which, "Sugartime", became a big hit by the McGuire Sisters.

Tommy had started singing on the radio in Shreveport when he was eight and made his big debut at the age of twelve on the Louisiana Hayride, which at that time was similar to the Grand Ole Opry show. Colonel Tom Parker, Elvis Presley's manager, got Tommy a contract with RCA Records and he cut his first record in 1951. In 1955 Tommy started to appear alongside Elvis Presley in shows all around the country. In 1956, he became an 'overnight' sensation when he got the lead role in the TV production of the "Singin' Idol". They had originally wanted Elvis, but he wasn't available and recommended Tommy for the role. Tommy got a five-year contract with Capitol Records and after his appearance on the show, received thousands of fan requests for information and pictures. Within twenty-four hours, he was offered contracts by four motion picture companies, and was hired to do the film version of "Singin' Idol". He made several hit records, sang at the Academy Awards and was the subject on "This Is Your Life", all before the age of twenty-one. He made eight films, many records and married Nancy Sinatra before his career faded and he disappeared from the public eye.

When Tommy was touring in the late 1950's, at the height of his fame, he spoke to Otis and Otis told him to call me before he came to Lubbock. He did, and we had a nice talk and made plans to meet when he played the college auditorium. When he arrived, I met him at the hotel and we went to dinner. It seemed like everyone in the restaurant came over to ask for an autograph. We spent the next day driving around town and talking. He was a delightful person and didn't take himself too seriously. I called a girl I knew, Janie Norris, and asked if she would like to go to dinner with Tommy Sands that evening. She was excited and of course said yes. Janie was a real beauty, and had been chosen the most beautiful girl on campus every year she was there.

That night I drove Tommy to the auditorium for his show. The approximately four thousand seats were sold out, and crowd was wound up. Another musical group opened and then Tommy went on and sang for about an hour and a half. The crowd loved it, standing up throughout Tommy's two encores. When Tommy came off the stage, he showered and changed before I took him out the back of the building and drove him quickly away.

Tommy did not want to go out alone with Janie, so he asked if I would join them for drinks and dinner. We had a wonderful time. Everyone was relaxed and it was clear that Tommy thought Janie was terrific. During the course of the evening, they talked a lot and at one point she mentioned that although she liked where she went to school, she felt a little isolated because she didn't have a car. After we dropped her off, Tommy told me she was the most beautiful girl he had ever seen, better than anyone he had met in Hollywood. He left the next day, but told me to call him anytime. Two days later, he called to tell me he was sending Janie Norris a new car. When I spoke to her later that day, she was overwhelmed. But strangely, Tommy never called her again.

I saw Tommy one more time, in 1961. I was going to Hollywood, so I called Tommy. At the time, he was filming "Babes in Toyland" for Disney

Studios, with Annette Funicello and Ray Bolger. He invited me to come visit the set, where I met Walt Disney and Tommy's costars. I was invited to have dinner with Tommy and his wife at that time, Nancy Sinatra, but was unable to go because of other commitments. I haven't seen him since, but remember him as a truly nice guy.

While at Tech, I lived in a rented house with three other guys: Jim Owens, Jerry Herron and Tom Chapman. Tom and I have maintained a relationship over the years. He got a masters degree at Stanford and married Linda, one of the most beautiful young ladies I've ever met. He became a teacher and then principal at the high School in McMinnville, Oregon. He retired about five years ago and travels with Linda. Jim Owens was from Alpine, Texas and had attended Sol Ross Junior College before coming to Tech. He always dated the prettiest girls and never had any money. He sponged off almost everyone but they didn't seem to mind. Jerry Herron, I haven't heard from since. He was not the brightest bulb on the tree, and almost got Tom and me killed.

Jerry started seeing a nice young lady and she began to spend a fair amount of time at our house. One day, the doorbell rang and Tom opened the door to a policeman with a very impressive gun. Tom later said he felt like he was looking into the mouth of a cannon. The policeman asked if his wife was there. Tom and I were stunned into silence. In fact, we knew that Jerry and the girl were in the back bedroom at that moment. Tom finally said that he did not believe there was anyone else in the house. The policeman asked if he could look around and pushed his way into the living room. We didn't know what to do, but we knew damn sure we didn't want to tangle with the cannon. The policeman proceeded to the back bedroom. We closed our eyes and waited for the sound of the gun. But nothing happened. The policeman returned, saying he was satisfied that his wife was not there, and left. We didn't know what had happened, but were thankful for whatever miracle had occurred. Jerry showed up a couple of hours later and told us that he and the girl had heard the doorbell and the ensuing conversation and had climbed out the back window. He thought it was hilarious and just laughed while we glared at him. We told him that we never wanted that girl in our house again. Shortly afterwards, to our relief, Jerry moved out. We learned an important lesson from this incident: never date a married woman, particularly one that is married to a policeman.

During the Christmas holidays of 1958, I went to Dallas to see some friends and attend the Cotton Bowl. At a Christmas Eve party, I met a very attractive young lady named Gretchen, who went to SMU. She was from Dallas and her family was of Swedish origin. She was a 5'9" blonde with a good sense of humor and I enjoyed being around her. We saw each other several nights in a row and when it was time for me to leave to go back to school; she informed me that she was going to transfer to Texas Tech. I was floored but happy with her decision.

Gretchen arrived at Tech and immediately told me that she wanted us to go steady and not date other people. I agreed and for about three months we literally spend all our free time together. I would meet her in the morning for coffee and we would say good night with a phone call around eleven. We got along well together and enjoyed a variety of activities, like bowling – which I was pretty good at in those days, with a 186 average. It was an intense relationship. One day, she said we needed to talk. We sat down and she proceeded to tell me that she wanted us to become engaged and she wanted to have it happen in Dallas in front of her parents. I thought about it for a few days and decided that it was a good plan for everyone.

We went to Dallas and I proposed in front of her parents. They seemed thrilled and took us out to dinner at the Baker Hotel to celebrate. Gretchen seemed ecstatic and was so happy on our way back to Lubbock. We arrived back on Sunday and on Monday we went through our usual schedule and then talked to each other quite late on Monday night. The last thing she said to me on that night was how much she loved me and that she wanted to spend the rest of her life with me. I told her how happy I was and I was looking forward to a wonderful life together.

The next morning, I went to the dorm to pick her up for coffee as I had for the past few months and a friend of hers showed up in the reception area and told me that Gretchen didn't want to see me again. I asked the girl why, but she didn't have any idea. She was puzzled because the night before Gretchen had told her how happy she was, but this morning, Gretchen had seemed depressed and simply told her to tell me not to call her again. I was in shock!

I never spoke to Gretchen again. My attempts to contact her were blocked. I saw her once at a pizza place but when she saw me she immediately left. I received a note saying that she wished to have any pictures I had of her back – and that was the end. I never saw her again. A year later, I heard that she was in a mental hospital in north Texas. Years later, I heard that she had married a fine man in Wichita Falls and they had three children. I haven't thought about that episode in many years, but it was one of the strangest occurrences in my life and I will never be able to fully explain it.

CHAPTER 18

I am glad that while I was at Texas Tech, I had the chance to be nearer to my parents again for a short time. Mother had begun to feel under the weather in about 1956. She had already lived with quite a lot of pain for some years after falling and injuring a hip, but this was different, and she seemed to know it. She had always felt she had a close personal relationship with God, and regularly prayed for all of her children and, of course, for Dad. She said that God talked to her and was capable of healing her ailments. God had been her companion through all the low points in her life and was what kept her going when nothing else seemed to go right. This time, though, her pain would not abate.

Dad finally took her to the doctor and the diagnosis was uterine cancer. She went to see every minister we knew and prayed with them. She felt sure that God would help her. Sometime in 1957 it was decided that she would have an operation to remove the cancerous growth. When the surgery was over, they recommended chemotherapy and radiation, which were tried with some success.

Bates came to town and spent quite a lot time convincing Mother to try an experimental drug to which he had special access. For a time it seemed to help, and we all began to breathe a little easier. Mother was happy for a while and, after I returned from my time in the military in September 1958, I got to spend some quality time with her. We relived a lot of experiences and laughed a great deal.

Then, in late 1958, she took a turn for the worse. We all sensed it was the end. Jeanetta came back from Los Angeles, putting her career on hold to tend to mother. That winter was difficult. Mother's pain was so great that all the medicine in the world did not seem to ease it. At night, I would hear her begging God to let her die, crying herself to sleep. After several months of this suffering, she passed from this earth. She weighed only eighty-five pounds when she died, having lost more than half her weight. I remember crying out of sheer relief that she was finally at peace.

As I have written, Mother had a tough, but loving way. She always encouraged each of us to do our best. She was not a doting parent, but she loved us without limits. When I was about seven years old, I was riding on the church bus when a woman who thought I was being a little unruly whacked me on the head, telling me to sit down. When I got home, I told mother what had happened – I certainly didn't want her to hear from anyone else that I had been out of line. She immediately went to the phone and called the woman and proceeded to tell her to never touch one of her children again. She said, "If one of my children does something wrong, then I will whip them 'til they can't stand, but I don't allow anyone else to punish them". That was Mother. I will always miss her. Sometimes it would be really nice to still have her around to give me a big hug and tell me everything will be all right.

She was a fun-loving, hard working woman. I was told that she was very pretty when she was a young lady. Mother was forty-two when I was born and had raised three other children before I came along. She could be a tough disciplinarian and almost always dished out the punishment when it became necessary. She had had a hard life and she was more emotional during my childhood. She had a nervous breakdown when I was ten or eleven, and spent some time in the hospital recuperating. After that she was never very emotionally strong, but she was very loving and more patient with me. She loved me dearly because I was the baby of the family. While she had a good sense of humor, she was very naïve about the world, which I attribute to not leaving home very often, except to go to church.

Her death changed my life. I never again enjoyed the same faith in God that I had before. I could never reconcile God's plan with the pleading of a woman who had utterly believed in a loving and compassionate God. Having watched her all my life and seen the absolute devotion and the work she had done for her belief, I truly thought that she had been abandoned. Since that time, I have reconciled this disappointment, and found a belief in God that allows that there may be a destiny for each of us that does not always seem to make sense. I don't believe God gives us things, or that we should ask him to intercede or do our bidding. I hope that I will have the wisdom to make the right choices for myself and for those around me, and that when I am gone, people will say that that I was fair and tried to do my very best.

PART SIX

OUR
NATION'S
CAPITOL

In May 1959, my former roommate Jim Owens and I decided to go to Washington, D.C. We had enjoyed our time at Texas Tech, but we were restless veterans and wanted to explore a new part of the country.

When I arrived in Washington, Jim and I rented an apartment in a midrise building on Wisconsin Avenue. It was an unfurnished one-bedroom place, and I didn't have the means to buy furniture or much else, so I decided to call my older brother, Tex, to see if I could borrow some money. I asked him for about $200 to pay the down payment on some furniture for the apartment. His answer came immediately. Tex said, "If you are ever in a position where you need my help for an emergency or for food, I will be the first to help you. If you are in danger or you are desperate, I will be there for you anywhere in the world. But don't ever call me asking for money for something like this". Then he hung up. I must say I was surprised for a little while, but after thinking about it, I realized that self-sufficiency was a good lesson for me to learn – although I was glad I had a safety net in case of trouble. In fact, I never asked him for monetary help ever again.

I wanted to continue my college studies, but I would need to support myself while I was in school. I transferred to American University because it was the only college in Washington with a schedule that would allow me to work while studying. I would love to have attended Georgetown University, but they would only allow full-time students. American conducted night and early morning classes at their uptown campus, which was housed in several row houses a couple of blocks away from the White House and Executive Building.

Jim and I arrived without jobs lined up, but we had total confidence we would easily land some. Jim was from Alpine, Texas (where Dan Blocker, who played Hoss in the television series "Bonanza", had been one of his classmates at Sul Ross Junior College). He approached the congressman from his west Texas district, who helped him get a position on the Capitol police force.

I was taking two classes in the morning, which started at seven a.m. and ended at nine a.m. Since Congress did not meet until noon, I thought it would work great if I could find a job there, so I perhaps naively decided to march down to the United States Capitol building and see what I could find. I knew the congressman from our district in Texas, George Mahon, but he had already extended his patronage to a number of others. I took a walk through the Capitol and saw Texan Sam Rayburn, who was the Speaker of the House of Representatives. I walked up to him and told him that I was also from Texas and was very pleased to meet him. We talked for a few minutes about my attending Texas Tech and about west Texas.

He invited me into his office in the center of the Capitol, where I told Speaker Rayburn that I was a veteran of the Korean conflict and had come to Washington to attend American University, but that I needed a job in order to attend. He picked up the phone and called a man named Fishbait Miller, who oversaw the doorman, elevator operator, page and other patronage jobs in the House. He told Fishbait to assign me as either a doorman or an elevator operator. That way I would be free in the early mornings and evenings to go to school. When I so brazenly approached the Speaker, I had no idea that he was considered an intimidating and unapproachable man. I was blissfully ignorant of that fact that he was one of the most powerful men in Washington and that most sensible people were petrified when he walked in a room. But ignorance worked in my favor in this instance!

I met with Fishbait and he initially assigned me to work as a doorman in the gallery area. My salary was $5400 a year, which sounded like a million dollars to me. It was a boring job at best and I didn't care much for it, but it had some fun little benefits. The main one was meeting all the famous people who sat in my gallery area – including Jacqueline Kennedy, several governors and a number of other politically important people. The gallery where I served was similar to a balcony section in a theater, and it overlooked the House of Representatives. I saw a lot of the action on the floor of the chamber.

My gallery was adjacent to one that had been the location of a violent attack by a group of Puerto Rican nationalists in 1954. Unhappy that Puerto Rico had recently become a US commonwealth, they came to the Congress and, from the gallery, shot up the House chamber. They wounded five congressmen, one seriously. At the time I was there, you could still see the repaired bullet holes in the tables and walls of the chamber.

House of Representatives, January 1961. Nixon is certifying the election of John F. Kennedy.

I later became the operator of the Speaker of the House's elevator, which I enjoyed a great deal. This job was quite an honor, as the only people who were allowed to ride that elevator were the Speaker, the President, members of House and Senate, members of the Supreme Court, the Joint Chiefs of Staff, members of the President's Cabinet and visiting dignitaries. I was honored to carry five past, present or future US Presidents, French President Charles de

Gaulle, Willy Brandt, who later became Chancellor of Germany, the King of
Nepal and many more.

The elevator was adjacent to Speaker Sam Rayburn's office and traveled
four floors. It had a rich brown hardwood interior and could carry about ten
people at a time. There was always traffic on the elevator but after Congress
adjourned for the day, which was usually anywhere from one to five p.m., my
workload lightened up, and by five-thirty I was off to attend evening classes
from six to eight p.m. After that, I would return to my apartment and study
until about eleven p.m., until it was time to go to bed and get up early the
next day to do it again. It was a tight schedule, with barely enough time to
eat! I would pick up any food that was convenient so as not to throw the
whole day off.

In the elevator, because the quarters were tight and the stakes high, I was
often privy to things that I was surprised I was allowed to witness. During
this period of time, Lyndon Johnson was the Senate Majority Leader. His
biggest supporter was Sam Rayburn. The two of them controlled the legislative agendas in the House and the Senate. Johnson was always pleasant to
me and I worked alongside his daughters during his campaigns for office.
When Johnson became Vice President in 1961, he came to the elevator one
day and asked me to take him up between floors. I did so immediately and
we talked for a few minutes. Then someone buzzed the elevator and Johnson
told me to go down and pick them up. When we arrived at the basement
level, there stood Barry Goldwater, the Republican Senator from Arizona
and future Republican Presidential candidate who would oppose Johnson
in 1964. Goldwater got in the elevator and Johnson told me to take it up
between floors again. I did so and then turned my attention to the nearest
wall. Johnson began to berate Goldwater for some action Goldwater had
taken with regard to an important bill that was before the Senate. He told
Goldwater that he expected a reversal of that action immediately or Johnson
would make sure that certain items Goldwater needed would be denied.
There was a heated discussion before they came to an agreement. Johnson
told me to take them to the House floor level, which I did. They got off the
elevator, Johnson patted me on the back and that was the end of it. I was

flabbergasted. I had never seen two senior statesmen have at it, let alone use such heated language in their conversation. It was the first fight I would witness between famous powerful men but it would not be the last.

I became familiar with many of the congressman, and a few of them were quite colorful. Kenneth Gray, a representative from Illinois, was an amateur magician. Every time he had a bill coming up for a vote, he would ask Speaker Rayburn if he could perform a magic trick on the floor of the House as a way to gain attention. Rayburn always said no, because he thought it would belittle the process. Gray always looked like he had just stepped out of Esquire, fashionable but somewhat overstated. He drove a red Cadillac convertible and always wanted to be noticed. One day I told him how nicely he was dressed and he looked me and said, "My boy, flattery will get you anywhere. It got me elected to this office and has kept me here for twelve years".

In my opinion, one of the nicest congressmen was Adam Clayton Powell, Jr. He was a tall handsome man who had been a Baptist minister in Harlem. He had a huge congregation and was always re-elected by a large margin. He and I would talk from time to time and after a while, he started to bring me two martinis whenever there was a roll call vote while I was working. He would hand both of them to me, then rush onto the House floor, cast his vote, and immediately return, taking one of the martinis with him and leaving one behind for me. He had a great laugh and I enjoyed him very much. Years later, he was accused of misappropriating committee funds, and the allegations cost him his seat in Congress.

I also became a witness to some of the congressmen's personal failings. Some of them clearly had real problems with alcohol. They would often sneak into the cloak room where no one could see them in order to drink between votes. If the House session went too late in the evening, some representatives had to be hauled back to their offices to sleep it off. Sometimes these gentlemen would become quite belligerent and take it out on the poor working folk – meaning me. One evening a congressman from west Texas started cursing me out and continued for some time. During this tirade, Congressman Cleve Bailey, a Democrat from West Virginia, got in the elevator and took the drunk congressman to task. The Texas representative immediately began to backtrack and apologize. Bailey told him that there was no excuse for yelling at an elevator operator, particularly with that language. He told the man that because of his actions he would not be allowed on any significant committee in the House of Representatives. Clearly that would ruin the man's congressional career. Cleve Bailey apologized to me and told me if anything of that sort ever occurred again he wanted to know about it. The next morning the hung-over Texas congressman came to see me shortly after I arrived at work. He apologized to me, begging my forgiveness and promising he would never do anything like that again. I told him that I appreciated his apology. I made sure Bailey knew of it, but I'm not certain that it helped.

My job certainly enhanced my schoolwork, and vice versa. The teachers at the downtown campus, where my classes were conducted, were often congressmen, senior government employees and prestigious visiting professors. For instance, my economics class was taught by a Director of the US Federal Reserve Bank and a congressman on the Foreign Relations committee taught our course in diplomacy.

One of my summer term classes was titled, "Public Affairs Laboratory". It was held once a week for three hours, during which we met with senior government officials. You could ask any question you liked, as the sessions were off the official record. We met with Senator Goldwater, Senator Russell and three other US senators. We met with Vice President Lyndon Johnson, the Secretaries of Defense, State and Treasury, two members of the Supreme Court and several congressmen. The class was limited to twenty participants, who had applied from all over, including Harvard, Stanford, Yale and Michigan. Many students asked unpopular and penetrating questions, which sometimes evoked angry responses. If the public figure tried to evade a question it just got worse. It made for thrilling and educational theater that to this day remains my favorite academic experience.

At the end of the term, we had to write a paper on a subject that had come up in the course of our interviews. I chose to write about the People's Republic of China. I conducted many hours of interviews with a congressman from Minnesota named Walter Judd who I had met at my job. Congressman Judd, a thin man of medium height, was a medical doctor who had worked as a missionary in China for ten years. He told me wonderful stories of sitting around the campfire, debating the future of China with Mao Zedong and Zhou En lai when they were rebels on the run from Chiang Kai-shek. They apparently came to consider Judd a friend, despite the fact that he was an American missionary. Thanks to Congressman Judd, my paper was an in-depth look at a fascinating side of Chinese history that had never been heard.

Walter Judd became an advisor and counselor to me. I learned a great deal from his experiences, which demonstrated the value of perseverance in one's beliefs. He taught me a lot about politics and how to deal with the very difficult congressmen with whom I was sometimes confronted. In 1981, Walter Judd was awarded the highest civilian honor, the Presidential Medal of Freedom, by President Reagan.

Congressman Judd had been great friends with President Truman; they had traveled around the country together, making speeches in favor of the formation of the United Nations. Later, however, Judd and Truman had a major philosophical split over the issue of Truman's firing of General MacArthur. Dr. Judd felt MacArthur's dismissal was a terrible mistake that ultimately prolonged the conflict in Korea, and perpetuated certain political dynamics that eventually led to US involvement in Vietnam. Judd, like MacArthur, felt that the US had not been aggressive enough in Korea or, later, in Vietnam, saying "if we pull out of Vietnam in an indecisive way, it won't end the struggle, it will prolong and expand it, and more people will be killed ... The only way to end a war...is when you prevail to the point the enemy has to stop his aggression".

I believe that Judd was right in a number of ways that apply to our current political situation. The Muslims may think we are weak because we pulled out of Vietnam and Somalia and did not retaliate as strongly as we might have for Muslim attacks on our troops in Yemen, Lebanon and Saudi Arabia. There was a desire by many in this country for the US to get out of Iraq, but I believe that withdrawal would only translate into even more American deaths in the future, because it could be interpreted as a lack of dedication to our political commitments.

Life in Washington was intense. Where you worked and who you worked for was of supreme importance. I didn't have time to socialize outside of work and I didn't date much because of a scarcity of time and money. I did go out with one girl who was pretty important in her own mind. I asked her to dinner and she immediately told me we should go to a restaurant in Georgetown called Espionage. I was ignorant of the fact that it was the most expensive restaurant in D.C. We first sat at the bar for a drink where we met a man there that turned out to be a US Senator (I think from Washington state). We talked for quite some time and he inquired where I worked and what I did. He knew I was a struggling student. When we moved on to dinner, I almost fainted when I saw the prices. Hell, I didn't even have a credit card. I didn't know what to do. I took the waiter aside and asked him if they would take a check. He looked at me and smiled and said, "Mr. Lewis, the Senator has already paid for your dinner". I would have kissed the Senator if I could have found him again. Needless to say, I never dated that girl again.

Jim and my relationship soured over the year we lived together. Jim was quite a leech. Whatever you owned became his by proxy. He stole a number of things from me and used my car almost constantly without asking or without any thought of my own transportation needs. Even worse, Jim was a girl magnet and he had no qualms about locking me out of the apartment while he enjoyed his relationships. One of our best friends was a young gay man from Tennessee who lived across the hall from us who would always make up a rollaway bed for me when I got locked out of the apartment. We always took him out to dinner to pay for the favor.

The Washington Senators were my new hometown baseball team, and I continued my lifelong interest in the sport by following them faithfully. The Senators were owned by a man named Griffith, who was a real miser. As a result, the team roster wasn't terribly strong, and the stadium facility was in sad shape. Griffith Stadium was nearly falling down, and was located in the worst part of town; it was actually scary walking home from games after dark. Despite Griffith, the team did have a handful of exceptional players, including Bob Allison, Bob Lemon, Harmon Killebrew – a terrific home-run hitter – and pitcher Camilo Pascual. But even with their efforts, the team never had a great season while I was in Washington, although they did have some exciting games. I had never been to a major league baseball game before, so I loved having the opportunity to attend home games and see some talented players while I was in the Capitol.

Strangely, it always seemed that the Senators couldn't seem to win against teams with mediocre records, but somehow had a knack for knocking off the league leaders. I tried never to miss a game against the Yankees. For some reason, the Senators often had the upper hand against the Yankees. The 1961 Yankee roster included Mickey Mantle, Yogi Berra, Bobby Richardson, Clete Boyer, Moose Skowron, Elston Howard, Whitey Ford and Roger Maris – who set his home run record of sixty-one runs in 1961. Some consider that team, which would go on to win the World Series, to be the best in baseball history.

One game I remember as particularly exciting. At that time, before the designated hitter rule, pitchers still had to go to bat. As I recall, Mantle, Maris, Killebrew and Lemon all hit home runs, and the Yankees were leading at the bottom of the ninth. With two outs and two men on base, Camilo Pascual, the Senators' pitcher, hit a home run to win the game. The Yankees couldn't believe it. The Washington crowd went wild. During my time in Washington, each and every game between these two teams felt like a classic. I couldn't have picked a better time to be a spectator!

CHAPTER 20

While I was in Washington, I had the good fortune to make the acquaintance of and was befriended by more than one congressman. One was George Mahon, who was the first congressman from the 19th congressional district in Texas after it was formed. He was first elected to Congress as a Democrat in 1934 and served in the next twenty-one succeeding Congresses, under eight Presidents, over a period of forty-four years. He was the chair of the House Appropriations Committee from 1964 until his retirement in 1979. A brilliant man, he faithfully memorized one new word and its meaning every day of his professional life. As you can imagine, his vocabulary was phenomenal, and his writing skills were unequaled. He was a friend of my brother, Tex, and remained a friend of mine until his death in 1985.

Congressman George Mahon and JPL

Mahon was a fascinating man, and had lived through fascinating times. During World War II, George was head of the House Subcommittee on Military Expenditures. He had set a policy that no expenditures could be approved by Congress until he knew how the money was to be used. One day he received a call from President Franklin Roosevelt asking him to come to the White House. When he arrived, he was ushered in to see the President; Roosevelt had a favor to ask of George. He said that Mahon would be receiving an appropriation request for $250,000 and wanted him to approve the request without any questions. George said that it would be against his principles to do such a thing. Roosevelt assured him the money was for a project of highest secrecy, but understood George's requirements and agreed to brief him on the project. Shortly thereafter, George approved the expenditure. The money was for the Manhattan Project, which developed the atomic bomb. Years later, George was prompted to tell me the story of his meeting with the President because that day he and I had lunch in the House cafeteria and he had came across a personal note from Roosevelt in his safe, thanking him for his support.

During Mahon's tenure as chairman of various congressional committees, his committees never had a minority report on any measure, meaning that the minority Republicans always agreed with the measure that passed. Talk about bipartisan action! I don't think we've seen that level of cooperation in Washington in the last thirty years.

A senior Republican congressman on many of those committees was Gerald Ford, a Republican from Michigan who later became President upon Richard Nixon's resignation. Ford once told me that George Mahon had the most integrity and vision of anyone he had served with in Congress. I can remember George taking visiting constituents over to the floor of the House (when it was not in session), where he would engage them and discuss his positions on the issues our country faced. Many times, his voters would tell him in no uncertain terms exactly what they wanted him to do on a certain bill. George Mahon would look at them and explain why he felt that, in good conscience, he could not vote for (or against) the legislation they wanted (or didn't). He took the time to describe why he felt his position was the best choice for the country or his district or his state. He was well-regarded and popular, and during his years in congress, I don't recall anyone even running against him.

He knew most of the towering political personalities of his day. In many of our meetings, we would discuss such people as Eisenhower, Patton, George Marshall, MacArthur, Churchill, Roosevelt and Truman. He would give me his personal recollections of each of these men, their strengths and their weaknesses, their courage under fire and their steadfastness of purpose. I tried for years to get him to write his autobiography, but could not convince him. Congressman Mahon was my friend for many years, and served as a great role model and influence on the shape of my life. Mahon demonstrated integrity, honesty and how to stand up for what you believe. I learned a lot from watching him deal with people both humble and powerful. He never changed his approach regardless of the position of the person involved. He lived in a quiet manner with his wife in a small apartment they had occupied since 1934. He had simple tastes but a thirst for learning. All who knew him looked up to him, even the Presidents of his time. Watching him was a great education.

Another big influence was Democratic Representative Charles Bennett, from Florida. Like Mahon, he served in Congress for forty-four years, including a number of years on the House Armed Services Committee. He was a warm, friendly man of great wisdom. His district was the Jacksonville area of Florida. A co-sponsor of the Americans with Disabilities Act, he himself was disabled after contracting polio during World War II, when he was a guerrilla fighter in the Philippines. He used a wheelchair or a cane to get around, but believe me, it was never a handicap. He had a great sense of humor, took me under his wing and always gave me good advice.

Just before I left Washington, I was offered a number of posts from sitting congressmen and senators. Charlie called me to his office, sat me down and talked to me about the importance of leaving Washington. He believed that there were a number of people in administrative positions around Washington that would never achieve their potential because they felt the need to stay close to those in political power. He admitted it was pretty heady stuff to spend time around those who ran our nation, but he wanted me to promise to move on and seek my future elsewhere. I thought it over and decided to take his advice.

Several years after I had left town, Charlie called and invited me to visit him in his Washington office. At the time I was in San Francisco, but I flew to D.C. and we had lunch. After lunch, we returned to his office, where he told me that his son was a dentist in Jacksonville who had no interest in politics. He told me he had decided to run for the Senate seat that was opening up in Florida and he wanted me to run for his seat in Congress. He said that he had held the office for so long and had such political capital that he could essentially deliver it to me if I was interested in running. What an offer! I was flabbergasted. I told Charlie that he had extended to me the greatest honor and compliment in asking me to succeed him. I very much appreciated his confidence in my abilities. But I reminded Charlie of his speech to me when I was working in the Capitol. I told him that I had taken his advice and sought my future elsewhere. I was excited about my business future and I felt I should stick with it. I also didn't believe that I could genuinely get excited about kissing all the babies and attending all the Kiwanis Club luncheons that would be required in order to get elected. Charlie just looked at me for a few minutes before getting up and hugging me. He said he could not fault my judgment, that he would pull for me always and would be there if I needed his help. As I left the congressional office building and got in my car, I had tears in my eyes. What a wonderful man. He subsequently decided not to run for the Senate seat after all and remained in Congress until 1992. I never had a chance to see him again before his death in 2003 at the age of ninety-two.

CHAPTER 21

Sam Rayburn was a giant in politics, one of most powerful man in Washington over many years, and amazingly, I had an opportunity to get to know him.

Speaker of the House Sam Rayburn, 1961. Photo taken by JPL.

Rayburn was born in 1882 and was elected to the Texas legislature at the age of twenty-four. During his third term there, he served as Speaker of the House. In 1912 he was elected to the United States House of Representatives as a Democrat from the Fourth Texas District. After the 1912 election, Rayburn had no Republican opponent for reelection at any time during his forty-eight years in Congress, where he served continuously until his death in 1961. He became the majority leader in 1937 and Speaker of the House in 1940. Rayburn served as Speaker during the Roosevelt, Truman, Eisenhower and Kennedy administrations. He was a close friend of Lyndon B. Johnson, and was instrumental in Johnson's ascent to power. His integrity was legendary; he accepted no money from lobbyists and paid his own way everywhere.

Rayburn, or "Mr. Sam", as he was known affectionately, was a short man with a stocky build and bald head. The hair on his hands, coarse but sparse, reminded me of bristles. He gave the impression of being a very gruff man with no sense of humor, and scared the stuffing out of most of the congressmen and staff; however, to those of us who worked around him frequently, he was always kind. Early in his career, he had been married for about three months before it was annulled, and since that time had remained a bachelor. He spent much of his time away from work alone and I got the impression that he was often lonely.

At night, he was driven home to his apartment just off Dupont Circle by his chauffeur, George. George had driven for whoever was the Speaker of the House for twenty-six years; for the past sixteen years, that had been Rayburn. Sometimes, at the end of the day, Rayburn would ask me if I needed a ride. If I said yes, he would take me as far as Dupont Circle, which was halfway to my apartment. George would escort Rayburn from his office in the Capitol to the limousine parked in the porte-cochere. George or I would take the Speaker's arm and he would get into the limo, his head down and his Stetson hat in place. That way no one would try to stop him on the way out and in many instances the public did not even recognize him.

When we all got in the car, Rayburn would usually initiate a familiar exchange, saying something like, "George, don't drive too fast on the way out!" George would reply with, "Don't tell me how to drive, Mr. Sam. I'll do whatever the hell I want!" This banter would go on for several blocks. If you didn't know them or their relationship you would be stunned. Mr. Sam loved George and vice versa. When Mr. Sam would get lonely, he would invite George over to watch television. When Mr. Sam wanted to go see the Washington Senators play, he and George would go together. Their relationship was important to both of them and they took care of each other. I always wondered what George's wife must have thought about the situation!

The Speaker often asked me during these trips if everything was fine with me or if I needed anything. I could never think of a single thing that I wanted or needed. Years later I would joke that I probably should have said that I wanted Rhode Island, because he probably could have given it to me.

Rayburn was a enormously powerful force in the House, and other congressmen were afraid of him. He decided committee assignments and the order in which bills came to the floor; if you became an enemy, Mr. Sam could bury you and your ideas, assuring that you would not get reelected. I recall a time I overheard two members talking about the Speaker. One said that he wasn't going to let that bald-headed so-and-so tell him what to do. The other congressman nodded. At that moment, Rayburn came through the doors – both congressmen fawned all over him and patted him on the back. As Mr. Sam walked past me, he winked, almost as if he had heard the whole conversation.

I often witnessed the strong influence Rayburn had on his fellow lawmakers. Once, when I was in Rayburn's office, Congressman Charles Mathias from the Sixth Congressional District of Maryland came in to see the Speaker. Mathias was a freshman congressman and was very upset about a bill that had been introduced on the House floor. Mathias said, "Mr. Speaker, this bill is an appropriation for the Feather River project in Northern California. From what I can see it appears to be a payoff to some construction company in that state. In all good conscience, I cannot vote in favor of this expensive development".

Mr. Sam looked at him a moment and then said, "Congressman, it is important that you do what you think is right. There is no one in this body that would want you to go against your scruples". He paused for a moment before adding, "As I recall, you ran in the sixth district of Maryland on dredging the rivers in your area in order for them to be cleaner and more capable of handling barge traffic. Isn't that correct?" Mathias said that was indeed true.

Mr. Sam asked, "There are 435 congressmen in the House. Of that number how many do you think are interested in dredging rivers in your district?" Mathias replied that he didn't think any of them would be interested in the rivers in his district. Rayburn continued, "That's what I would suppose. If you vote against the California congressman's bill then the odds are he would vote against yours. In addition, other members would not trust your support. If you don't get your bill passed you probably will not be re-elected. You just have to weigh all the issues and vote the way you feel is best". Charles Mathias voted for the California project. He must have learned his lessons well, because a few years later he was elected as a Senator from Maryland.

Another time, a bill came to the floor of the House that was designed as a relief measure for several depressed areas of the country. The main targets were certain coal-mining areas in Pennsylvania, West Virginia, Tennessee and Virginia. The bill was initially drafted to alleviate unemployment in those four states, but by the time the bill came to the floor of the House for a vote, it included aid to about thirty other areas of the country. I remember asking the Speaker why in the world he would allow congressmen to attach amendments to the bill that would dilute its effectiveness. He said, "John, that's the way politics works. You have to get a consensus in order to get the bill passed. In this case, 85% of the money will go to the four original areas. So we got what we needed but we had to give something up in the process". Rayburn was a man of integrity, but he was also deeply practical, and knew that he sometimes had to make compromises in order to be effective.

But that's not to say that Rayburn didn't relish a good victory. I recall the time Mr. Sam got into a match of wills with the Hon. Howard Smith, the Chairman of the powerful Committee on Rules. Smith was a politically strong congressman from Virginia, a conservative Democrat who had been a leading opponent of civil rights laws for black people. The Speaker wanted to add members to the Committee in order to assure passage for some of the Kennedy Administration's legislation. Smith was against packing the committee. After the floor vote, the Speaker came back into his office and said to me, "That will teach that S.O.B. to mess with me!" Rayburn had won the vote 218 to 217. Not what I would call a resounding triumph, but it did the trick.

I learned a great deal just by observing and talking to the Speaker. He had been deeply entrenched in the political process for almost forty years by the time I worked for him. One time, I asked him why there was so much confusion on so many legislative items. Mr. Sam replied, "John, the government in this country has been going to hell for over 150 years and it's still the best in the world. You have to give people the chance to speak their mind and they'll generally make the right decision".

Mr. Sam was not without his flaws. He had a tendency to pat pretty girls on the rear, and somehow always got away with it. He was in his late seventies at the time and seemed fairly harmless, and I suppose no one wanted to call him on it. He did help me out when I found myself on the receiving end of some unwanted attention, though. I had begun to have a problem with a congressman from Ohio. Every time he came into my elevator, he would try to put his hands on me in some intimate places. It made me angry, but I wasn't sure what exactly to do about it. I asked the Speaker if I could talk with him, and told him about what was happening. I said I didn't want to make a scene and embarrass the congressman in any way, but wanted some guidance on how to handle it. Rayburn told me, "John, the United States House of Representatives is truly representative of the population as a whole. There are a number of homosexuals who have been elected to this body and we have to learn to deal with them. You do what you have to do and I will support you". The next time the congressman from Ohio approached me, I told him to leave me alone or I would tell him in a louder voice next time. He never bothered me again.

My father came to Washington for a visit one summer, and I knew that he thought that Rayburn and Johnson were just about the finest men he knew. I asked Rayburn if it would be acceptable if I brought my father by his office to see him during his visit. He asked me for the dates of the visit and after consulting his calendar he said that he wanted me to bring my Dad by at eleven-thirty on a particular morning. I told him I would.

When Dad got to town, I told him about the appointment and he was thrilled. We arrived exactly on time and were invited into the Speakers office. To our surprise, Lyndon Johnson was there and the Speaker told me that the three of them – Rayburn, Johnson and Dad – would be going to lunch and that I should meet them back at the office at one-thirty. I couldn't believe it – and neither could Dad. He was thrilled. I returned to the office on time but they didn't get back until two. They were laughing and having a great time.

After we said our goodbyes and left, Dad turned to me and said, "Those men really like you. They told me what an important role you played here". He was beaming from ear to ear, and I didn't have the heart to tell him that I was just a gofer and an elevator operator. But my already significant loyalty and respect for these two men had been raised another notch. I would always be grateful for the time they took to please an old man, who would talk glowingly about them for the rest of his life.

CHAPTER 22

In January 1960, public transportation altered my life. I was riding from downtown Washington to my apartment on Wisconsin Avenue when a young lady on my bus caught my eye. She was small, with dark hair and blue eyes, and I was instantly attracted, but didn't have the nerve to speak to her. She got off at Connecticut Avenue, which was not my stop, so I did too. I walked along with her to the next intersection before working up my courage and introducing myself. I found out that her name was Ann Lorrayne Skoda, and she was originally from Johnstown in upstate New York. She had attended the University of Maryland, graduating with a degree in nursing. She was working in the heart research area of the National Institute of Health in nearby Bethesda, Maryland. I asked if I could call her later; she was a little nervous but reluctantly agreed.

Ann Lorrayne Lewis, 1964

I called the next day and made a date to meet for a drink the next evening. As you might imagine, she was still a bit apprehensive when we met, but over the course of the next few hours, we got to know each other. I should just admit up front that I misrepresented some facts about myself. If Ann was telling the story, she might tell you that I outright lied, but I think that's a little harsh! I told her that I was attending law school and working on the Hill, when I hadn't even finished my undergraduate degree... My means may have been suspect, but my motive was pure: I was nervous and wanted to impress her.

In any case, the pretense didn't last long – as we got to know each other, I told her about my four years in the military and then came clean about my educational progress, or the lack thereof. She took everything in stride and we grew even closer. I discovered that, in addition to her striking smile, she had a great sense of humor, and a positive approach and enthusiasm for life. I soon realized that she was a true gem of a person, and I missed her terribly whenever we were apart. I became certain that she was the one for me and proposed to her that summer; luckily she felt the same about me and accepted. We got married in September and took a short honeymoon to Bermuda.

Our wedding, September 7, 1960.

The honeymoon was a bit of a disaster. We had originally booked a cruise to Nassau, but there was a hurricane in the Bahamas, so at the last minute the captain of the ship redirected us to Bermuda. On the second day out, the edge of the hurricane reached our ship and we had high winds and stormy seas for the next two days. Nearly everyone got seasick except for the captain and me. Ann was terribly ill. At meals it would be the captain, me and a very small group of wobbly passengers that would change daily. By the time we got to Bermuda, Ann felt so weak that we did very little sightseeing. It was not a auspicious start to our relationship. After we returned, we moved into an old carriage house just off Connecticut Avenue, near the Maryland border. I'm sure it was over a hundred years old, and at first we were completely charmed by it. When we signed the lease, the weather in Washington was mild and the carriage house seemed comfortable and perfect. Then winter arrived. We could actually feel the wind coming right through the walls. It was colder than blue blazes. Suddenly, our heating bill was more expensive than our rent. We stuffed newspaper and rags in the openings but we still froze. The place became less and less charming every day, and I think we left before the following winter.

Our family backgrounds are very different. Ann had a happy childhood as an only child in Johnstown, which was known for making Knox gelatin and gloves. Her mother, Cora, was a Buckingham before she married and the English influence was evident in the conservative attitudes exhibited by her and her siblings. Ann's father, Steve, was born the US but his parents came from Czechoslovakia, a heritage that was apparent in his work ethic and his love of certain foods. Steve was a big lovable man who adored his daughter. He was always very good to me and was positive in his attitudes. Cora was much more opinionated and didn't shy away from expressing her views. I'm still not sure that she ever approved of Ann's choice of a husband! Ann's extended family included an Italian uncle, whose influence came in the form of great food and lengthy meals. My parents had grown up and lived almost all their lives in Texas. There was no ethnic diversity in my family tree, and thus not much variety in food, politics and religious beliefs. I really enjoyed all the different aspects of Ann's family life and learned a great deal from all her aunts and uncles. We have now been married for over fifty-two years. How can I describe such a long-standing, all-important relationship? In all respects Ann is a person that people invariably like. She would never do anything to hurt anyone. We have experienced ups and downs financially, emotionally and physically but we are a team that works together. Ann has always encouraged me to take chances in my career and has never complained when things don't go well. Because of my work, we moved eleven times in our first thirteen years and she never protested. In our time together, we have traveled all over the world, enjoying the company of each other. Ann has been a good partner in all of our endeavors, with a great sense of humor and a wide-ranging curiosity. She is compassionate, and always willing to listen to the problems of others. She has always taken good care of me and given me good counsel, and I hope she would say the same of me. I still find her as attractive as the day I followed her off that bus. I love her with all my heart and would be lost without her. We will be together all the days of our lives.

CHAPTER 23

While my personal life was undergoing some big changes, so was the country as a whole. 1960 was an election year, and the activity in the Capitol really picked up. The crowds were unusually large because both of the party candidates and their running mates could be seen in action in the Senate. Richard Nixon, who was then Vice President, would be the Republican nominee for President and Senator Henry Cabot Lodge, Jr. the candidate for Vice President on his ticket. Senator John F. Kennedy was the Democratic nominee for President and Senator Lyndon Johnson his Vice Presidential nominee. Everyone wanted to get into the Senate gallery because there were times when all four of these men would be in the chamber simultaneously. The lines were often four across, spanning the entire rotunda, and getting around in the Capitol became very difficult. And when the President came to the Capitol for any reason, especially for something big like the State of the Union Address, the crowds multiplied exponentially, and reporters showed up in droves.

Autographed photo of Richard Nixon

During those times, it was part of my function to stay in the hall outside the Speaker's office with the Secret Service agents. They wanted the halls cleared of all nonessential personnel before the President was to walk down the hall and enter the House chamber. I was expected to know on sight the various members of Congress, the members of the Supreme Court, members of the President's cabinet and the Joint Chiefs of Staff. I had a handbook with pictures of each of these individuals, but just being around many of them on a daily basis made it easy to memorize their faces. When anyone I didn't recognize came into the hall, I would politely ask their name and destination. If the information didn't sound right, I would tell them that it was a restricted area and ask them to leave. Generally that would be the end of it, and if they refused to leave, the Secret Service would escort them away.

I did this during one year of the Eisenhower presidency and two years of the Kennedy presidency. It surprised me how many kooks managed to get into closely guarded areas. Most people who attempted to get close to the President were just curious, and willingly obeyed when they were told to move. But I do recall an instance when a man showed up in the hall, standing in precisely the spot where the President would be walking shortly, with a box a little larger than a shoe box under his arm. When I approached and asked his name, he refused to give it to me. I told him he needed to leave the area, which he did. But as the President's appearance became imminent, I looked around and spotted the strange man with the box again. I don't know how he got there, given the tight security. He must have come from upstairs in a circuitous fashion. The nearest Secret Service agent nudged me, so I again approached the man and told him to leave. He told me he wanted to stay right there so that he could be close to the President. In the blink of an eye, two Secret Service agents appeared, one on each side of the man. They lifted him off the ground and carried him away. I don't know what happened to him, but he certainly didn't come back!

Because I worked around the Speaker, the President and several ex-Presidents, the Secret Service had checked me out very thoroughly. One time, their familiarity with me created a potentially risky situation. I was on the Senate side of the Capitol, trying to help manage the multitude of people trying to get near the presidential candidates. A member of the Secret Service approached and asked if I would be willing to help them for a moment. Rather naïve, and trying to be friendly, I agreed. They asked if I would just walk slowly forward toward the center of the Capitol, facing the long line of people waiting to get into the Senate galleries. As I started forward, I felt a man's hand on my shoulder, I glanced back and realized it was Richard Nixon. With his left hand on my left shoulder, he was reaching between us with his right hand to greet people. We walked in lock step for about twenty minutes, covering about one hundred yards. Nixon then left me and descended the stairway in the center of the rotunda to an office he occupied in the basement. I turned to the agent next to me and asked what that was all about. He told me that anyone who might want to shoot or harm the Vice President would not harm an innocent bystander. That was the last time I ever let anyone use me as a human shield. The agent assured me that I was never in any danger, they were watching very closely and nothing could have happened. I asked him not to do me any more favors.

I found Nixon very distinguished-looking in person, of medium height and with salt-and-pepper hair. He had a nice smile and gave the impression of being friendly. But after being around him several times, I realized that his eyes were cold and that while he was shaking your hand, he was already looking past you to the next person. If you were not of interest to him, he made no effort to connect.

Perhaps my fondest memories of a politician are those of John F. Kennedy. I saw him quite frequently when he was a Senator. He would sometimes come over late in the evening to see the Speaker, and would come to my elevator first to talk awhile. We talked about all kinds of things. I think it was a kind of distraction for him. At the time, I was taking a course in economics from a Governor of the Federal Reserve. When Kennedy heard that, he was intrigued. He didn't agree with this particular Governor and decided that I was going to be his means of challenging this man. He gave me a question to ask the Governor the next time I went to class. I did as I was told, and the professor paused a moment, then just looked at me and smiled. He knew where I worked and he knew the source of the question. He immediately launched into a dissertation of an answer. I frantically took notes. At the end of his response, he said that he wanted to outline a question for me to ask my friend. The next time I saw Kennedy, he asked, "Well, what did he say?" I took out my notes and told him, finishing with the question given to me. Kennedy launched into a critique of the teacher's answer, and then gave me another question to ask him.

This exchange went back and forth for several weeks. These questions concerned money supply, credit restraint, interest rates and so on. The other students started to realize that they were witnessing a debate between Kennedy and the Federal Reserve, and could hardly wait for the next class to hear the next installment. I sure got a kick out of being a willing conduit for the dialogue, and I know that Kennedy and the Governor both loved every minute of it.

After Kennedy was elected President, I saw him much less frequently, but when he came to the Capitol he was always friendly, inquiring after me and Ann. He was a naturally gifted, very social politician, with a greeting for almost everyone. This was very different than his predecessor, Eisenhower, who would walk down an aisle of people without even looking to the left or right. Eisenhower always looked straight ahead as he probably did when he was a general. But Kennedy not only greeted people, but he also remembered their names, the names of their family members, and what the person did for a living. I was told that the President had people to prompt him on the names of the people he might meet, but I know they never had to prompt him on folks like me or any of the other workaday staffers he saw regularly. He never forgot any of us. I often wish I had a gift like that; I have trouble remembering names and it can sometimes be embarrassing!

Kennedy's physical appearance was quite striking as well. He was a handsome and impressive individual, about six feet tall, with wide shoulders and a tan. Even though we now know he had health problems, he always appeared hale and hearty to me. One time, when I knew the President was going to be at the Capitol for the State of the Union address, I asked Ann if she would like to see him. She said she would like that, so I took her with me that day. I had asked the Secret Service ahead of time if Ann could be allowed to stand in an isolated spot outside the elevator, so that when Kennedy exited its doors to leave the Capitol, she would be the only person he would see. They agreed and we put her about ten feet from the elevator, where the President would have to walk toward and within about two feet of her in order to make his exit.

When I took Kennedy down in the elevator after his speech, he saw Ann and walked right up to her, held out his hand and said hello. Ann was absolutely stunned. She just shook his hand with her mouth open, unable to say a word. I have kidded her about this ever since, but most people react in a similar fashion when they come face-to-face with the President. Kennedy had a special charm, but the power of the office itself is impressive. People remember a single glimpse of or handshake by the President for their entire lives. After Kennedy became President, I must admit that I saw him in a different light and reacted differently to him.

Just once, Jack Kennedy came by with his brother Bobby. Bobby was shorter in stature than Jack Kennedy and I didn't think he had the presence of his brother. I remember that, while we all talked in the elevator, Bobby put his feet up on the rail that circled the elevator, supporting himself with his elbows on the rail across from him. You have to be pretty agile and strong to hang like that for very long. It was a brief encounter, but he seemed like a nice fellow.

During my brief time in Washington, I encountered no less than six former, current or future American Presidents. Of these, Truman may have been the most intimidating, but only because I was ignorant of proper protocol...

Quite often in Washington, the political parties have what I would call 'political revival meetings'. Politicians and big money donors would gather for dinner, drinks and speeches. Often, contributors would send money but not show up for the meeting, but the party wanted a full house, so they would invite people like me to help fill the room. It really was like a revival meeting. The speakers would say something and everyone else would respond, "amen" or "that's right, brother!" It was always done tongue in cheek and there was lots of laughter. A good time was had by all.

I worked for the Democrats, so I was invited to their meetings. One time, former President Harry Truman spoke, followed by Sam Rayburn, Lyndon

Johnson, John Kennedy and several other party leaders. After the meeting, I was asked to deliver a message and an envelope to Truman at the Mayflower Hotel early the next morning. Truman always got up early and took a vigorous walk before breakfast. I got there early, but not early enough. Truman had already finished his walk and was eating breakfast in the hotel dining room with three other gentlemen. I didn't really know what to do and I grew a bit impatient waiting. That was a mistake. I went into the dining room and approached the table. When Truman saw me, he told me to wait outside until he finished breakfast.

Though he wore thick bifocal glasses and was not a tall man, Truman was imposing. Solidly built, he always stood very erect and with great dignity. Knowing that Truman had been a powerful contemporary of Churchill and Stalin, had negotiated with them and had played a key role in ending World War II gave him a powerful aura. An aura I had plenty of time to contemplate as I waited for him out in the lobby of the hotel.

Forty minutes later, Truman came out and very loudly and angrily asked me what I wanted. I told him who had sent me, gave him the package and delivered the message. He dismissed me very curtly and I went on my way. I was embarrassed and even though I knew I had acted inappropriately, I was hurt by Truman actions. The very next day, Truman came to the Speaker's office and, as soon as he saw me, made a point of shaking my hand and saying it was nice to see me. There was never another word spoken about the Mayflower incident, and he was always pleasant to me the subsequent times I saw him. I always felt it was a heck of a gesture for him to be so nice to someone who had clearly been wrong.

When I first arrived in Washington, Eisenhower was the President. A legendary figure, Eisenhower had been a five star general and had headed up the Allied forces in Europe during World War II. He was first elected in 1952 and was re-elected in 1956. I only saw Eisenhower on two occasions: the first was when he came to the Capitol to make the State of the Union address in 1960, and the second was at the Kennedy Inauguration in 1961. He never spoke to me, but he didn't speak to a number of people around him. Like Truman, he walked with his eyes straight ahead. A career military man, he had a serious, stern appearance, although a great many people who knew him well said that he had a very friendly personality, a great sense of humor, was a good companion and loved dirty jokes. He was well liked by most everyone who knew him, but to me he seemed unapproachable and I was a bit in awe of him.

Presidential Inauguration of John F. Kennedy

Because of his friendship with Sam Rayburn, I saw Lyndon Johnson quite often before he became President. My impression of Johnson was as a tall, gregarious and moody individual. He had been narrowly elected to the House of Representatives in 1937, and after six terms in the House, he was elected to the Senate in 1948. In 1954, he became the youngest Majority leader in Senate history. While I was in Washington, I witnessed Johnson vie with John Kennedy for the 1960 Democratic Presidential nomination. I worked on Johnson's campaign with his two daughters, Lynda and Luci. We stuffed envelopes, delivered signs and did every kind of odd job they could come up with, having a lot of fun with the whole process, but ultimately, Johnson lost the nomination to Kennedy.

Speaker Rayburn had been the Chairman of the Democratic Convention for several years and I was told that I would be asked to attend the convention in San Francisco as a part of his staff. But before the convention, afraid that

Rayburn would control the whole convention and block Kennedy's nomination, the Kennedy camp appointed their own Chairman. So at the last minute, I was told that I would not be attending the convention after all. The Speaker was furious and the Kennedy camp immediately set out to mitigate the fallout from their decision. As a result of Rayburn's negotiation, Johnson became Kennedy's vice presidential candidate. When Kennedy was elected President, Johnson became Vice President. When Kennedy was assassinated in 1963, Johnson was sworn in as President. He was re-elected in 1964, but dropped out of his re-election campaign in 1968 because of the lack of support for the war in Vietnam.

I never saw Johnson while he was President, but I did see him again after he had retired. In those later years, he seemed to be an unhappy man, often caught between emotional extremes. He had been demoralized and discredited by having to step aside as President, and was obsessed with his place in history. He died in 1973.

The sixth President I encountered during those years was Gerald Ford, although he did not become President until long after I had left Washington. At that time, Ford was a very well liked and able Congressman who had served as the minority leader of the House Military Appropriations Committee. He seemed to genuinely like people and was always friendly to me. He worked closely with George Mahon on all kinds of legislation and there was never a time that they were not able to reach a compromise. Ford was a large man, who had been a football player at the University of Michigan. He served in Congress for twenty-five years, and was the Minority Leader of the House from 1965 to 1973. He was the first Vice President chosen under the terms of the Twenty-fifth Amendment, succeeding Spiro Agnew, and, in the aftermath of the Watergate scandal, succeeded Richard Nixon, the first President ever to resign.

Years later, I saw Ford again on a golf driving range in Vail, Colorado. I spoke to him and told him that I used to know him in Washington. He looked at me a moment and said he recognized me from the years I used to run the Speaker's elevator. I was floored that he remembered me after so many years.

PART SEVEN

BACK TO THE REAL WORLD

CHAPTER 24

After two and a half years in Washington, I decided to return to Texas. I wanted to listen to Charlie Bennett's advice about getting out of Washington, plus there were financial considerations; the college credits at American University were very expensive and I could finish my degree back at Texas Tech for only $75 a semester.

We headed back to farm country. Ann had never been very far west of the Atlantic Coast, and she was a little shocked by the flat countryside, but she was game for the adventure. She got a job right away as a nurse to an eye surgeon who specialized in infant eye surgery. When I left home in 1950, I was really just a boy and the only jobs I could get were in supermarkets. I thought as a young man of twenty-six returning to Lubbock, I would find a greater choice of jobs. Unfortunately, when we arrived in town, I soon discovered that there were few jobs for college students, and even those were fairly low-paying.

I went to work delivering furniture for a store. It almost did me in. The back pains were awful. I really didn't have the strength to carry sofas and appliances into multistoried houses. I soon found a new job as a salesman in the men's department of the finest department store in west Texas. That had no heavy lifting and a great atmosphere, but it didn't pay well. After a few months, I took the best-paying job I could find, working as a janitor at the Ford dealership's truck repair and maintenance facility. My paycheck, added to my veteran's stipend, allowed us to live fairly well. My boss, a gruff, uneducated bear of a man, didn't have much use for a college student. He would yell, "Hey, you! Smart assed college boy! Get your butt in there and clean out that toilet!" He was convinced that college was a waste of time. Luckily, I didn't listen to him! In addition to working mornings and late afternoons, I was taking a full class load at Tech, usually twelve to fifteen hours of class load per semester. I was determined to graduate in January of 1963.

Tech wasn't as much fun this time around; my schedule was crazy, and the mix of the student body had changed. When I was there the first time, there was a preponderance of veterans, but now it was mainly young people just out of high school. The age difference seemed enormous and Ann and I didn't know many people our own age. In any case, we spent most of our time either working or studying and mainly saw each other some nights and weekends, but it was a happy and productive time. We didn't have a lot of money for extras, but we attended activities at the university and went to the Saturday football games, which were a big event in the town. Being back in Texas was good for both of us.

Ann was very supportive and encouraging of my crazy schedule, and was finding her own place in the community. She made friends with the people she worked with. The area was doing well economically and it had grown since I had last lived there. Though it was still an agricultural center, it had become the medical center for most of west Texas and eastern New Mexico.

It was fun to be living back in my old hometown again, and many people I had known were still there. Mom, Dad and I used to attend church at a tabernacle with a minister named Reverend Boyd McSpadden. He and his wife were both beautiful people – literally. He was very handsome and his wife looked like Linda Christian, a famous movie star who was at that time considered by many to be the most beautiful woman in the world. They had two children, Boyd, Jr. and Cheryl. When Cheryl was one year old, her mother asked if I would babysit her during the evening services. I was only nine or ten, but I guess I appeared responsible. I babysat Cheryl for about twelve months.

Back in Lubbock, around the time I was preparing to graduate from college, I was invited to lunch with a friend named Myron Garner who I met golfing. He was a successful lawyer and a very fine man with a great sense of humor. As we started to walk from his office to lunch, there was quite a commotion on Broadway, the main thoroughfare. We heard bands playing and saw people marching. Myron told me it was a parade in honor of the new Miss America, who was from Lubbock. We went to the curb and watched her go by; she was in a bathing suit, seated on the back of a convertible, waving to the crowd. She was beautiful. I asked Myron who the young lady was, and he told me her name was Cheryl McSpadden. Almost without thinking, I said,

"Well, isn't that something. I used to change that girl's diapers!" He looked at me strangely and said, "I would advise you not to remind her of that in the present circumstances". We both laughed and went on to lunch.

While in Texas, I kept up with political news, and I could see how my time in Washington had helped shape my opinions. In November 1961, I was saddened to hear that Sam Rayburn had died of cancer. A number of students at the college cheered at the news of his death but, having had a chance to watch him work up close, I felt sure that the country had suffered a great loss of leadership. I don't believe the House of Representatives has had the same quality of leadership since his death.

Not long after I had arrived back in Texas, I sat in my car and listened to President Kennedy address the nation during the Cuban missile crisis. There was a real fear in the country at that time that the Russians might actually launch a missile our way, just to intimidate us. The night after the speech, I drove out into the countryside around Lubbock and saw a surprising and scary sight. In every direction around me, I could see missiles that had risen up out of underground silos. Steam was coming off the missiles and they were bathed in strong light. There was nothing clandestine about it; it was almost as if the government wanted our enemies to see that this country was ready for battle. I had never known that there were so many silos on so many farms. It was an eerie spectacle, one that I will never forget.

While we were in Lubbock, Ann's parents decided to come visit us and see where their daughter was living. When we arrived at the airport to meet them, they had already formed an opinion on west Texas – and it wasn't positive. They didn't like the area, and their opinion didn't change when they saw our apartment. We had rented a place near the college, over a garage, which consisted of a bathroom and a large room containing the bed, the kitchen and a small table to eat on. To her parents, it looked pretty grim. They didn't want their daughter living in such an awful place and tried to convince Ann to come back east with them. Thankfully, they didn't persuade her to leave, but they weren't too happy with me. Actually, Ann and I didn't think the apartment was all that bad. It was cheap, convenient to work and school, and we had a good time there. Chalk it up to the rose-colored glasses of newlyweds!

Of course, people are often partial to the landscape they grew up with. Some time later, we took my father to visit New England during the loveliest time of the year. The weather was crisp and the trees were alive with glorious fall colors. We drove him through Vermont, marveling at how beautiful the colors and the countryside were. But when I asked Dad what he thought of the area, he paused for a moment and said, "Well, you can't see anything for all these damn trees. There's no way these people can make a living off this land". Of course, in his own way he was right. Everyone sees things a little differently.

Being back in Texas gave me more opportunities to spend time with my father as he was getting older. At the Texas Tech homecoming game, they always gave out awards to parents for things like the furthest distance traveled, the youngest parents, etc. In 1962, Dad got the award for the oldest father of a college student. He was seventy-eight years old. He got his picture on the front page of the newspaper, was kissed by a couple of young lovelies, and received a plaque to commemorate the event. He loved every minute of it.

Around this time, we took Dad to Mexico City for a week's vacation. We all went to a restaurant one night, and after a good meal headed to a bar near the hotel. There were a number of Americans there and Dad struck up a conversation with a schoolteacher from Tennessee. She was about half his age and they seemed to be getting along famously. Ann and I left him there and went back to the hotel. The next morning, there was no sign of Dad. We didn't actually start to worry until the next day, but we didn't know what to do. It's a little hard to explain to people how you have lost your seventy-eight year old father. On the fourth day, Dad showed up. Of course, I wanted to know where he had been, but he basically informed me that it was none of my business and that he didn't feel he needed to report to me. I told him we had been worried about him and he let me know that he had done fairly well for the better part of a century without my protection and he didn't need it now. Talk about a role reversal! Ann and I decided he was right and the conversation ended. We all enjoyed the vacation, but I think Dad enjoyed it the most!

CHAPTER 25

As my graduation drew nearer, I deliberated a great deal about what to do with my professional life. I knew I wasn't interested in politics but didn't have an obvious road I wanted to travel. I came to the decision that I wanted to get involved in international business; I didn't know much about the business world, either at home or abroad, but it sounded exciting to me. I did my research and found out about a school in Glendale, Arizona called the Thunderbird Graduate School of International Management that granted a very well-regarded graduate degree in international management. I applied and was accepted.

The year-long program started in January 1963 and, as soon as I had graduated from Tech with a degree in economics, Ann and I hightailed to Arizona so I could start school immediately. The curriculum consisted of graduate courses in marketing, management, government relations and economics from the standpoint of operating in a foreign environment with currency risks, governmental risks and cultural differences. In addition, we did intensive study in a foreign language, consisting of about two hours of class work and three hours of lab work each day.

I decided on French as my language. I can't for the life of me tell you why I decided to study French. I guess I had a romantic view of Europe. I had never been there, but thought that Europe sounded like a nice place to visit and work. The school's method of language instruction was adapted from the program developed at the Monterey Language School for the military and other government agencies. It uses what is termed the "oral-aural method". All classes were conducted entirely in the foreign language and the laboratory sessions consisted of listening to conversational tapes hour after hour, until the student begins to understand clearly what is said. The instructors were

Parisian and spoke rapidly. The idea was that it didn't help much to learn the language if you couldn't understand what was said to you in a realistic setting.

Before long, I became thoroughly sick of French. I studied very hard but I never crossed over that threshold where I began to think fluently in the language, although it did seep into my dreams and take over my brain. I felt like I was constantly translating everything back and forth mentally between English and French.

There were students who not only came to think in whatever language they where conversing in, but could do so in four or five different languages. I remember one student who used to walk around campus wearing a bow tie and carrying a small wicker basket. He had served as the interpreter at the peace talks at Panmunjom that ended the Korean War, and could read, write and speak Japanese, Korean and both Cantonese and Mandarin Chinese. If that wasn't maddening enough, he was also a genius at economics and spoke fluent French, Spanish and Italian. I grew to hate the guy, because everything was so easy for him. Meanwhile, I felt like I had to work as hard as I could just to achieve mediocre results. Language was not my strong point. The wicker basket guy was eventually hired by Ohio State University to help them fulfill a contract to reengineer the economy and governmental structure in Liberia. He got eight times the starting salary that anyone else in our class received. Oh well, I was never that excited about Liberia anyway.

When the summer break came, about fifteen of us were hired to go work at the World Trade Fair that was being held at McCormick Place in Chicago, at that time the largest exhibition hall in the world. Ann and I took off for Chicago, but decided to stop in Lubbock on the way to see my Dad. We hit the road in a new Volkswagen Beetle and as we were just leaving Santa Rosa, New Mexico, a hailstorm hit, pelting us with hailstones the size of golf balls. Ann and I got out a blanket and held it against the front windshield to prevent the window from falling in on us. I drove slowly until we got under an overpass that gave us some respite from the storm. It probably didn't last any more than fifteen minutes but it seemed like longer. By the time the storm had passed, the hail was almost a foot deep on the ground and our car had been totaled. We finally made it to Lubbock and limped in to the Volkswagen dealer. The formerly round roof of our car was now totally flat, as was the hood and the engine housing. Every window was damaged or gone. Our new car was in dire straits, but thankfully the engine was in good condition. The auto repair crew did a marvelous job and about a week later we were on our way to Chicago.

We rented a room on the east side of downtown and I reported for work. We all wore plaid jackets so everyone could recognize us. There was even a front page article in the Chicago newspaper with a photo of three of us in our jackets. About six of our group were used as interpreters and the rest of us worked as Information Officers. Several of the interpreters could translate between two other languages, such as German and French, French and Spanish or Italian and Russian with no problem. I was very impressed by many of my classmates. The fair went on for six weeks and we worked long hours, but it was worth it. It was a wonderful learning experience. Vice President Lyndon Johnson came to town to open the fair, but I didn't get a chance to see him; however, two members of his staff came by and told me they would tell him hello for me.

That fall, we returned to school and on November 22, 1963, I was just leaving a morning class when a classmate named Max Arehart came up and said, "Did you hear that Kennedy just got shot?" I said that sounded like some wild rumor, but that perhaps we should call the newspaper in Phoenix just to check. I called the newsroom and someone told me that it had indeed come across the tape that Kennedy had been shot in Dallas. We went immediately to the student union building and watched the story unfold on television. The President had been taken to Parkland Hospital, but there was no statement as to how serious his injuries might be. Memories of my encounters with him flooded my mind and I prayed that he would be all right. But before long, the news came that he had died.

I was stunned, and everything began to happen in a daze. It felt like such a personal blow on top of the obvious political tragedy, and I wondered what in the world would cause someone to want to kill Kennedy. In my eyes, he had been a man with a great sense of humor, a warm friendly nature and a genuine interest in humanity. In my opinion, Jack Kennedy was the last Democratic

President who was somewhat moderate and had the support of Congress for most of his program. Our country lost a fine man for no good reason. I think sometimes that fate takes someone from us in order to lock that person in our memories in a certain way. Forever more, we will think of John Kennedy as a handsome, delightful forty-five years old.

It was the end of an era, both politically and personally. My last semester at Thunderbird went by in a blur of activity. The work was intense but in addition, we started to interview on campus with companies for employment after graduation. I probably interviewed with twelve or so companies. I received interest from a few but the first firm job offer I got was from United California Bank in Los Angeles. It was the tenth largest bank in the country, and had a very good international division. The offer was for $6800 a year, which was a little above the average at the school. Ann and I thought we were rich. I wrote a letter of acceptance. Three of my classmates also received offers from UCB and accepted them; I was glad to know that at least I would have some friends there.

A great many of my classmates at Thunderbird went on to distinguished careers. The school is now rated as the best international business school in the world. It helped me get started in an interesting business that formed the basis for everything that followed in my professional life.

PART EIGHT

INTO THE CORPORATE WORLD

CHAPTER 26

Ann and I moved to Los Angeles and rented an apartment in Hollywood in January of 1964. Our place was in a low-rise garden apartment building, a type that is commonly seen in Los Angeles. The other residents were a mix of aspiring actors and aging has-beens. Ann got a job as a nurse in the OB/GYN clinic at UCLA. I rode the bus to work on my first day, not knowing what to expect.

New management hires were required to go through a year-long training program. After orientation, we were sent to different branches of the bank to learn as much as we could in a concentrated period about a variety of jobs and specialties, such as teller, mortgage lending, automobile loans, branch accounting and counting currency. The purpose was for us to learn the duties of each employee. I was assigned to the Hollywood and later the Santa Monica branch for this training. It was a whirlwind of new information and new faces; I had never seen such a menagerie of people in my life. After about three months, we returned to the head office.

JPL and Joe Rodrigo, International Division of United California Bank, 1965

We then took a bank credit course that lasted about six months. It was terrific because it gave us an opportunity to work on actual banking situations. We were making decisions about committing the bank's money to real borrowers. Each case was analyzed based on all the known information, and then we would be evaluated on the decision we had made. There were about thirty people in the course being assessed at the same time. It was very competitive and we didn't want to make mistakes, as our progress was continually being relayed to the division head.

After the bank credit course I was taken out of the program early and put into international operations. There, I was constantly being inundated with new tasks. Banker's acceptances, letters of credit, foreign exchange and loan documents were all very complicated and took a while to understand, but my supervisors were very thorough and very helpful. They wanted me to know not only what they did but also how to sell and process the product. I don't think I've ever learned so much in such a short period of time. This knowledge would be the foundation of my career for a long time and luckily I had great teachers.

At the end of my training, I was assigned to the European section of the International Division. That, too, was a real learning experience. My new boss had been a banker since before the Second World War and had started with Bank of America in the early forties, spending a great deal of time in Rome and at the Vatican. My first trip to Europe was primarily to Italy. I made calls in Florence and Rome. Even though I could not speak Italian, I used my French to talk with bank managers. I can't say I was terribly good at it, but we managed to carry on a conversation and I got a new account from the Banco Tuscano in Florence, a relationship that would last for many years. Apparently, I was the first American banker from California ever to visit them! They were impressed and treated me in a very friendly manner, showing me a lower conference room in the bank with paintings on the ceiling and walls by Michelangelo and other famous artists of that time. They gave me a beautiful book with pictures of the murals, although as soon as I got back to LA, the book became the property of the bank.

JPL in Rome, 1967

Back in Los Angeles, my job also entailed calling on firms who had any foreign activities. This led me to become acquainted with the motion picture studios, which made or purchased a number of movies overseas. Our bank might finance the cost of a film with a guarantee from the parent company, or issue a letter of credit for the purchase of movies from producers such as Dino DeLaurentiis. I primarily dealt with the financial executives, but I did get directly involved in a number of projects. We financed "Love Story", "Darling Lili" and "Paint Your Wagon", among other films.

There were two transactions I was involved with that were different from anything I had seen before. The first involved the head of the NAACP in Los Angeles. The man was a lawyer and very smart. It landed in my lap because it involved a letter of credit and probably no one else wanted to touch it. Since

I forget the man's name, I will refer to him here as Mr. Jones. Mr. Jones was referred to me by the Chairman of the bank. He said that he had arranged a loan to the state of Guerrero, Mexico, of $50 million in US dollars. The loan would be for twenty years with interest at 8% per year. Payment of both the interest and the principal would be guaranteed by the Federal Government of Mexico. There was one note drawn for the $50 million, due in twenty years, plus twenty interest notes due one each year. Jones had arranged a sale of the twenty interest notes to a labor union in Los Angeles in exchange for $50 million; in addition, the union would receive an insurance policy from an insurance company in Canada that guaranteed repayment of the $50 million note in twenty years. The insurance policy cost Jones $25 million and was in the form of an annuity. Jones wanted me to assure the insurance company in Canada and all the other parties involved that our bank stood behind this transaction. I refused to do any of the things he demanded and he threatened the bank with all kinds of ramifications if the deal fell through. I was sure it would fall through. So much for my opinion. The deal went through like clockwork, Jones pocketed a cashier's check for $15 million, shook my hand and left.

The second transaction involved James Arness, who had been the star of "Gunsmoke". After the series ended, Arness wanted to sell the thirty-minute episodes of the show to ABC with the proviso that he not have to pay any taxes on the transaction. The deal was structured so that Arness borrowed, as I recall, three million dollars from the bank. ABC guaranteed repayment of the loan. Arness put the thirty-minute episodes up as collateral to ABC for the guarantee. When the note came due, Arness refused payment and the bank collected on the guarantee from ABC. In the end, ABC got the programs, the bank got paid and Arness got what he wanted for the programs without being taxed. Under today's tax law that transaction wouldn't have worked, but it sure did at the time.

It's hard to live and work in finance in Los Angeles without having some dealings with the film industry, whether professionally or simply through some inadvertent run-in. One night, when I was leaving the CBS television studios in Hollywood, I noticed the guy parked next to me had a flat tire. He was trying to figure out where the jack was and as I passed he asked if I could help him. I recognized him immediately. It was Johnny Carson. I removed the spare tire and found the jack underneath it, and we worked together to get the tire switched out. It took a few minutes, during which we talked about all kinds of things. I was impressed by how friendly he was. When we finished, he thanked me profusely and we parted. I saw him on a couple more occasions when he was on stage and I always thought back to that one chance meeting.

One thing that I liked about being in Los Angeles was that I was nearer to Jeanetta again. Jeanetta had run into a dead end with her acting career, and was broke and discouraged. She had been livid at Tex because she thought that he should have gone to bat for her in Hollywood. She felt like he didn't care, but in reality he was working his rear end off and was gone from home almost constantly, starting a new company. I remember one time picking him up at the airport and taking him home to change the clothes in his suitcase just so I could turn around and drive him back to catch another plane. As I dropped him off, he had tears in his eyes and told me he was so tired he wished he could just go home. I tried to explain this to Jeanetta, without success. Tex had become the focus of her frustration, and Tex didn't understand her hostility. I knew he would help her if she would ask, but she thought he should call her and offer to help. He gave her shares in his new company but she would just send them back and refuse to speak to him. And I was stuck in the middle.

Jeanette, 1956

One evening she was at wits end and I encouraged her to reach out to Tex for help. She started to cry and it was clear she felt lost. I hugged her and told her that I would call Tex on her behalf if she would talk to him and tell him what she wanted to do. She nodded and I called. Tex came on the line and I passed the phone to Jeanetta. She told him that she wanted to work in the motion picture industry and asked if he could arrange for her to interview at Universal Pictures. He said he would call back. At that time, Tex was on the Board of Directors at MCA, which owned Universal Pictures. He called back in about thirty minutes and told her to be at Universal at nine a.m. the next morning.

The next morning, she went to the front gate of Universal and they immediately showed her to the main offices where she received a great reception from a top executive. He said he had two ideas that might interest her. He first outlined a position with Universal studio tours, which was just beginning. He said it had a great future and she could be involved with both the creative and the management side of the business. The other suggestion involved going through a year-long training program to become a script supervisor. She was a bit wary of the tour business and said she would be interested in the script supervisor opportunity. Presto, as if by magic she had her chance. It wasn't acting but it was part of the business. She went though the training and became a terrific script supervisor.

Around this time, I got a call from Eugene Arnstein, who was the President of the Motion Picture Producers and Directors Guild. Mr. Arnstein asked if I could have lunch with him. I said yes and he named a time and a place. We met and had a delightful time. He asked if I had any interest in the motion picture business. Obviously, I did and told him so. He told me that the guild was starting a film producer training program. He said the program would last two years, after which they would guarantee employment as an assistant producer for at least another two years. Then the person would be on his own. He said that the guild wanted me to be that person. I told him that it was a flattering offer and I would seriously consider it.

As soon as I left lunch, I called Jeanetta, and asked if I could get her advice on a matter. She told me to come on over. When I got there, a friend of hers, who was a successful actor, was visiting. I told them both about my meeting with Mr. Arnstein and asked what they thought of the offer. Their first reaction was largely negative. At that time, many film producers were Jewish, and they felt that because I wasn't, I would face difficulties. The conversation went on for some time and by the time we were finished they had scared me to death. The next day, I wrote Mr. Arnstein a letter that said while I was honored by his offer, I had decided to continue with the opportunity in banking I had at present. I thanked him for his consideration.

I later learned that I was offered the job precisely because I was a gentile. There had been a lot of criticism of the film industry because of the fact that very few non-Jewish individuals had become successful producers. They wanted to change that perception partly through this new program. I was told later that several thousand people interviewed for that position each year. What might have been! But you just can't look back, or you will make yourself crazy!

The next time I went to Paramount Pictures, the Chief Financial Officer asked me what I had decided about the offer by Mr. Arnstein. I told him the decision I had made. His opinion was that I had probably made a mistake, but it was already done. As we came back from lunch at the studio commissary, I saw a guy passed out on the steps. As we got closer, I recognized that it was Lee Marvin. I said something to my host as we stepped over and around Marvin. He said, "Well, it's after lunch and that's generally where you find Lee at this time of day". I knew that Marvin had fought and was wounded at Iwo Jima during World War II. He had been a true hero, and it was sad to see him in that state, although he went on to win an Academy Award in 1965 for his role in "Cat Ballou", so I guess it didn't hurt his acting too much!

Dad was out in the Los Angeles area now too. After Mom's death, he had moved out to Tex's ranch in Hidden Valley, which was about forty miles northwest of the city, near the town of Thousand Oaks. I guess everyone thought it would be good for him to have a change of scenery. Hidden Valley was a beautiful place, with rolling hills and expansive valleys. Ranchers in that area mainly raised race horses and a few head of cattle, but it had become popular with film stars as well. Some of the residents in the valley included

Bob Hope, Richard Widmark, Dale Robertson and Alan Ladd. Dad made friends with a couple of those guys and as soon as they found out he was a veterinarian he became a frequent guest of theirs.

I was so busy at work that by the weekends I was exhausted and didn't really want to think about driving out to see Dad, but every so often, Ann and I went out to visit him. We didn't go often enough, because he made it very plain that he was lonely. The guest house where he lived had knotty pine on the walls and ceiling. He looked at me one day and said, "Do you know how many knots there are in this room?" I said I didn't. He said, "Well, there are 1726. I've counted them a thousand times. I'm lonely and I want to go back home to Texas". I told him he could do what he wanted, but I now wish I had taken the time to go and visit with him more often.

Dad finally told Tex that he was so lonely than he wanted to return to Texas. Tex was not at all pleased. He told Dad that he provided a guesthouse for him to live in, paid for his gas and food and anything else he needed. He felt he had been very generous and he told Dad he didn't think he appreciated what Tex had done for him. Tex said later that Dad just looked at him and said, "I do appreciate what you have done and what you have given me. I gave to you when I didn't have the money to give. I borrowed to send you off to Washington and when you needed something I made sure you had it, even if I had to go into debt to provide it. I don't think I owe you anything".

Tex said he was devastated. He turned to Dad and said, "Please forgive me. I know you sacrificed all your life to give to me and I can never repay you. If there is anything you ever need, at any time, please tell me". So often we forget the unselfish gifts of others and think only of ourselves. At that time, Tex was one of the wealthiest men in this country and for just a moment, I think he had forgotten how he had got there

CHAPTER 27

In 1965, the bank decided to move me to San Francisco, so Ann and I moved north and rented an apartment on Pacific Avenue. It was a one-bedroom place, and again, I was able to ride the bus to work. They wanted me to call on various companies in the bay area that were involved in foreign trade. There was no shortage of international companies in the city.

In order to get to know as many businesses as possible, I joined the World Trade Club, the Merchants Exchange and the Olympic Club. The economy seemed to be booming. Quite early, on, I started financing high tech companies, and was involved with National Semiconductor, Memorex and a slew of other newcomers to the industry. I also helped finance the import and export of goods being exchanged with companies in the Pacific Basin. I got involved in the import of furniture from Denmark, electronic items from Indonesia and baubles from Singapore and Japan – a full spectrum of merchandise from all over the world.

One industry that I particularly liked was the coffee business. As I became acquainted with the various facets of the business, we began to finance growers in Brazil, Peru and Columbia. We would lend money for six months against the crop in the fields. After the coffee was picked, we would finance the crop in warehouses in the country of origin until it was shipped. We then financed the coffee on board the ship until it landed in Los Angeles, San Francisco, New Orleans or New York and was sold to the roaster. In other words, we financed the same coffee crop up to five times. It was great business for the bank. All this financing was done using bankers acceptances, which the bank created and then sold into the investment market; that way, they were never out any money and still earned a commission.

One of the best things about my stay in San Francisco was the fine people I became acquainted with. One was Robert Pecota, who worked in marketing at MJB Coffee. Bob was a smart guy and we became friends. He taught courses at University of California and at Stanford, and asked me to come out and present a seminar on international trade and the role that banking played in the field. I put together a presentation that I gave at both graduate schools. The questions asked by the graduate students were penetrating and showed a great deal of interest in the subject, and I enjoyed my first foray into teaching.

Bob quit MJB Coffee in the mid 1960's, sold his home in the North Bay and moved his family to Napa Valley. He, his wife and three children all moved into an apartment near Rutherford, and he went to work in the marketing department at the Beringer Winery. He also bought seven acres of property in the middle of Napa Valley and in his off hours and on the weekends he began to plant Cabernet Sauvignon grapes. After about three years of long hours and hard work, Robert Mondavi came to see Bob and asked if he would like to trade his seven acres, which were adjacent to the Mondavi vineyards, for forty-one acres with mature grapes near the town of Calistoga. Bob went up and looked at the property; in addition to the grapevines, the acreage also included a four-bedroom house and equipment for the harvesting and handling of grapes. He agreed to the trade.

That was the birth of the Robert Pecota Winery, which has been a success for the past forty years. Bob made about 40,000 cases of wine each year, mainly Chardonnay, Petit Syrah, Cabernet Sauvignon, Sauvignon Blanc and a sweet wine he calls Muscat de Andrea. Both of his daughters worked in the business, one in marketing and the other in the processing of the grapes. Bob worked hard in the summer and fall when the grapes are harvested and then spent much of the winter and spring traveling around the country talking to distributors and restaurants about Pecota wine. Three years ago Bob sold the winery and has retired. We have been friends for over forty years and I love to see him. We don't get together very often but when we do we remember the old days of hard work and big dreams.

Burt Fulmer was another adventurer I met in San Francisco. He worked for a coffee brokerage company called Leon Israel and Company. They would receive small samples of coffee from overseas growers. They would roast a small portion of each sample, taste it, grade it and then invite roasters such as

Folgers, MJB, Butternut and others to come to their office to taste the samples. Based on that tasting, the roasters would make a deal with the brokers for certain number of bags at an agreed-upon price. Burt has an infectious personality and you can't help but like him. This trait, along with his knowledge of the coffee industry, made him an effective salesman.

After having been with Israel and Company for a number of years, Burt decided to really take a chance and moved to Singapore. He felt that he had a chance to corner the Indonesian coffee market. I visited Burt in Singapore one time when his office was in a questionable area of town where the communists hung out. Burt said he got along with everyone, and wanted to keep a low profile. He spent a lot of time in Jakarta, Indonesia, and met anyone who mattered in that market, and lo and behold, after a few years, he had achieved everything he had set out to accomplish. Burt became a very wealthy merchant. Today, his son runs the Golden Mountain Coffee Co., the largest independent coffee importer in the US, with offices in San Francisco and Singapore. Burt's big gamble paid off in a big way, but that ending was never assured. It takes a lot of guts to leave what you know, travel halfway around the world to a hostile environment and make it all work.

I still talk to Burt on occasion. He's eighty years old and in great health. His adventure started forty years ago and he is still excited by what his son is accomplishing in the business. He is now on an advisory committee in Shanghai and goes there about three times a year. He's a good friend.

One of the finest men I met around this time was Ian Bradford, who was English by birth. As a young man just out of university, he was hired by Standard and Chartered Bank of Great Britain. The rules of employment at that time, in the 1930's, were very strict. A man hired to go abroad for the bank had to sign a contract that he would not get married for at least ten years. Ian's first posting abroad was in Indonesia, where the men all slept and ate in dormitories. He worked in Indonesia and Malaya (now Malaysia), and was moved to Singapore just before the Second World War. When the Japanese began to capture most of the countries in Southeast Asia, the British remained very smug about Singapore. The garrison there had large cannons that protected the harbor and the Straits of Malacca. No vessel could get by them. Unfortunately for the British, the Japanese did not attack Singapore from the sea; instead they fought their way down the Malay peninsula and came into Singapore from the back. The British could not turn the cannons around and lost the island nation quickly.

Ian was captured and taken to a prison camp on the Kwai River in Burma. He said they were beaten often and given very little food. The Japanese wanted them to build a bridge over the river. The Americans were assigned to bomb the bridge, but every time they tried, they missed the bridge and the Japanese would beat the prisoners. He said they used to curse the American planes every time they came over. Of course, a well-known movie, "The Bridge on the River Kwai", was made out of this episode.

After the war, Ian returned to Singapore, where he was made President of the Standard & Chartered Bank in Hong Kong. In the late fifties, he accepted a position as the President of the Hong Kong and Shanghai Bank in California. He was in his fifties before he finally got married; he and his wife had a baby girl who became the light of their lives. I once asked Ian why he waited so long to marry. He said, "I guess it was because after that ten year contract expired, I didn't meet any Anglo women until I moved to San Francisco". At that time, it would have been unusual for a traditionally minded Englishman to marry an Asian woman.

I may have learned as much about the banking business from Ian as anyone I ever knew. He was particularly smart about doing business in Asia. He taught me about always being above board in all my dealings but always allowing the Asian businessman to save face in any situation. You could refuse any request, but you had do it a way that did not reflect badly upon your Asian customer. Ian had lots of patience and was calm in any storm. He had a great sense of humor and was an exceptional teacher.

I have tried to appreciate and learn from all my friends, but sometimes, unfortunately, it takes a premature end to make you realize just how treasured a friend is. When Ann and I had lived in Los Angeles, we met a couple that became good friends. Ann met Miriam Hastings because they both worked at UCLA Medical Center and through Miriam we met her husband Wood Hastings. Wood was the head of Time Life on the West Coast. He basically was the person who decided where to advertise and what to sponsor, and he did the entertaining necessary to promote the magazine. More importantly he was the nicest person I ever met.

When I wanted to get into the Jonathan Club in Los Angeles, I applied and tried to round up sponsors. One night we were having dinner with the Hastings and I mentioned this to Wood. He said that he would take care of it. It turned out he was the President of the club, and I was made a member immediately. When he invited me to USC or Rams games, our seats were always in the best locations. When you talked to Wood, he always wanted to know how you were or what he could do to help you. He never once talked about himself or what he was doing. He was the greatest companion, always in a good mood and I don't think I ever heard him complain about anything.

One day up in San Francisco, I picked up the paper and was astonished to read that Wood Hastings had passed away. He was only thirty-eight years old and had seemed in good health the last time I had seen him, about six months earlier. I flew down to Los Angeles for the services. I got to the chapel early and as I sat down, I thought to myself what a shame it was that more people would not be there to honor such a wonderful man. But as I waited for the services to begin, I noticed that more and more people were showing up, until finally every seat was taken, and speakers had to be installed outside to accommodate the thousands of friends who would not fit inside.

The memorial began, and a man I didn't know got up to speak. He said, "I'll bet everyone here thought you were Wood's only friend. That's because when you were with him, he never talked about himself and he never talked about anyone else. He only cared about you. Look around you, there are thousands of friends here who you did not know existed. I loved Wood and I'll bet you did too. When Wood was diagnosed with incurable cancer seven months ago, he told no one, not even his wife. He suffered in silence. Many of you saw him in the last seven months and he always asked about you, but he never told you that he was dying of cancer. When he got to the point where he was going to be incapacitated, he told Miriam about his condition and then stopped seeing his friends that he cared about so much. I feel so fortunate to have known

Wood and hope that I can live my life more like him every day. God bless each and every one of you".

Every time I think of Wood, I try to be less selfish, less of a complainer and think more of the people that really matter to me. Sometimes I wish I still had Wood around to talk to and pat me on the back, but that's selfish. Instead, I try to remind myself to be more like him in my dealings with others.

San Francisco was a very different environment from any place we had lived before. The hippie movement was in full stride and topless dancers were in almost every bar in the Broadway area. One of the unique attractions in the city was the "Hungry i". During the fifties and the early sixties, it was a very popular night spot. When you walked in the first thing you saw was a brick wall and about 8 feet in front of the wall was a grouping of small tables. You sat at these tables and you could have a limited menu meal and drinks. The entertainers would come out and perform in front of the brick wall. When we were in San Francisco we went to see Woody Allen, Johnny Mathis, Bill Cosby and a number of other acts make their debut there. For many performers it was their start in the entertainment business. Barbra Streisand, Shelly Berman, Mort Sahl, Lenny Bruce, Jonathan Winters, Dick Cavett, Phyllis Diller, the Smothers Brothers and Joan Rivers all launched their career there. In other cases the Hungry i helped many others build their career. The Hungry i closed not long after I left because it's popularity waned.

While I was in San Francisco, Jeanetta began work on the Steve Allen Show, a variety/talk show similar to the Tonight Show (which Allen had actually created and hosted in the 1950's). Jeanetta had a number of duties, working as the floor manager and a sort of assistant producer. One of her tasks each week was to choose a "girl" for each program. The show was on six nights a week so she had to pick six girls from a Saturday morning casting call. She said that about 1500 women would show up each week for the audition, having come from all over the country to get their break in Hollywood. The only requirements were that they had to wear and look good in a bikini and be pretty. If they were chosen, their appearance on the show would last about thirty seconds; they would walk out in their bikini and hand something to Steve Allen and he would make some humorous comment. Every time Jeanetta would say how tired she was, I would offer to help by taking over this particular responsibility from her. I think she always thought I had an ulterior motive. Sometimes when you try to help people, they just don't appreciate it!

They used to film two or three shows each night for later viewing. Between shows, the crew would always go across the street to a small roadhouse-style restaurant for dinner. It had to be fast because they only had about a forty-five minute break. I remember one morning the television and newspapers were full of the terrible news of the night before, when some maniac came into the roadhouse and killed about twelve people that were dining there at the time. I had been with the cast a number of times and I knew that was where they always ate. I called Jeanetta immediately, and was so relieved when she answered her phone. In a stroke of good timing, they had all decided to try a new place for a change that night.

During my time in northern California, I was able to get in some good golfing practice. I was not terribly good, but I was enthusiastic and loved to play the great courses. I played Pebble Beach Golf Links, Cypress Point, Spyglass, Stanford University course and the Olympic Club a great many times. In 1966, the US Open was played at the Lake course at the Olympic Club, and I had the opportunity to follow Ben Hogan, Arnold Palmer, Jack Nicklaus, Sam Snead and Billy Casper at various times over the four days of the competition. On the final day of the tournament, Arnold Palmer was leading by seven strokes after the front nine and everyone assumed he would win going away. On the back nine, Arnold faltered and Billy Casper played magnificently, ending up tying Palmer and forcing a playoff the next day which Casper famously won.

In later years I became a good acquaintance of Billy's and I told him I had been there on the days he tied and then beat Palmer in the playoff. He looked at me and said, "John, I've heard that story from about 400,000 people over the years and there were only about 40,000 who were actually there. You now make it 400,001". I insisted I really had been there, but he never quit kidding me about it.

CHAPTER 28

In May of 1966, Ann was seven months pregnant with our first child. We were still living in the apartment on Jackson Street, where I hosted a regular Friday night poker game. Six of us would get together to drink a lot of beer and bet a little money. We were in the middle of a game when Ann came in and asked to speak to me in the bedroom. There, she told me that she thought the baby was coming. I told her it must be false labor, because she wasn't due for another two months. Besides I had a good hand and didn't want to lose the pot. A few minutes later, she came back in and said she wanted to go to the hospital. Thinking I would be back before long, I made everyone promise not to look at my hand and I took her to the hospital.

I suppose I shouldn't have debated the subject with an OB/GYN nurse. Almost immediately, Ann went into full labor, and around midnight she delivered our baby, who we named Michael Steven Lewis. While she was in labor, the guys showed up with the card table and beer and we continued the game in the waiting room. I don't know if it was the cigar smoke, the beer or the laughter that tipped off the head nurse, but she came storming in and broke up the game, throwing everyone out but me.

Michael weighed 3 pounds and 11 ounces and was the tiniest baby I had ever seen. Because he was premature, he had to stay in the hospital for about five weeks before coming home. In the meantime, our landlord informed us that we would have to move because babies were not allowed in the apartment building. I found an apartment in San Mateo that would allow children and by the time Mike came home, we were living in our new place.

We didn't really have a master plan in terms of our family, and we just took the changes as they came. San Francisco didn't seem particularly geared towards families with children, but we did our best. Ann had to quit her job, which reduced our family income by about a third, but we happily rearranged our lives to accommodate our new addition. Michael became the center of our family.

Later that year, Tex invited Ann and me to fly with him in his plane down to Harlingen, Texas, where Dad was living at the time. He brought Jeanetta and picked us up in San Francisco, and we all headed down, with Dad's new grandchild in tow, to celebrate Dad's eighty-second birthday. We had a good visit and talked about old times and old friends. Dad seemed glad to see us all – since he had returned to Texas, he had been nearly as lonely as he had been when he was in California. Many of his old friends had died, and it's hard to make new friends in your eighties.

Before we left, Dad took me aside and told me his stomach had been hurting quite a bit. I asked if he had been to the doctor and he said no. He didn't want to go because he suspected it was serious. I told him he needed to go in order to determine the cause.

We flew back to San Francisco, bid farewell to Tex and Jeanetta and went back to our daily routine. About two months later, I got a call from Tex. He wanted me to come down to Temple, Texas, where Dad had entered the Scott and White Clinic. They had examined him and the news was not good. I knew they wanted me to tell Dad the bad news.

When I arrived in Temple, I met with the doctors and then sat down with Dad alone. As soon as I walked in, he looked at me and said, "I knew they would call for you if the news was bad. I guess I'm going to die". I bent down, kissed him on the forehead and answered the only way I could. "Yes Sir, you are. You have cancer throughout your stomach and there is nothing they can do to help".

Dad said, "It just makes me so mad, because I am in such good shape otherwise". I pointed out, "Dad, you have lived an incredible life. You came from the time of covered wagons to our landing on the moon. What enormous changes have taken place during your lifetime". He just looked at me and said, "That may be true, but I like it here and I don't want to go".

He had a very hard time of it and was just skin and bones when he died in November. It was a very hard time for me. Dad had been my best friend for much of my life. And even though he didn't understand what I did for a living, I would call him and use him as a sounding board when I was uncertain or confused. Sometimes he would simply say, "John, I know you will do the right thing for yourself and those around you". His words always made me feel better. I miss Dad every day, and wish I still had a father to talk to. It is so important for a man to have someone that thinks he will succeed regardless of the odds. I loved my father very much and still dream about him.

Dad always taught me that a man's word was his bond. He felt you needed to maintain a good reputation and good credit. Every year or so Dad would go to the bank and borrow a hundred dollars. He would put it in his safety deposit box. Six months later, he would take it out and pay the bank back plus a little interest. He had the best credit in town.

Losing my father and gaining a son in the same year really put me face-to-face with the stark realities of life. It was time for me to step up and become a father myself, all the while working on my good reputation and credit.

CHAPTER 29

In the fall of 1966, the powers at my bank decided that I should return to Los Angeles and join the Latin American section. The head of that section was Hugh Mangum. Hugh was an alumnus of the First National City Bank of New York, which, at that time, was the largest bank in the world. While with that bank, he had worked eight years in Buenos Aires in the fifties, during Juan Peron's regime, and he had many colorful stories about that period. Buenos Aires was a dangerous and exciting place during those years; it had also been a time of great growth for the banking business in that region. Having worked in South America for so long, Hugh was fluent in Spanish and well-known in most of the Latin American capitals. I looked forward to learning a lot from him.

Most of our bank's business came from Mexico and Central America. I was responsible for all our bank's business in South America, with the exception of Venezuela. I prepared by going over every piece of correspondence and every file we had on all our South American customers, and researching all of the previous business calls that had been made in that region. I also got busy studying Spanish. Finally, after several months, Hugh scheduled a trip to South America to introduce me to people in a number of countries.

We started our trip in New York, talking to various international bankers and getting current on information about the countries we were going to visit. We needed to know about political developments as well as economic news. Then, we were off to South America; our first stop was Brazil.

This was my first time in South America, and as soon as we landed in Rio and retrieved our luggage from customs, Hugh took me aside. He looked me in the eye and said, "John, I have been to all of these countries many times and I know my way around. Just follow my example and you will be fine. The first thing to remember is to keep your eye on your luggage at all times". As he finished his statement, he turned around to find that his luggage was gone. It seems funny now, but it wasn't at the time!

Flabbergasted, Hugh immediately contacted airport security. We didn't know what else to do. With no leads and little hope, he finally decided that, since all of his clothes and all of his files had been in his luggage, he should probably just take the return flight home. Now I panicked. Here I was in a country I had never seen before, where I did not know one single solitary person, and where they spoke Portuguese – not even the Spanish I had been studying! Hugh assured me I would be all right and headed over to the Varig Airline counter to reserve a seat home. You cannot imagine the level of anxiety in my head! As I stood there, a man ran up to me and asked if I was Mr. Mangum. I said, "No, he is the gentleman standing at the Varig counter". The man ran to Hugh and said they had found his luggage. Man oh man, what jubilation – I wanted to kiss this man. Apparently, Hugh's bags had been mistakenly put on a flight to Sao Paulo and the plane had been taxiing when they made the discovery; they had brought the plane back to the gate and retrieved his suitcases. We retrieved the luggage and took a taxi to the Lama Palace Hotel on Copacabana Beach. After checking in, we went to the bar to settle our nerves and celebrated the start of my first Latin American tour.

As would be the case in the future, we called on about eight companies or banks each business day. In Brazil, each meeting started with friendly greeting and then we would be served a very strong coffee served in a small demitasse cup with sugar. This was the customary greeting in all the South American countries we visited. Unfortunately, they would refill your cup every few minutes, and it was considered impolite to turn down the offered coffee or the refill, so after about two or three business meetings I would be really wired. After eight meetings I couldn't close my eyes even if I tried. This went on for five business days. The calls were interesting as we explored every conceivable avenue for us to do business with each group. We were received well on most visits, but made no concrete transactions.

Between meetings, Hugh showed me around Rio and took me to some restaurants he thought I would enjoy. He made sure I ate several of the local favorites as well as some native dishes, such as Feijoada. This is Brazil's national dish, a dark bean stew that contains nearly every part of a pig. The taste was terrific but I enjoyed it more if I made a conscious effort not to think too much about the contents.

On Sunday, we traveled to Sao Paulo and took meetings for three more days. Sao Paulo, the commercial center and largest city in Brazil, was a city of about ten million even in 1966. There were skyscrapers everywhere, similar to New York but spread over a larger area. I found it awesome. The citizens of Sao Paulo are called Paulonistas, and they are generally more serious and businesslike than the Cariocas, in Rio. The Cariocas are more fun loving and would rather go to the beach than work and they very often do just that.

We left mid-week and traveled to Montevideo, Uruguay, for two business days. Uruguay is a small nation with a government based on the Swiss model. It's a nice country with some beautiful areas, but lacks a lot of economic development. Hugh knew most of the people we met with, and introduced me as the new area head for South America. I was glad to finally be able to put some of my Spanish to use. The tone of the calls was very friendly and we felt they were very successful.

Again, we left on a Sunday and headed to Buenos Aires, Hugh's old stomping ground. While the meetings were cordial, they were not as friendly and we did not socialize while we were there. Hugh explained that, as a result of the Germanic influence on the culture, the natives of Buenos Aires were particularly difficult to cultivate socially. Whatever the reason, I was never invited to an Argentinian home in all the time I traveled there. However business was good and we had several active customers in Argentina.

We went from there to Santiago, Chile, and then on to Lima, Peru. Lima was one of our best visits and the people were very warm and outgoing. Next we went to Bogota, Columbia, where we encountered quite a few good clients and a very friendly atmosphere. We hadn't even gotten to Bolivia, Ecuador or Paraguay yet, but it was time to go back to Los Angeles. The trip was about five weeks long, and by the time I got home I was exhausted. My future trips all lasted from five to six weeks and were strenuous.

Hugh thought the trip had gone well and he wanted me to start planning the next visits. He was complimentary about my skills and was told by the

people we met that I was 'simpatico', which means 'friendly', and was someone they would enjoy working with. The only complaint was that my Spanish
was not very good. It never got any better.

Hugh was a great teacher and fun to work with. He was a connoisseur of
a great many things. He had a discerning palate that allowed him to know
wine as few people do. He could sample a wine and tell you the year it was
bottled and the varietals of grape it contained with accuracy. He knew good
scotch and could identify the area of Scotland that produced it. He had a
wide knowledge of food from all over the globe, including the details of its
preparation. I was in awe of these abilities. I learned so much just from traveling with him and he was always generous and never pretentious about his
knowledge. He always treated me as a contemporary, never as a subordinate,
treating me with respect in front of existing or potential clients.

He seemed to know people all over the world. One of his great interests was Formula One Grand Prix auto racing. He was part of a committee
headed by retired General Curtis LeMay, who had been Commander of the
Strategic Air Command when I was in the Air Force, that was pushing to
establish more venues for Formula One in the US.

Several movie stars who were avid racers were part of a group that often
met to talk about racing over at Hugh's house. I sometimes would go over to
Hugh's house to find James Garner, Steve McQueen and Paul Newman playing pool and discussing the future of US racing. Garner had been involved in
several races and had actually won the Sebring 500 in Florida driving a Lola.
I rode in the Lola several times and it just looked and felt like speed. McQueen
and Newman took part in several races and even won some regional contests.
When those three guys were at Hugh's, there were always an abundance of
good looking girls; when I was there, I guarantee that not one of those girls
even knew I was in the room

Hugh obviously traveled in some fancy circles, but I still thought he could
be a bit of a name-dropper and would tease him about it. Many times Hugh
had told me what good friends he was with Jackie Stewart, then the premier
Formula One driver in the world. Stewart had been the world champion
three times and was always the man to beat whether in Monte Carlo or at

Watkins Glen. One time, I was waiting in TWA's Ambassador Lounge at JFK airport in New York, on my way to London. I was settling into my seat when the guy next to me said hello and asked where I was headed. I told him London and asked the same of him. He said he was on his way home to Switzerland. I introduced myself and he did the same, telling me his name was Jackie Stewart. What an opportunity! At long last I would catch Hugh in an exaggeration! Hardly able to contain my glee, I asked Stewart whether he knew Hugh Mangum in Los Angeles. To my eternal disappointment, he said that Hugh was one of his best friends in the world.

We talked about racing and he told me about the time they were making the movie, "Grand Prix" with James Garner. There was a scene in the movie, which I remembered, when the cameras showed a car veering off the track and people rushing to try to rescue the driver. Stewart said that the footage was from a real race, and that he was the one in the car. The gasoline tank ruptured and he was covered in gas. If there had been a spark from anything he would have been toasted. He said he saw a helicopter coming down and thought they were coming to his rescue. Instead, they were filming the movie. He yelled at them but they couldn't hear him.

After Stewart caught his plane home, I called Hugh and told him what had happened and how I thought I had finally caught him. He just laughed. I will always remember Hugh and the things he contributed to my life. Over the last few years, I tried to track him down, but his name is nowhere to be found. He may well be gone. He was about seven years older than me which would make him about eighty-three. If he indeed is gone, then the world has lost a wonderful man.

CHAPTER 30

Over the next few years, I spent a lot of time in South America. It was a time of much political and social change, and my travels always felt exciting and a little dangerous. During one trip to Brazil, there was an attempted coup by a rival political party and I watched as tanks rumbled down the streets. I returned to my hotel and simply stayed inside until the coup was defeated. Thankfully, it didn't take long! In Lima, Peru, I woke up one morning to find the square outside the hotel filled with soldiers with guns and rumbling tanks. I took the day off and cancelled my calls.

On what turned out to be my last visit to Peru, I went to lunch with the president of the largest bank in the country. We were at a private club and the Peruvians at the table started talking seriously about how the President of Peru should be assassinated. I decided to excuse myself from the table, telling my hosts that I should not be a party to such a conversation. They agreed and I left. I immediately returned to my hotel, packed my things and got a seat on the next plane leaving for Miami. While I was checking in at the airport, I heard my name being announced on the intercom. I went to my gate, where the police hustled me into a nearby room. They took my passport, briefcase and tickets and told me to sit down. For the next thirty minutes, they asked me questions about where I had been and what I was doing in Peru. I thought my goose was cooked for sure. Then, suddenly, they returned my things to me and told me to board the airplane. As I was leaving the room, one of the security people told me that I should probably not come back. I haven't set foot in Peru since. I know good advice when I hear it.

The Peruvian government wasn't the only one that took an interest in my travels. After I started traveling to South America, and later to other parts of the world, I would receive a visit from a CIA agent after I returned from each trip. He informed me that I was expected to help my country with information about the countries I was visiting. He told me that they would only ask economic questions about each country: did I know anything about any gold shipments in and out the various countries? Had I acquired any knowledge about industry difficulties or union unrest? Did I know of anything that might cause an economic upheaval? In most cases I had nothing to tell them. After a while, the questions began to stray to political topics as well: did I think the country was stable and, if I was worried about the atmosphere in the country, then why? I did pick up a lot of interesting information on these trips, but I don't think I ever told them anything terribly useful.

But ultimately, the things that have stayed with me from those years are not the politics, but the personal relationships I formed on my travels. Early in my travels to Rio, an acquaintance introduced me to a woman named Adelaide Garcia. She was about sixty years old, and was both very nice and very rich. She owned, among other things, the Volkswagen rights in Brazil, which meant that no one else could sell the number-one selling car in Brazil. She also had the right to all orange juice sales and, from what I gathered, many other things. Her husband, who had started all these businesses, had died several years before. She also had a son named Paulo, who was about twenty-one years old, handsome and in great demand by the ladies.

For some reason, Adelaide took a liking to me and would often invite me to dine with her family or, on occasion, with her alone. She did not speak a word of English and we communicated with the few words of Spanish and Portuguese that I had learned. She ultimately became the single most important person behind my business success in Brazil. For instance, one evening at dinner she asked me how business in Brazil was going. I told her that I was having absolutely no luck in meeting the Minister of Finance, a contact that was especially crucial for me, as the only way you could get government business was through the Minister. She didn't say anything then, but the next day I received a phone call from her secretary telling me to be at a certain restaurant at 7:30 that evening.

I went to the restaurant spotted Adelaide in the back, sitting with a distinguished looking man. When she saw me she motioned for me to join them, introducing me to her dining companion, Delfim Netto, the Minister of

Finance of Brazil. I was quite surprised, but very pleased, as you might imagine! The Minister said that he was pleased to meet a good friend of Adelaide's, and wanted me to come and call on him the next day. We had a cordial dinner and the next day I went to see Mr. Netto; he agreed that our bank could to be a lender to a government hydroelectric project. It was the best loan in the country, and my superiors in Los Angeles were ecstatic. They had tried for years to break down this barrier and I had been the one to do so.

This was the first of many introductions that Adelaide arranged for me. They all led to new and very lucrative business for our bank. She introduced me to Colonel Stroessner, who was the son of the dictator of Paraguay, and our discussions lead to new business in that country. She also gave me people to call in Argentina and Peru. She was an incredible contact and a generous friend, telling her secretary and maid that anytime I was in Rio that I was to have the free use of her home. Her home was in the Edificio Chopin, right next door to the Copacabana Palace Hotel and the most expensive location in the city. She occupied an entire floor and furnished it entirely with European antiques.

Adelaide Garcia was not a particularly attractive woman and I think she was lonely. I tried to take her to dinner or for cocktails whenever I was in Brazil, and was attentive to her whenever we were out. We spent a good deal of time together, but I don't believe that I ever made physical contact with her except to hold her arm getting in or out of a taxi.

Our relationship came to an abrupt halt for all the wrong reasons. There was currency control in Brazil at that time and residents could not obtain foreign currency for any reason. That meant that they could not leave the country unless they had some source of funds outside of Brazil. One day in Los Angeles, I received a call from Adelaide. She had a friend on the phone with her and she asked if I could lend her $20,000. She said she would pay me back as soon as I came to Brazil on my next trip. At the time, I made about $12,000 a year and it cost that much for Ann and me to live. I told her that I would talk to the bank and see if I could make some kind of arrangement that would meet her needs. She said she wanted me to give it to her, because there would be no record that the Brazilian government could follow. I told her that if I had that kind of money, I would be happy to give it to her, but that

I simply didn't. She did not believe me. She thought I was a wealthy banker and that I was just unwilling to help her. She hung up on me.

I wrote to her, trying to explain my position. I even wrote to her son, but I never heard from, spoke to or saw her again. The truth is that I could not have even borrowed that much money. It was a tremendous loss, as she was a good friend and had been so kind to me.

It was around this time – while I was earning this salary – that I found myself accepting Henry Ford's quiet, under-the-table assist! If I could not lend Adelaide the money she wanted, I certainly could not afford to take a billionaire and several of his wealthy friends out for dinner and drinks! As I described in the prologue, I found myself in the spring of 1968 celebrating Carnival in Rio with Henry Ford II, his lovely wife Cristina and the Morera Salles family.

After Ford bailed me out of my jam, he invited me to join him for a night-cap at the Morera Salles' home. I accepted, and Ford's driver took the three of us to a large mansion in a very exclusive neighborhood. We received a warm greeting and I had a chance to roam around a bit. I discovered that the house was built around a large, square courtyard; on the inside, there was a large swimming pool and a beautiful garden. On the first floor of the house, there was a living room, a large den, a parlor, two dining areas, a kitchen, an office and an entertainment center. In addition there were servant's quarters in the back. I would guess the area to be about 8,000 square feet. The upstairs was the same size. I did not go into the bedroom area but I did see another entertainment center, a smaller dining area, a complete kitchen and another large living room. It was very impressive! I learned that people like Henry Ford do not stay in hotels unless there is no other option. When in the US, he stayed in one of his numerous homes around the country. When he was in Brazil, he stayed with the Morera Salles family. He had similar arrangements all over South America and in Europe.

Henry was tickled when I told him that my half brother, Tex, used to work for him. He was very lavish in his praise of Tex, saying that he was one of the smartest men he had ever known. After an aperitif and a lot of conversation, Henry asked if I had any free time over the next few days. I told him I would be in Rio for the week and he invited me to spend it with the four of them. I said I would like that very much. When he walked me outside at the end of the evening, Henry told an assistant to put a car at my disposal and that they would pick me up at the hotel at four the next afternoon. When I got back to the hotel I was very excited with this new and unusual turn of events!

The next evening I accompanied Cristina Ford and Elizinha Morena Salles to the Carnival parade. The parade takes several hours and is comprised of various samba schools representing the various parts of Rio and its suburbs. It is always unbearably hot during Carnival and that year was no different. We began by watching the parade from the second story of an air conditioned building, which suited me just fine. Henry didn't show up over the course of the evening and I never asked about him. After a while, the women got bored and decided they wanted to walk along the parade route and see the costumes up close.

Now Rio is not the safest place today, but it was very dangerous at that time. There were so many people living in extreme poverty, and the crime rate was astronomical, especially for robberies. I was not convinced that a walk was a terrific idea, but went along. We started down the street and the crowds were unbelievable, jam-packed all along the parade route, making walking a real struggle. The two women walked on either side of me, each taking one of my arms. They were having a great time, chatting and laughing. Out of the corner of my eye, I saw a man moving rapidly toward Cristina, but before I could react, a large man came out of nowhere and bashed the approaching man with some sort of club. The intruder hit the ground like a rock, his head bloodied. Two more guys came over, picked him up and carried him away. Cristina and Elizinha never even noticed that anything had happened; they just kept talking without missing a beat. I was left rather stunned, as it had all happened so fast! As we continued strolling through the crowd, I noticed several men in plainclothes walking just behind and to our sides. I guess I should have known that the police were not going to allow anyone to hurt Cristina Ford because it would have made the news all over the world.

The rest of the evening passed without incident. At one point, Cristina asked me if I would like to be as rich as Henry. Not an easy question to answer. I told her that it would be nice to have a lot of money but I was not sure I would want the hassles that seemed to come with it. It's hard to discuss this subject with someone who had never been anything but rich and beautiful, but she said she liked my answer and she thought I was very smart!

The next day was a big ball at the Copacabana Palace Hotel. I had to rent a tuxedo and the car picked me up at eight p.m. I met Henry and Cristina in the lobby and we entered together. Photographers descended upon us and Henry hid behind me. The press was always trying to generate a story, so they would try to sneak some nearly nude girl behind or next to Henry and then call his name in order to get what looked like a compromising photo. To combat this, Henry simply put his arm around my neck and each time his name was called he would swing me around in front of him. The press sure didn't want a picture of me so they would jeer and Henry would laugh at them. They never caught him with his guard down. The life of a famous person!

One evening, we were invited to a party at a private residence with socialites and jet-setters from all over the world in attendance. At one point in the evening Prinz Johannes von Thurn und Taxis came up to me and, looking down his nose, said "What are you doing here? You don't belong here". I was flabbergasted and didn't know what to say. He was one of the richest men in the world. His owned so many castles, estates and other assets that it took several months to even inventory a portion of his worth when he later died. His date was the current Miss Universe and he was obviously an unmitigated snob. Henry Ford, who had been dancing nearby and apparently had overheard the remark, came up and in a loud voice said, "John, don't pay any attention to this queer. He is someone that everybody knows to be a fool". Ford then turned and faced von Thurn und Taxis and said, "How dare you question a friend and guest of mine. Get away from here". The Prinz got red in the face, then turned and quickly left the party. West Texas, one: Germany, zero! I was grateful to Ford for stepping in when I was too stunned to speak.

I spent seven great days with the Fords; it was fun and educational and by the end of it I had made a new friend. When it was time to part, Henry and Cristina asked if I would like to accompany them to their home in Martinique for a week or so. I told them that I was flattered but unfortunately I had to work. They said that no one would complain if I mentioned who I was with. I said, "I don't think so. I'm pretty low on the totem pole and they expect me to be working when I'm down here". They seemed truly disappointed. I got the impression that they were a bit bored and lonely. In any case, Elizinha gave me their personal phone numbers and told me I could stay with them anytime I came to Rio. I never took them up on it, but I thought it was a kind gesture.

One of the secrets of getting along with people like Henry is to avoid talking about what they worry about or their business life. Henry was an interesting person. He had turned Ford Motor around in his youth. He was 28 when he took over and the company was losing a million dollars a month. In Rio, Henry was looking for someone more interesting than the very rich people he was staying with and socializing with. We talked about Rio, what I did down there, where I lived and everything around us. Also, he liked my brother a lot and while we didn't talk about their relationship, I think it kind of gave me the aura of a friend. We kidded each other constantly and he loved it. Time magazine had him on the cover later with the statement, "No one calls him Henry". He was surrounded by yes men who were afraid of him. I wasn't afraid of him and I was irreverent around him. We laughed constantly. He had foul speech and I even kidded him about that. I never mentioned Ford Motors or Detroit. We concentrated on where we were and what we were doing.

The truly rich and famous are very different from you and me. They are catered to constantly. After we spent an evening together, he decided that he wanted me with him for the next few days. He spoke to a man outside and immediately I had a car and driver at my beck and call. All that is taken for granted. He knew I wasn't a wealthy person and that's why he came to my rescue when I tried to pay a bill I couldn't afford. The key thing is, he didn't want anyone to know that he had bailed me out. Cristina, his wife, had always been wealthy. She didn't flaunt it, but she never had to think about money. That's why she asked me if I would like to be rich like Henry. It was a naïve question but it was sincere. She was a lovely and beautiful woman and was always at the best parties in the world whether Henry was there or not. She was spoiled but she was very kind and affectionate to me and I think she truly liked me – at least for the moment. She was the one that asked me to go with them to Martinique. They were kind of lonely in some ways and they wanted someone to laugh and play with. I have never believed that I could acquire riches of that magnitude. That wealth is generally inherited. Henry was not an entrepreneur. He was a manager of enormous family assets. A great story about Henry was about the time when he was on a trip to Eastern Europe during the Cold War. Obviously, the communists knew who Henry Ford was and as a capitalist he was to be disliked. As the plane landed in Poland, East Germany or whatever their destination was, Henry immediately grabbed the suitcase of Ralph Bunche, who was a black man, and proceeded to carry it off the plane. The greeters were stunned that Ford would carry the baggage of a black man, as he knew they would be. A look into a complex personality.

I saw an article on Henry Ford after that in some magazine. There was a picture of Henry in the doorway of a plane waving. Now I wasn't there but I know what he was saying. He would be pointing to some Russian bureaucrat and he would be saying, "Look at that goofy looking guy there. What an A--h---!". He was totally irreverent and he didn't like pretense.

Henry gave me his private numbers at work and at his home in Grosse Point. He said he wanted to see me again soon. Shortly after I returned home, I received a long personal letter from him. We wrote and talked to each other for about two years. They always seemed happy to hear from me. Then the relationship began to erode over time. Carnival had been an experience of a lifetime, but it was in the past and I didn't know what to say to them any longer. Henry and Cristina got a divorce not long afterwards.

When I got back to work, everyone asked me how the trip had gone and I first told them about the business successes I had had, and the opportunities I had uncovered. I then mentioned that I had met Henry Ford. They thought I was lying to them, so I just dropped the subject. About a month later, Time magazine put out an issue with Henry Ford on the cover. One of the secretaries in the office came over excitedly and opened the magazine to the article on Ford. There was a picture of Henry and Cristina coming down the stairs at the ball in Rio and there I was, right between them. Great memories!

Henry and Christina Ford with JPL trailing

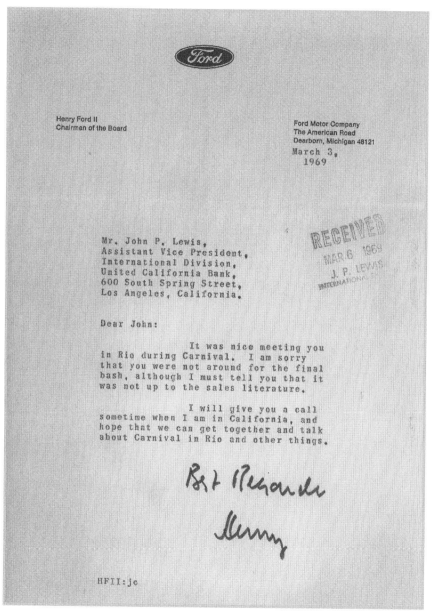

Letter from Henry Ford

CHAPTER 31

Back in Los Angeles, Jeanetta's career as a script supervisor was going terrifically, with jobs on both television series and movies. She also had a new boyfriend, Bernie Koppell, who later became known for his role as the doctor in "The Love Boat". She worked with Roddy McDowall on the set of "Planet of the Apes". Jeanetta also worked on most of the early Woody Allen films. She went to New York to make a movie called "Madigan" with Henry Fonda and Richard Widmark, who she said was a horse's rear end the whole time. And then she headed to Miami to work on a film called "Don't Drink the Water" with Jackie Gleason and Estelle Parsons. I stopped in for a visit to the set on my way back from a trip to South America. The film was a comedy and it was fun to watch them work, although Jackie Gleason was not the friendliest person. He sat by himself and basically didn't talk with the cast or crew or anybody when he wasn't filming.

Roddy McDowall, promotional photo sent to Greg

Woody Allen. Photo taken by JPL.

Henry Fonda and Richard Widmark relaxing on set of "Madigan"

Robert Taylor. Photo taken by JPL.

I was traveling so much during this period, and it was always a welcome treat to get back to Ann and Michael in LA. Ann and I developed a love for college basketball and got season tickets to the UCLA Bruins games. We went religiously whenever I was in the country, and our beloved Bruins won the NCAA championship the first year we followed them. That team was small in size, with their tallest player being center Keith Erickson at 6'7". They played number one-ranked Michigan for the championship. Michigan had a big team that was favored to win by a large margin. Gail Goodrich was a guard for UCLA and Sports Illustrated said that he was the most over-rated player in the country. UCLA started the game playing a full court press on defense (this defensive strategy was used for the first time in a championship game) and Michigan turned the ball over seventeen times in the first half. The Bruins won by twenty points; Goodrich scored thirty-five of them. What a game!

We cheered the Bruins as they won three national titles with such players as Lew Alcindor (later known as Kareem Abdul-Jabbar), Mike Warren, Len Shackleford, Kenny Heinz, Kenny Washington, Mike Bibby and a slew of great players. One year, Houston beat UCLA in the Houston Astrodome before the biggest college basketball crowd to date. Alcindor was hurt and UCLA only shot 30% from the floor; Houston, with the terrific Elvin Hayes on the team, won by two points. The press immediately pronounced the Cougars the best team in the country. The two teams met again in the semi-finals of the National Championship in a game that most pundits said would be won by Houston. Ann and I were there and watched as UCLA surged ahead by forty-four points in the second half. At that point, the starting five Bruin players simply raised their hands in the air and walked off the court. The reserves finished the game. It was the best-played basketball game I have ever seen. The coach of UCLA was the legendary John Wooden, whose teams won ten NCAA championships before he retired. We had such a good time at the games, and we were lucky to witness a stellar Bruins era!

Linda Carter, autographed photo sent to apologize for missing a lunch appointment with JPL

During the times I was back in Los Angeles, my bank wanted me to give talks to community groups about international trade, discussing what it meant for the US economy and the state of California. One of my least favorite things to do is to make speeches, but the bank thought it would be good publicity for us, so I did it. We had requests from civic groups all over Los Angeles and Orange counties. Most of these were Kiwanis, Elks and Rotary clubs and Chambers of Commerce from various cities. The audience was usually twenty-five to forty people and it was usually at a luncheon meeting. I must have given my speech a hundred times, and it was always well received because it was on a topic that was unfamiliar to most people.

My speech giving came to an end for good after I spoke before the Rotary Club of Bell, California. We had just finished our meal when the president of the club introduced me to the group. I got up to the podium and was opening my notebook to begin when someone set off a giant firecracker just behind me. It was like a cannon going off. I'm sure my heart stopped. The group began laughing hysterically. I slowly closed my notebook, went back to my seat, got my briefcase and walked out of the building. The president of the club came running after me and asked me to come back. He said they were just having a little fun. I begged to differ. It was the last time I met with such a group, and I didn't miss it one bit.

PART NINE

CITIBANK & PVO

CHAPTER 32

Towards the end of 1968 and into 1969, the economy was becoming overheated and the Federal Reserve Bank began raising the interest rate. In addition, bank regulators were beginning to put pressure on banks to make fewer loans, and even get rid of some of the loans they had on the books. It was a painful time for those of us who had been seeking new customers, because as credit became tighter, we got more calls, and yet could do less than ever for prospective clients.

Just as it seemed that business would be stagnant for a while, I received a call from First National City Bank (Citibank), which was headquartered in New York. They asked me to meet with their executives in San Francisco. I went up and talked with a gentleman named Terry Hyman, who was slated to be President of a new bank subsidiary that would be headquartered in San Francisco. They wanted someone who was both familiar with the customer base on the West Coast and had international experience. They offered me a job with a 40% increase in salary, more responsibility and a raft of new of opportunities. After talking it over with Ann, we decided to accept the new challenge and head up to San Francisco once again. It was an exciting development, but it was hard to leave all my friends at UCB. No matter how hard you try, it is difficult to maintain relationships with people at a distance.

JPL, 1970

It was an especially tough time for Ann to make this transition, as we had just had a second son in February, who we named Gregory Allen. Ann was caring for two children under three and trying to move at the same time. Never let it be said that my wife is not a trooper. We went up to San Francisco on a scouting mission and found a three-bedroom house to rent. It was an older row house on three floors, and there wasn't much room for the boys to play, but we would enjoy the place, determined to make the best of a city that, for all its charms, is not the best place to raise children. The schools are bad, the weather is cold and damp much of the year and, unless you are near Golden Gate Park, there isn't much outdoor green space.

But San Francisco in the 1960's was definitely a wild place to live. Nude dancing became all the rage in the City. There were clubs everywhere, each trying to outdo the other. It was a novelty, and almost every visitor to the city wanted to check it out, especially the Asian businessmen that flocked to the West Coast. I once took eighteen jute manufacturers from India to see a place called The Roaring '20's. The Roaring '20's had minimally-dressed waitresses but the big draw was a young girl who descended on a swing from the ceiling completely nude. I had warned the Indian visitors that the policy was looking but no touching. But when the girl descended, they got carried away and decided to try to take the girl off the swing. I melted into the wall as bouncers swarmed them. They were taken away, but I didn't bother to ask where!

Street culture was blossoming. I remember a musician that played the violin at one of the corners across from Union Square. He played beautifully and the public rewarded him with generous donations in his violin case. One day, the San Francisco Examiner did a feature story about him, in which they mentioned that he had previously played with the Boston Philharmonic Orchestra. They also printed that he now was making between $3,000 and $4,000 a week busking, more than he had made in Boston. The next week there were musicians on every corner, trying to get in on the action.

One time, a businessman told a group of us in a meeting that the night before he had witnessed four individuals walking down Broadway completely nude: a male midget with a wooden leg, a tall skinny woman, a tall skinny man with an eye patch, and a very obese short woman. It will tell you something about what a crazy time it was that no one in the meeting doubted his story. The "love generation" had arrived, but business went on as usual.

Working at Citibank was a great experience. I was part of a huge worldwide bank that functioned, for the most part, as a well-oiled machine. If you had an international customer, then you were the controlling entity for that company wherever it did business. You, along with the other bankers over-seas, would decide what level of credit or services the company needed world-wide for the next year. I would coordinate with New York to get approval for a world credit facility. Once it was approved, then I was responsible for allo-cating its use. For instance, if a subsidiary of the customer in Brazil needed a ten million dollar loan for expansion, then the account officer in that loca-tion would contact me and ask for an allocation under the approved facility. If there was room, then I would approve the loan and it would be deducted from the overall total available. It was a great system that had been worked out over the years.

Terry Hyman, the president of the new subsidiary, was just a little bit older than me. He had a Harvard MBA and was on a fast track at Citibank. They had moved him from an assignment in Manila to take over the new bank. While I don't think he had been the top man during his stay in Asia, the bosses in New York liked him and felt he could do almost anything. I started out as an Assistant Vice President. Terry also gave me the author-ity as head of the Credit Policy Committee and as the Foreign Exchange trader for the bank with large credit limits in each case. Soon after I joined the organization, Terry became very defensive with his superiors in New York and spent most of his time on the phone playing politics. He didn't come out of his office very often, so we ran most of the activities of the bank with his blessing. Business was good and we were growing by leaps and bounds.

One of the coworkers under my leadership at Citibank was a young man named Stephen Van Rensselaer Spaulding III. He spent every morning from 7:45 to 8:15 am opening his dividend checks. He had a three-year old son who had more income than I did. Steve had gone to an Ivy League school, I believe it was Yale, and his demeanor was a little bit patrician, but he had a good sense of humor and was always fun to be with. One day, I looked at Steve and said, "You know, I'm a hell of a lot smarter than you are, so why do you think you have all the money and I don't?" Steve just laughed, and with a twinkle in his eye said, "John, you are a pain in the ass, but if you were rich you'd be unbear-able!" He probably was right.

I had some interesting customers in San Francisco that were quite successful. One was a company called Determined Productions that had been formed by a woman who had obtained the rights to all of the Peanuts characters from their creator, Charles Shultz. Everything – from clocks to rag dolls – that bore the image of one of the Peanuts characters had to be licensed through her, and in most cases she actually had them made. Her sales were phenomenal and the profits margins were in the 40% range. It was a great business.

We also had the banking activities of a company that had the rights to the Encyclopedia Britannica in all Spanish speaking countries. The sales were in the $500 million range and the profit margin was 48%. Since the company was headquartered in Venezuela, it paid no tax on sales in any other country. The owner lived in California part of the time but never paid any US tax. I had never seen anything like the profitability of those two companies!

For a time, I had a customer in San Francisco named Christiansen who owned a company called Copenhagen House of Danish Furniture. The firm did well but never made much money. He was a new customer, so I went to see Mr. Christiansen and told him that he was taking too much money out of the company and that I was concerned about the future of the business. He asked me what he should do. I told him he needed to reduce his staff and limit his salary to $2000 a month. He said he didn't know whether he could make ends meet at that level of compensation, but said he would try. I met with him quite often and, as the company increased its sales and profits, I would tell him to give himself a raise. This continued for quite some time, until the company was really doing well, at which point I told him he didn't need my input any longer. He continued to expand, opening additional stores and, after a few years, buying the furniture factory in Denmark. He became quite a success story and I was glad to have been able to help him develop his business.

While I was working in the San Francisco office, we had a strange and upsetting situation arise. A girl who worked in our operations section came to our office crying and said that she had received a number of obscene and threatening phone calls at work. We immediately called in an investigator

and he quietly set about trying to determine who was calling. The girl continued to get calls, which she said were all from the same man and she repeated
the conversations. Terry decided to call in the FBI. Because we were a feder-
ally-chartered bank, the FBI thought we were within their jurisdiction. They
tapped the phones and put in tracers; the calls continued but for some reason
they were never taped. The girl seemed scared to death. The other employees
were beginning to distrust each other and work was beginning to suffer. One
day, it occurred to me to wonder if this girl had ever had this experience in a
previous job. We called her previous employers and found out that in fact it
had happened to her at two different companies. The FBI called her in and
she confessed to having made the whole episode up. A psychiatrist told us
that she had likely done it to draw attention to herself. I can't remember what
happened to her after that, but she came close to tearing our bank apart.

I did a fair amount of traveling for Citibank, but instead of South America,
my main focus was now Asia. The bank, with operations in almost every
country in the world, sent me early on to a conference in Manila, Philippines,
that was led by the Xerox Corporation. They had devised a very educational
workshop for sales and marketing techniques organized around questions
that could not be answered by a yes or a no; instead, the questions led the
customer towards a particular product. The conference lasted for about ten
days, after which I was scheduled to visit a few of the other facilities in Asia.

My first stop after Manila was Singapore, where I knew a few people. Bert
Fulmer, my entrepreneurial friend who was trying to corner the Indonesian
coffee market, was there and introduced me to several businessmen in the
area. I spent a few days at the main Citibank facility and it was all very impressive. I also visited Malaysia, Taiwan, Korea and Thailand, in each case visiting
a customer and touring plants, such as steel plants in Korea and assembly
plants in Taiwan, which in many cases we had financed.

The Mattel toy plant in Taiwan, where they made Barbie dolls, was fascinating. The facility was huge. There were dormitories for the roughly four
hundred young female employees who were not only housed but fed and
clothed. Each assembly line had a particular function – painting Barbie's
face, washing and perming her hair, making her clothes – and the factory

was a beehive of activity. The individual elements were then sent to plants in Mexico and other countries where the dolls would be assembled, put in boxes and shipped all over the world. Literally millions of these dolls were manufactured and assembled every year.

I then traveled to Hong Kong and Tokyo, where I met our key people and was introduced to our operations in each city. These were our two biggest operations in Asia, with several hundred employees in each location. Time was spent in each place bringing me up to date with what was transpiring in the various economies of the region, so by the time I returned to San Francisco I could speak with some knowledge of Asia. Much of the business activity in California had some connection with the Asian market. Asia was not an easy place to travel in the sixties. As in South America, there were not many hotels to choose from; the food, in some cases, was not too exciting and it could be difficult to get around in some of the cities. The one advantage was that the air transportation in a number of countries was being run by European airlines and so was fairly reliable. Some countries, like Indonesia, were dangerous.

Ness Industries was an early customer of the San Francisco bank. Gordon Ness was considered quite an entrepreneur. He was written up in all the business magazines and had a large auditorium named after him at Stanford. He had opened the first electronics manufacturing facility in Indonesia. They were making calculators with light emitting diodes (LEDs), which, at the time, were state of the art. The next time I was in Asia, I went to Indonesia to see the Ness plant, which was in the capital city of Jakarta. Indonesia had recently been through a period of political upheaval and civil war, and although the new president, Suharto, was encouraging economic development and foreign investment, there was still much corruption and unrest. In Jakarta, I could not walk down the sidewalks at night because they were full of sleeping people. I didn't even leave the hotel after dark. Ness's plant seemed to be running fairly efficiently, despite these issues, but was always being shut down by a more local problem. There is a strong mystical tradition in Indonesian culture, and the plant had a Dukun, or traditional witch doctor, on staff. Hundreds of workers, mainly women, were housed and fed at the factory, and one or more of them would go into a trance on a fairly regular basis; the witch doctor would have to perform a ritual that would break the trance. This ritual could take some time and until it was finished, the production line would be shut down.

But Ness Industries started having bigger problems in 1971. They began to have competition from newer technology and more efficient production methods, and the stock hit the skids. Ness could not pay its bills. I told the chief financial officer that our bank would not renew their loan facility because of these problems. We needed a plan to help us see what they intended to do. Instead of a plan, I got a call from Gordon Ness himself, inviting me to lunch. He took me out on his yacht and, after we had eaten, told me that he really needed someone with my abilities to work with him. He talked about the enormous potential of his company. Then he offered me a job with a big title and three times my bank salary. He sat back and smiled at me, seemingly certain that he had stunned me. I was stunned, but not in the way he intended. I told Gordon that I was flabbergasted that he would have the audacity to make such an offer in order to influence my decision. I told him that the company's loan facility was cancelled immediately.

Several days later, he went to see Walt Wriston, the Chairman of Citibank, in New York and spoke to him about my inflexible attitude on his loan. Mr. Wriston phoned me, with Ness on the call, and asked if I could explain my position. I told him in detail about the financial condition of the company, the competition they were facing and their continued reluctance to provide the bank with a workable plan for the future of the company. Mr. Wriston told me how much he appreciated my elucidation, that my decision was well-founded and that he concurred with me. Then, while I was still on the line, he informed Ness that my decision was final. I had great respect for Walt Wriston even before the call but the experience made me realize the importance of backing your people if you are going to manage a worldwide multi-billion dollar corporation.

While I was in San Francisco, Jeanetta was hired to work on a new series shooting in the city called, "The Streets of San Francisco", which starred Michael Douglas and Karl Malden. I was able to see her often and many times would stop by the set during lunch. They often put me into the scene they were filming that day, but as far as I know, I never showed up on the screen – I must have poisoned the scene! It was a happy set to work on. Malden was a terrific guy and Douglas, then a newcomer, was learning from Karl. So there was no arguing or bitching and lots of laughter. Michael Douglas was dating an actress from Dallas, Brenda Vaccaro, whose parents owned a restaurant just off of Oak Lawn.

Ann and I had moved to Moraga, a small town on the east side of the bay from San Francisco. It was a pretty village and was near a redwood forest that would never be developed. The rest of the surroundings served as a watershed for Oakland and San Francisco. It was the prettiest area we ever lived in.

Shortly after moving there, a friend of ours mentioned that he knew a young woman from Sweden who had just arrived in the US who was interested in living with a family as an au pair, helping to take care of their children. We interviewed her and told her that we were interested in her staying with us but could not pay her very much. As I recall, we offered her about $250 a month, plus room and board. For some reason, she decided to accept our offer.

Her name was Juliana auf Ugglas, and the first day after she had moved in with us, I asked her what town she was from and if she would tell us about her family. She said she was from a small town near Malmo, Sweden. She said she had a picture of their home and her family, went into her room and came back with a Swedish magazine that was similar to "Look" magazine in this country. She handed to me and said, "This is where I live". I asked, "What page is it on?" She said, "That's it, on the cover". The building on the cover looked a lot like Versailles. It was enormous and very beautiful and of course prompted me to ask more questions. It was obvious she didn't need the small salary we were paying her, but she said she was eager to learn while she was with us.

The children loved Juliana from the start. She was a lovely young lady with blonde hair and blue eyes. She was about 5' 10" with a winsome figure and a winning personality. She also had a way with children. She was loving, but also was not reluctant to discipline them when it was required.

Juliana was invited in one instance to attend a luncheon in San Francisco at a single men's club that met on Tuesdays; they would invite a group of single woman to be their guests at each luncheon. The club had about thirty members, all of whom were in their thirties and were successful in business. After this event things became pretty hectic for Juliana. She would increasingly ask us if she could have a night off and unless we had prior plans we tried to accommodate her. All of a sudden, there were Rolls Royces and Mercedes pulling up in front of our house to pick up Juliana. We would often pick up the paper the next morning to find a picture of her at some social event the prior evening. She also had a habit of sunbathing in our yard in a small bikini, which definitely entertained the men in our neighborhood.

She stayed with us for a little over a year before announcing that she was returning to Sweden. The boys cried when they found out she was leaving. We were all going to miss her a great deal. Ann and I took Juliana out to dinner to give her a send off and tell her what she had meant to us. She told us that on the evening when she came to live with us, she had been very apprehensive because everyone in Sweden told her that the American husbands would present a problem for a lovely young girl like herself. She said that she was surprised that I had never even touched her and she wanted to thank us both for a wonderful experience.

Several years later, Ann and I went to Sweden and Juliana's family entertained us royally. We were feted in several manor houses and cordially thanked for taking good care of their daughter. Juliana later married and had three children, and we received Christmas cards from her for many years.

CHAPTER 33

In 1971, I was approached by the Larry Apple, the President of PVO International, a client of mine at the bank. Larry, a good man who had been the CFO before becoming President, asked if I would consider becoming the Chief Financial Officer of that public company. He offered me a 50% increase in salary. Now I had never been CFO of a public company and I told him so. I also told him that I didn't know the many facets of the position. He said he wanted me in the job and he could help with the tasks I didn't grasp. I told him that I would have to sleep on it.

When I got home, Ann and I put our heads together and drew up the pluses and minuses. Citibank had been very good to me and had given me authority and opportunities. On the other hand, I wasn't sure what my future would be there and no one had addressed it. PVO had a rocky history and would be more of a gamble. It was a chemical and food company with 3500 employees and thirteen plants in eleven countries. It had a commodity risk, but this would give me a better industrial background. We decided to go for it.

PVO gave me a contract that was very generous and I tendered my resignation to Citibank. It was really hard to leave the bank. It was a world-class organization but sometimes you can get lost in such a large, corporate environment. I was game for a change.

PVO dealt in vegetable oils and the products those oils produced. We made foods such as artificial cheese, polyunsaturated margarine and cooking oils. We traded large quantities of safflower oil, sunflower seed oil, rape seed oil, coconut oil, cottonseed oil and about thirty other plant oils in lesser quantities. We made oil-based chemicals for all types of uses, such as paint thinners and mixes and soil additives to halt erosion. The company was public and had about $250 million in sales, which was a good-sized company for that time. It had large facilities in Boonton, New Jersey, Saint Louis,

Missouri and Richmond, California. The company also had 13 plants in eleven foreign countries.

I soon realized I was truly in over my head. If it had not been for Larry Apple, I would have drowned. Larry had worked for Harold Geneen, who was Chairman of ITT and known as one of the toughest CEOs in business. He knew so much about managing a business, especially from a financial viewpoint. He taught me how to read the stacks of financial printouts from our operations all over the world. His assumption was that everything inside of the company with a number attached to it would be my responsibility. If a division wanted to acquire new equipment or do anything that cost money then it was my decision. Did it fit in the budget? Was it necessary? What would be our return on the investment? New hires had to be approved by me. I was a one-person salary committee who decided if an employee got a raise and if so, how much. In other words, from Larry's perspective, I was essentially the chief operating officer, which is the way my job was described to the other officers. In retrospect, giving me such a huge responsibility allowed him to focus on the strategic decisions that needed to be made about the direction of the company.

One unfortunate side effect of this position was that it made me unpopular with almost everyone at the company. If an employee got promoted or got a raise or bonus, it was my policy that the division head or supervisor should be the one to convey the good news and to reap the good will of their employees. If the person did not get a raise or promotion, or if they were to be let go then I was the one who would tell them and take the blame for the action. When I walked down the halls, many people would not speak to me, even ducking into offices in order to avoid me. This made me unhappy but it had the overall effect of making the employees work harder for their immediate supervisors.

There were so many working units in so many places, and problems seemed to flare up all over. Most of the time they were the result of human error, but we still had find out what was wrong and fix it. I traveled quite a bit and spent many hours reviewing printouts and operations in order to troubleshoot problems. The President backed me up regardless of the situation. If he had an item that he did not like, he would call me in and we would discuss the matter, but it was always done in private. If he hadn't dealt with me in such a supportive and insightful way, it would have been an almost impossible position. He taught me how to face adversity and handle it.

In one instance, I needed to figure out why we were losing a million dollars a month in our Boonton, New Jersey plant, which had about 950 employees. We did our best to uncover the source of the losses, even bringing in the FBI to investigate. Their report to us said that tank cars of oils and chemicals were regularly disappearing from the railroad sidings surrounding the plant. They intimated that there was a large Italian influence in the area and in the plant. While they did not say the Mafia was involved, I was told by the supervisors that they believed that was the case. I decided to take drastic action. I wrote the names of all the operational personnel on a blackboard and drew a line though the names of family members and others that because of their family connections and personnel files I thought might be connected. I had long conversations with Larry and he finally agreed with the plan. I issued severance notices to two-hundred and eighty-six of our employees the next day.

The union went crazy. I told them that if we did not take this action, we would have to close the plant and fire everyone. They knew that the company could not continue sustaining the losses, and that this was our last resort. Everybody was angry at me, including the Governor of New Jersey. But from the day I took that action, the losses stopped. Obviously some or all of the group that had been severed had been stealing from the company. Not an easy solution and probably not one that could be done today, but it was effective.

We hired a very nice gentleman named Meyers, who had an interesting story. He had been in charge of the Campbell's Soup plant in Sacramento for several years but had not advanced because of his dedication to his daughter and her dream. Each day, he would drive his daughter a hundred miles to and from a special swimming class before going to work. After work he would return to pick her up. His daughter, Debbie Meyer, won three gold medals in the 1968 Olympics at the age of sixteen, and then told her father she never wanted to see him again. She felt he had ruined her life by making her train all the time, and said she had missed out on growing up and had never even had a date. As you might imagine, he had been crushed. We subsequently hired him to manage our Philippines subsidiary, and he and his wife moved to the Manila area. The last time I saw him, he was still sad about his daughter. But about six months after they moved, his daughter called them and said she loved them and wanted to reconcile. After all that, a happy ending.

There was a very funny incident while I was in this job, involving my secretary, a nice-looking woman named Barbara Brandfass. Ann and I had a party at our house one night and invited friends from work as well as from our neighborhood. Barbara, who was quite well-endowed, was wearing a low-cut dress, and one of our neighbors could not stop giving her leering looks. After this had continued for a while, Barbara turned to him and asked if he wanted to play strip poker. His face lit up and he immediately said yes. Barbara got some cards and started shuffling. Our neighbor's wife was apprised of the impending game and immediately came in to tell her husband that they would be going home. The husband told her to go ahead and he would join her later. She insisted that they leave that instant. As soon he was gone, Barbara started laughing and put away the cards.

The next day Ann perpetuated the joke and called the neighbor to say that it had been too bad he had to leave the party so early, because Barbara had lost every hand and was nude shortly after he left. He brought the subject up every time we saw him after that, and no one ever told him the truth!

PVO was doing well but the stock price never seemed to go up much. After earnings improved, a group in New York started a proxy fight to take over control of the company. Larry thought the hostile group would probably win. He called me in and told me I had done a good job in a tough position and he was proud of me but he wanted to give me a little space. He decided that he would relieve me of my position before the onslaught and management were subsequently fired. Business has some ugly sides to it. As for me, I got the education of a lifetime in the space of about two years.

I interviewed with all kinds of companies, both in the Bay area and elsewhere. Some of them spoke to me at length about a position and salary, but I didn't like any of them. Then, I received a good offer from the First National Bank in Dallas. Ann and I visited and liked the city, so we decided to leave California and return to Texas.

PART TEN

NEW DIRECTIONS

CHAPTER 34

The First National Bank in Dallas was a large regional bank with interests concentrated in oil and gas related businesses and real estate transactions in roughly a three-state area. Most of the senior officers were born and educated in Texas and were not very open to outsiders coming into their ranks. Although I was a native Texan, I was considered an outsider by some in management because I was coming from the outside. I was hired primarily for my international experience, but arrived to find myself working in a division headed by a banker who was sorely lacking in international experience or knowledge. The first comment made to me was that I could not be effective in international banking because I did not speak a foreign language. It would have done no good to remind them that I had been the largest international business producer at any regional bank in the United States – their viewpoint had been formed long before I arrived. The head of the International Division neither understood nor enjoyed doing business outside the US. He thought the risk was too great and wasn't interested in listening to my dissenting opinion on the matter. Needless to say, this made my job a bit tricky. However, I did manage to extricate the bank from a loan they had made to a group in Monterrey, saving them quite a lot of money.

Because of the bank's unnecessarily conservative attitude towards foreign business, I was transferred to the Energy Division after about six months. Since energy was the main focus of the bank's business, the department was well-supported and I enjoyed my new activities. I found the customers in the oil and gas business to be very friendly and I liked working with them. After about a year, I received a call from the president of the bank, Rawls Fulghum, asking me to come to his office. When I arrived, two other men were already there, discussing a problem they had. Rawls welcomed me and introduced me to Dink Dalton, the Chairman of the Placid Petroleum Company and Walter

Fraker, the CFO and chief legal officer. They presented their situation: they had received a hydrocarbon lease in the Dutch sector of the North Sea and, after extensive drilling, had discovered large gas reserves off of Holland and needed to both develop these reserves and build a pipeline under the sea to Germany. Obviously Mr. Fulghum remembered my experience in international finance.

The question was then posed to me: could I put together a loan package that would initially give them sufficient funds to build the pipeline and then provide a larger loan to develop the field, based only on undeveloped gas reserves? At that time, this kind of project had not been accomplished before anywhere in the world; no one had ever made a loan with the collateral still underground, in unconfirmable quantities. Estimates have gotten more accurate, but back then, it was still a bit of a gamble as to what would eventually be uncovered. I told them that while I had not done an oil and gas project, I had been successful in structuring large development loans in several parts of the world, and felt certain that I could put this venture together with a consortium of foreign banks. Dalton said that Citibank had told him they were the only bank that could handle a project of this magnitude. I said that I was one of the very people who had accomplished the funding of similarly large projects at Citibank and I felt I could do the same here. After some more questions and discussion, Dalton decided to have us lead the project.

Rawls Fulghum was very excited. This was one of the most complex and difficult transactions the bank had ever undertaken. After the Placid team had left, he reminded me that the bank's reputation was on the line. I told Fulghum that the project would take time and a great team in order to succeed, and I would need his backing. He promised me his complete support.

One of the first things I did was to get the law firm of Graham and James in San Francisco on board. They were one of the best international law firms in the country at that time. The challenges we were facing involved foreign government interference, foreign exchange risk, political risk in Europe and the Middle East and explaining the hydrocarbon reserve risk to banks that were not familiar with that industry. Another thing that was necessary was for me to become conversant in oil jargon and familiar with the physical features of the gas deposits and what would be required to develop them. I got petroleum engineers who worked for the bank to travel with me to several oil and gas drilling and production facilities and educate me.

I spent a lot of time with the Placid team as they developed the project plans. They literally spent hours explaining to me the facilities that had to be built to produce and process the gas. At the same time, I was working with the pipe-laying company to understand the procedure for laying forty miles of 36″ pipe underwater to a receiving station in northern Europe, where the gas would then be sold to Dutch and German utilities in Dutch Guilders and Deutschmarks. The pipe was to be installed under one of the most stormy and violent bodies of water on the planet, the North Sea. The foreign exchange risk could be substantial given that three currency rates were involved, and the first loan, for the pipeline itself, was for about $160 million.

Having educated myself, I then had to sit down with a colleague and write a descriptive brochure of the whole process, outlining the things we needed from other participants in order to achieve our goals. The project was named Noordgastransport. When we were finished writing I had to have the engineers, lawyers, bankers and the company approve of the product. We did this and got the go-ahead to move forward.

I went to talk to friends at Morgan Guaranty Bank in New York, which I considered the best major bank in the world. We discussed the transaction and I asked if they would like to co-lead the project with us. They enthusiastically said yes, even though they knew the difficulty of the proposal. We brought them up to date with the facts and details of the deal and jointly planned our next steps. Together we visited other banks in order to identify those that might be interested in joining a syndicate to make the loan.

We then took the petroleum engineers on a road show, visiting each of the interested banks in order to answer all their questions and show them the details of the project. This took about a month, in Europe and at home. Finally the syndicate was committed – the banks that ultimately joined us were Christiana Bank and Den Norske Creditbank in Norway, Deutche Bank in Germany, a bank in Belgium, National Westminister Bank in England, a

French bank, Chemical Bank of New York and two other US banks – and we negotiated the loan documents with Placid and the Dutch government. The project was approved by all parties and the pipe laying finally got underway, about a year after the entire process had begun.

One glitch along the way had been that the Dutch Central Bank wanted the loan to be in Dutch Guilders. I wanted the loan in dollars because oil is a dollar-based commodity. Even though Placid was to be paid in German Marks and Dutch Guilders, the US dollar would always determine the exchange rate. I prevailed, and in the end, because the Guilder and Mark increased in value against the dollar, Placid received two dollars in value for each dollar it had to pay, which translated to big savings for the company.

The bank got a lot of very favorable publicity from the transaction and we were soon besieged with calls from other oil companies who wanted our advice and help on their projects. Over the next few years, I was asked to participate in development projects all over the world. I was considered a real expert in these types of transactions on the basis of the Dutch venture.

I traveled several million miles, working on developments in Indonesia, Malaysia, Thailand, England, Scotland, Ireland, New Zealand, Norway and Australia. In addition, we were the lead on the development loan for the Placid gas field. At one time I was in England for thirty out of thirty-six months. I would have much rather been home with my family, but I couldn't back away from the job I was being paid to do. I tried to diminish the distance with calls and presents, but it was difficult for all of us.

During the Placid project, I became acquainted with a fine man who lived in The Hague. His name now escapes me, so I will just call him the Doctor. He was the president of a bank that specialized in middle term credit for industrial development in Holland. He was in his seventies, with grey hair and a perpetual smile on his face that I will always remember. I met with him several times because he had a lot of government connections and we wanted to avoid any problems that might arise on the project. One night, I asked the Doctor if he would join me for dinner and he agreed. I met him at the restaurant and as we walked in, I noticed that everyone was looking at the Doctor. When we were seated, everyone in the restaurant stood up and looked in his direction. He nodded his head in recognition of their gesture. I was dying to ask him about the gesture but I assumed it was some sort of local honor in The Hague and said nothing.

About a week later, we were scheduled to have dinner in Amsterdam. Again, we met at a very nice restaurant and as we sat down everyone in the restaurant stood up and nodded toward the Doctor. He nodded back. I looked at him and finally asked him why everyone honored him wherever we went. As he answered me, there were tears in his eyes. "During the war, I was the head of the Dutch resistance against the Germans. I had a large price on my head and I lived on the run until the Germans left Holland. These friends are all trying to thank me for what I did". He then added, "It was a long time ago". I was truly moved by both his actions, and by the response of the community, even so many years later.

The Placid development loan was for $240 million dollars, and was easier to put together because the transport pipeline had been finished. We did suffer one setback when the pipeline suddenly materialized on the surface of the water off the coast of Holland. The laying vessels went back in and put heavier weights on the line, solving the problem.

I went over to visit both the pipe-laying project and the development project. When you went out to the drilling rig, you could travel on a barge across a rough North Sea and then be lifted about ten stories riding what is called a donut, which is a circular piece of material about five feet in diameter, with a four and a half foot hole in the center. The part you stand on is only about 6" in width. Ropes suspend the donut from a hook, which is attached to a steel cable. This cable lifts you the hundred feet or so to the floor of the production platform. It was as scary as it sounds. Even scarier was descending the ten stories back down to the barge because it looked like a toy boat from that height. The only other way to get on board the rig was by helicopter, which was usually a rough ride as well, due to the winds above the North Sea. I went out once when it was snowing heavily. That experience will wake you up fast!

Jan Van Dyck was the President of Dutch State Mines, a government subsidiary that would be half-owner of the pipeline we were financing.

He wired me in Dallas and asked if we could meet in Maastricht, which is located in southern Holland about sixty miles east of Brussels. I flew to Brussels and took a train to Maastricht. Jan picked me up and took me to a very old hotel and restaurant at the top of a hill. He told me that this had been the most northerly Roman settlement in ancient times, and was the highest point in the area looking south across the entire valley. Every military force in history wanted control of this high point. For that reason, the Nazis had placed a command post there.

Behind the hotel, there were a number of caves that the Germans used to store ammunition and food supplies during the period they held the area. After lunch, we walked back into some of the caves, which were incredibly deep and dark. He said the Germans had been reluctant to stray back too far into the caves, which is why they never found the passage through the mountain, about a hundred yards farther into the caves, which had been used as an escape route for allied pilots and escaped prisoners. Even deeper into the mountain, there is a cave that was used during the war to hide all of the art that the Dutch took out of the Rijksmuseum in Amsterdam, including works by Rembrandt and Van Gogh. All of that right under the Germans' noses, and they never knew!

I spent a great deal of time in the Netherlands for this project, and really got a chance to see a lot of the country, though I most often stayed in the Hague or in Amsterdam. One time in Amsterdam, as I was walking down the front steps of the hotel, a young man approached me, said that they were making a movie at the hotel and asked if I would be willing to help them. I asked how, and he said that a grey Mercedes would be driving around the corner and stopping in front of the hotel entrance. An actor would get out of the back seat, open the front door, take out a suitcase, say something to a man in the back seat and then turn and walk up the steps into the hotel. He wanted me to walk from the corner to the hotel, timing it so that I would arrive on the front steps at the same time as the actor from the car. I said that would be no problem.

I went to the corner and when they yelled "action!" I started to walk toward the hotel. On cue, the grey Mercedes came tearing around the corner toward the front of the hotel. Just out of view of the cameras, men with buckets were throwing water on the car's windshield, which had its windshield wipers going full blast. The actor got out of the car, closed the back door and reached in and got a suitcase off the front seat. He then wheeled about and started up the stairs to the hotel. As I got closer, I realized that the man leaving the car was Robert Mitchum. As we started up the stairs together, Mitchum looked at me and said, "You're not going to believe this, but that dumb bastard driving the car has got his window down, and is soaking wet from all the water they're throwing on the car". I couldn't keep from laughing; Mitchum was laughing too. The director immediately yelled "CUT!" and told everyone we would have to retake the scene.

We all went back to our starting places and the scene started all over again. As I walked up to Mitchum during the retake, he looked at me and said, "The window is still down. I just can't believe he's that dumb". When we were done, Mitchum invited me to have a cup of coffee with him in the hotel. The actor who had been in the back of car came in and joined us. It was Leslie Nielsen. That was the first time I had met either of them, but I would meet Leslie again years later. The film was called "Amsterdam Kill", and when I went to see it the next year, my scene had been cut from the movie – just as I always was cut from the films Jeanetta was working on. Some things apparently stay the same, no matter what country you are in!

Some time later, Indiana University invited me to lecture at its Graduate School of Business on the Noordgastransport project. I went up to the main campus in Bloomington and met the Dean of the school. That evening, a professor and three students took me out to dinner. During the course of the dinner, I apparently made a major faux pas by using the term gal (as in: "I think she is a fine gal") during the course of the conversation. The professor immediately took me to task, saying that it was inexcusable to refer to any woman as a "gal". He felt I should apologize to the women present. I was taken aback, and told him that the term was not meant to be derogatory, and was used in common speech in the area of the country where I lived. I felt there was no reason to apologize. He was livid and immediately took me back to my hotel room.

The next day I presented a case study on the Dutch project. During the lecture, I discussed the risks involved in the development and how those risks could be hedged. I discussed the reserve risk in developing the gas reserves; the political risk between the producer and the countries of Holland and Germany; the currency risk that was inherent in lending in dollars and being repaid in Deutchmarks and Guilders; the contract risks that would arise between the producer and the Dutch government because of the dollar denomination; the risk involved in laying a forty-mile pipeline under one of the roughest seas in the world; and lastly the risk of putting together a financing package with banks from six countries with six different currency hedges. At the end, I asked if there were any questions. There were none, even from the professor. I realized they hadn't understood a thing I had said. Afterwards, the students came up and asked me to explain certain fundamental concepts to them, which I did gladly. I was told later that the project became a case study at Harvard Business School, but I never saw the case so I can't say for sure.

The bank's project work continued to expand. In Malaysia, we got involved with an oil development for Exxon. We worked to finance several fields in Ireland, England and Scotland and assisted in the development of the Northwest Shelf gas discovery in Australia. We also helped fund a large liquid natural gas (LNG) project on Kalimantan in Indonesia. It involved several million dollars for the development of the gas field and several billion dollars to build LNG processing facilities. In addition, several LNG tankers had to be built, which would cost about three billion dollars, and finally the Japanese had to spend four or five billion dollars for plants in Japan that would convert the LNG back into gas that could be distributed in their country. This project was successfully completed and the payback on the loans occurred in about two years.

Two other projects took a great deal of time. Delhi Petroleum wanted to build a pipeline in Australia connecting gas fields in the northeast to a point just north of Adelaide, where it would go to a new ethylene dichloride plant. This pipeline would traverse the harshest part of the outback. The existing Australian laws would not allow a bank or other financer to attach the proceeds of the sale of the gas. In other words, the gas could be paid for and none of the money would go to the parties putting up the money. We asked the Bank of New South Wales to partner up with us and, with their help, got a law firm to lobby the Parliament to change the laws in a way that would allow us to finance this project. Parliament changed the laws and the deal was done. We also worked on an ethanol plant in New Zealand.

During my tenure at the bank in Dallas, I had a number of terrific customers. One that I enjoyed the most was Tenneco. The Chairman was Jim Kettleston and the Executive Vice President was Ken Reese. Jim had been the Chairman of J. I. Case before he came to Tenneco and Ken had previously been the President of the Firestone Tire Company. They were both tremendous leaders and ran a marvelous company. I took several trips with them to some of their subsidiaries. They owned Newport News Shipbuilding and I had the pleasure of going through nuclear submarines, a nuclear carrier and a giant liquid natural gas tanker. When I was there, there were 25,000 people working on the carrier and the LNG tanker. It was like a town unto itself, with all the same problems that a town that size would have: drug dealers, theft, rape, assault and prostitution. It had its own police force.

We also went to Tennessee, where they owned Container Corporation. After taking me on a tour of the large container plant, they took me to a clearing nearby, where an assortment of the large bulldozers, tractors and other heavy equipment they manufactured were on display. They told me that I could operate any piece of equipment there and do whatever I wanted with it. It was a childhood dream come true! I tore down trees, dug ditches and raised havoc for about an hour. What great fun!

Sadly, Ken Reese died of a heart attack one morning while out running. His secretary called me immediately, saying he would have wanted her to. I was heartbroken. He was such a great friend and counselor and I will always miss him. The older I got, the more friends it seemed I was losing.

CHAPTER 35

I had been traveling so much; it was time to get away and spend some time with my wife. Ann and I went to Hawaii for a vacation and stayed at the Kapalua Resort. It a very romantic place and we enjoyed the time together. I tried to get a tee time at their golf course but being a single, they wouldn't give me one. I had to wait until someone else wanted to play and there was an opening for me. One day I stopped by and they told me that a gentleman from Chicago was coming to play and asked if I would I like to join him. I said yes and asked what he did in Chicago; they told me they thought he was part of the Mafia. I was game; at least it wouldn't be a boring! A few minutes later, a long Cadillac limousine drove up and out stepped a round, bald-headed man. They told him I would like to join him and I introduced myself. He grunted and said his name was Bruno.

I drove the cart and Bruno didn't say much for the first few holes. On one of the holes, I hit a good drive down the middle of the fairway and asked Bruno what club he would recommend I use for the next shot. Without looking up, he said, "Nine iron!" I took out a nine and, as fate would have it, hit a shot that ended up only a foot from the flag. I said, "Bruno, you chose the perfect club".

He looked up, smiled for the first time and said, "I'll tell you the same thing they told me when I joined the family. Stick with me, kid, and I'll have you fartin' through silk!" He laughed and clapped me on the back. I didn't have the nerve to ask him which family he was talking about!

Ann and I also took a few days to go visit Jeanetta in Nashville, where she was working on a movie called "W.W. and the Dixie Dancekings". It was a comedy with a lot of music, and starred Art Carney, Jerry Reed and Burt Reynolds – who Ann thought was extra special. We drove to Nashville and went out to join my sister on the set, which was several miles out in the country. When we arrived, we were asked to park our car and then walk to the set. They were in the process of filming a scene, so a red light at the top of a small hill was on, which meant we had to pause, so as not to interrupt the scene.

When the light was turned off, we headed over the hill and down to a small house where the actors were waiting for the cameras to be moved for another set-up. When we got within about twenty yards of the set, Burt Reynolds came running toward us; he grabbed Ann in his arms, told her she was beautiful and bent her over backwards as he gave her a big kiss on the lips. Ann was utterly speechless. She could only stare at him as he beamed a big movie-star smile. Finally, the US, but with full pay for quite a while we realized that Jeanetta had arranged the greeting. She had known that Ann really liked Burt Reynolds and got a big kick out of the whole affair.

Jeanetta walked us down to the set to meet Art Carney and Jerry Reed. Everyone was in a great mood and we had a chance to chat before the next scene. During the next break, Burt and Jerry were sitting on two director's chairs and they drew me right into the conversation. Out of the corner of my eye, I saw a young girl headed across some pasture land toward us. She had gotten around the police barriers by going through some nearby fields. After she climbed over the last barrier, she came over and stood behind Burt's chair, coughing and clearing her throat. He didn't pay any attention to her, so she got increasingly more dramatic with her noises, but Burt still ignored them. The day was overcast and chilly, and the girl was skimpily dressed in a skin-tight t-shirt and a very short skirt. As the hour grew later, she started to shiver, and she reached over and took Burt's coat off the back of the chair he was sitting on. He immediately turned around and said, "You better not put on that coat because it's a magic coat". The girl giggled and said, "If it's magic, what will it do? Make me disappear?" Burt said, "If it would make you disappear, I would have had it on your back about thirty minutes ago". The girl, missing the whole point, just giggled and security finally came and asked her to leave. Jerry Reed almost fell down laughing.

The next day it was drizzling and the temperature was a little cooler but they decided to film anyway. The crowd was larger than the day before, even with the miserable weather. Midday, the cast headed back into town for lunch. When Burt's limo got to the highway barrier, he told the driver to stop. The fans surged to the car and started yelling. Burt rolled down the window and motioned to a woman in the crowd to come forward, which she did. She had a small, very young baby in her arms, covered with a only a light blanket. Burt said, "Lady, you need to get that baby to shelter and out of this rain. What do you want? Why are you here?" The woman said that she just wanted to see him and perhaps get a picture. Burt said, "Lady, if you promise to take that baby right home, I'll give you all the pictures you want". He turned to his assistant in the front seat and told him to give the woman several signed pictures. With that accomplished, he rolled up the window and we went on into town. Burt's fans were nothing if not devoted!

I had been traveling a lot for work, but so had Jeanetta. She had been hired to go to Sri Lanka to be the script supervisor on a movie directed by John Derek. It was his version of "Tarzan" and starred his wife Bo Derek, who we all remembered from "Ten". Apparently the movie was going to be filmed in an area of the jungle known to harbor Tamil Tigers guerillas, who were then waging a violent secessionist campaign against the Sri Lankan government. Not surprisingly, everyone was a little on edge on the first day of filming; when everyone arrived, John Derek called for the crew to gather on the set for the first scene, and everyone got a shock, but not the kind they had been worried about. When the door to Bo Derek's trailer opened, she stepped out completely nude. Jeanetta asked whether John Derek was intending to film a porno flick; he didn't like her comment and that's when the trouble started. Before long, he had fired the entire production company and they all returned to the US, but with full pay for quite a while; I believe it was six weeks. He eventually hired a new crew and made the film, but it was not a success and even earned several Golden Raspberry Awards nominations in the categories of worst film, worst actress and worst director of that year!

While Jeanetta was out of the country on location one time, there had been a wind and rain storm and a limb off of one of her trees had fallen on a Camellia bush on her neighbor's property and apparently the bush died. When she returned from her job, he came to see her, irate, and told her that he was going to ruin her career in Hollywood. He was a small-time producer who had produced one movie a few years earlier, and was clearly not a happy man. She offered to buy him a new bush but he just cursed at her and said he would get revenge.

Jeanetta called me and asked if I could come and talk to the guy. I went over to see if could patch things up. I rang the neighbor's doorbell and a short, stout man came to the door. I said, "I am the brother of the lady next door to you and...". He immediately yelled, "I ought to kick your ass right now. You get your ass off my property and don't come back. I'm going to ruin your smart-ass sister. She'll never work again in this town!"

"The lady next door would like to reimburse you for any loss you have suffered. Please let us repair any damage to your property". I said. He said, "You heard me – get off my property!" I looked at him and said, "My sister has three brothers and we do not like her being threatened. This will not have a happy ending for you". He slammed the door.

I went back to Jeanetta's place and told her that I would take care of this matter. I called Tex and told him what had transpired and how we had tried to solve the dilemma without any luck. Tex said that he would see what he could do. The next day, an attorney named Clarence Price showed up on the neighbor's doorstep. Clarence told the neighbor that he represented Jeanetta and he wished to reach an amicable settlement over the matter that was bothering the neighbor. The neighbor began to rant and once more he repeated his threat concerning Jeanetta's continued employment in the motion picture industry. Clarence just said, "Not only will you not be in a position to threaten Miss Lewis, but I can assure you that you will not be working in this town again. Miss Lewis' brother is on the board of Universal Pictures and an advisor to MGM. So I think this time you over-stepped your capability".

Clarence had a ten-foot fence erected along the side of Jeanetta's property that completely closed off any view the neighbor previously had. I suppose the moral of the story is that you really should know who you are threatening before you open your mouth and start yelling.

CHAPTER 36

It was an exciting time for me at work. I was on the line trying to solve large problems in order to fund large projects and we succeeded most of the time. First National Bank became InterFirst Bank during this time, and the new regime was not that interested in what I was doing. The banking business in Texas and the Southwest was booming and my projects weren't considered an essential part of their operation. They put me in charge of Multinational Energy, where I led a group that was responsible for new accounts or increasing current business with major oil companies in the US. We established new relationships with Exxon, Mobil, Cities Service, Phillips 66, Chevron, Amoco, Marathon, Union, Arco and Tenneco, increasing our business by $400 million. I knew or met the Chairmen of all the major oil companies and enjoyed those relationships. The bank was still unimpressed, probably because they could make more from smaller companies, from whom they could derive a higher profit margin.

I visited Hong Kong on business quite a few times, and it was always fun to see Bob and Jenny Theleen, who were the bank's Hong Kong representatives. Bob is an inventive and talented dealmaker. On one trip, the three of us took the hydrofoil to Macao, where we had been invited to attend the farewell dinner for the Chief of Police on Macao. Since Macao was a Portuguese colony, the Chief was Portuguese and was on his way back to Lisbon. It was a wonderful evening. The meal consisted of a number of Chinese delicacies like hundred-year-old eggs, real shark tail soup and fried milk that I found hard to enjoy. But even though the cuisine was not my cup of tea, the surroundings were great and the people first class.

In 1980, Bob and Jenny Theleen arranged an invitation for me to come to the People's Republic of China. I was asked to present a seminar in Beijing on ways the Republic of China could best finance the development of their energy reserves. I prepared a paper that I thought was very comprehensive and would be useful to the Chinese attending. I was accompanied by two attorneys who specialized in corporate law; Jenny Theleen spoke both Cantonese and Mandarin and would act as our interpreter during the seminar.

When we arrived, we were put up in the Beijing Hotel, which had been built in the 1920's and enlarged by the Russians in about 1950. Our rooms were rather drab; they were in the oldest portion of the hotel and parts of the ceiling actually fell on us during the night. We were supplied around the clock with hot water for tea in a large thermos bottle. It was pretty primitive and seemed to be a sign that the Chinese were not ready for the rest of the world. Most of the foreign companies had their offices in the newer part of the hotel and ended up using those rooms for living quarters as well.

I was struck by the fact that there was absolutely no color anywhere in Beijing. Both men and women wore dark grey or dark blue Mao jackets and matching pants. There were no signs, no neon and not many cars. Almost everyone commuted by bicycle. We went to a shopping district of the city to shop where there were no sidewalks, only dirt streets.

The ten-day seminar began the day after I arrived, and there were about thirty people in attendance, most of whom seemed to be between fifty and seventy years old. These were people that had lived at least a portion of their lives under a capitalist system, before the communist regime had taken over. I thought they would be just the audience for what we intended to speak about.

After the niceties of the introductions were over, I started on the lecture material. Almost immediately, there was a question. What was interest? I was taken aback, but I gave a practical illustration and explained that it was the cost of borrowing money, that interest was the earnings accruing to a lender. The next question was "what are earnings?" Oh boy. I knew my presentation would be worthless because it assumed basic knowledge of business and clearly, that had not been a safe assumption. I switched gears, and for the next week and a half, I basically taught a basic business and MBA course. We had to explain the term "Eurodollar", what the time value of money was, what depreciation was, what we meant by the words escrow, collateral, value, development period, well head and proved reserves. After all that, I tried to explain how the Chinese would go about borrowing money and what a state guarantee was.

JPL lecturing in China, 1980

At the end of the first evening, all of the participants came up to where I was standing; many put their hands on my arms and told me how much they had learned. It was a show of kindness and affection.

Before I left for the trip, I had talked to a China expert about etiquette and protocol and was told that the Chinese did not like any type of physical contact. This was the first of several things that turned out not to quite be true. Another thing I was told was that when the Chinese proposed a toast and said "ganbei" you were supposed to drink your liquor bottoms up.

Well, the evening of the first seminar day, we were invited to a banquet at an ornately decorated building. There were about six tables of eight people each and each place setting had three drinks lined up before it. One was beer, one was a plum wine and the last was a liqueur that was very strong and tasted like old tires. Seated next to me was the Minister of the Interior, who at about six feet was unusually tall for a Chinese man. He stood up and gave a welcome to the American visitors and then he said "ganbei" and drank some of his drink. When I heard the word "ganbei", I immediately drank my liqueur down. The Minister, who had spoken only Chinese until that point, looked at me and in clear English said, "Oh my, don't drank that stuff like that, it will kill you". I said, "I was told that it was expected of the visitors here". He replied, "Who told you that?" I said, "The China expert we talked to in New York". He said, "Not much of a China expert, because she is wrong". That was it; he never spoke English again during our visit.

The banquet was quite elaborate, and the toast was just the first of many – it was a good thing I was warned. At each table someone would give a toast and say something good about China and then one of our group would make a toast and say how much we enjoyed our visit to China and the make a positive statement about the US. Then it was "ganbei" and another drink. This went around all of the tables. We all had a great deal to drink, and finally one of the female Chinese interpreters slid off her chair and ended up under her table. Talk about job hazards! After the meal, since I was the guest of honor, they dressed me up as an emperor, had me sit on a throne and took pictures. I looked awfully silly but everyone seemed to have a good time.

"Emperor" Lewis in Dowager Queen's Palace, 1980

Somehow we recovered from that night, and the seminar continued. Classes went from eight a.m. to six p.m., with a break for lunch. Everyone grew more relaxed and the questions began to flow more freely. We covered all the basic business fundamentals and they seemed to understand as we proceeded through the various subjects. Each day we became better acquainted and acted more like friends. The Chinese began to laugh a lot in the class and the mistakes they made became less embarrassing to them. During the

234

last class, the Minister talked to us about their plans for granting concessions to drill in Chinese waters. He gave us some insight into their thoughts and asked me to please keep the information confidential.

During this trip, my hosts took me to the Ming tombs, the Forbidden City, the Great Wall and the Dowager's palace and hosted me at four banquets. They also took me to a show where the audience was principally made up of Chinese military personnel. There was a magician that did amazing tricks – like making a live fish appear on the end of a line that he had thrown out in the audience – that made the soldiers scream and laugh with delight.

When the seminar was over, we were scheduled to go to Shanghai. We said our goodbyes and a warm feeling of friendship permeated the room. As we shook hands, I knew I would miss these students and always remember this experience.

After arriving in Shanghai, we went to a hotel that was the best in Shanghai at that time – I cannot remember the spelling but I believe it was called the Jai Jiang Hotel. It no longer exists. We went to reception to check in, and our interpreter informed us that they only had one room reserved in my name. Since there were five of us, I explained through the interpreter that one room would not work. They insisted that our entire group had to stay there. The argument went on and on and finally I gave up and said we would just have to make do. Some of us could sleep on the floor. We were all a little upset as they escorted us to Room 1200. It turned out that Room 1200 was actually the entire twelfth floor. We had eight bedrooms, each with private baths, and our own dining room, complete with private chef. It was magnificent. Why they could not explain to the interpreters the real extent of room 1200, I will never know. But once we were there, no one in the group wanted to leave.

We had another communication problem when we set about trying to confirm our flight to Hong Kong the next day, only to learn that the plane was full. Again, an argument concerning our confirmed reservations ensued, with no answer or solution. I told our interpreter to get reservations out of Shanghai on any plane, to any destination. Several hours later we got on a plane to Tokyo with connections to Hong Kong.

As we were checking in at the terminal, an old Chinese man in front of me had his watch taken off his arm by one of the security personnel who wanted it. While we were waiting for our flight, the old man approached and introduced himself to us in English. He had been a physics professor at Beijing University, but had spent the last ten years in prison. I asked why he had been put in prison. He said, "It was all a mistake. I had been a member of an engineering fraternity at Cal Tech when I was in college. At my trial they said it was an anti-communist spy organization and I was a traitor. Now they have admitted their mistake, so I am a free man and I am going to visit my son who lives in Louisiana. He is a professor at LSU".

I asked, "What was prison like?" The old man replied, "It was very bad. The guards told me that I would never leave there alive. I learned to carry material equal to my body weight for five miles each day. You don't think you can do it but you can if you want to live". He weighed only about 120 pounds. We said goodbye to him as we boarded our plane and wished him well. I have learned through seeing a great deal of the world what the true meaning of freedom is. I feel so blessed to live in this wonderful place.

The next year, I received an invitation to return to China and renew discussions. I went to Beijing and met with many of the same people to talk about their plans for development of their energy resources. They wanted my opinion on some of their approaches to foreign participation and were very complimentary, saying that I had respected their confidences and they felt they could trust me.

Beijing had changed in just the year since I had been there. There was a lot of color everywhere. There were bright signs advertizing commercial products. Children were wearing very colorful and flowery clothes; some of the men were beginning to wear suits and the women dresses. The shopping areas with the dirt streets had disappeared, the shops had been moved to nicer surroundings and the prices had gone up. The new China was beginning to appear.

In 1994, I went back to China with Ann. The changes were incredible. Before we left, I had told Ann what to expect in China, based on what the country looked like in 1980-1981. We both realized very quickly that my description had been way out of date in many ways. The hotels in Shanghai and Beijing were some of the most modern structures we had ever seen. Those cities were colorful and full of life. Service was not very good but the food was much better than my earlier visits. She was fascinated by the mass of humanity and the constant hustle and bustle of the country. Outside the two major cities, the changes were less apparent. The towns, streets and people looked more like the China I had visited years earlier. Bathroom facilities, especially for women, were still very primitive.

The differences between the more modern parts of the country with which foreigners have more contact and the more rural, undeveloped parts were quite stark. When Ann and I left Xian for Shanghai, there was some problem with the regularly scheduled flight we were booked on, so they put all the passengers on buses and transported us to a military air field somewhere outside of town. Because it was a military facility, they escorted us into a small building and told us we were not allowed to go or even look outside during our stay. You can imagine how enjoyable it was for a couple of hundred people to be cooped up in a small building with nothing to drink and very primitive bathrooms!

After about two hours, a couple of Chinese officials came in and announced that they were ready for us to board the airplane. They separated us all by height – Ann and I were split up. They loaded the tall people first; we were seated in the back of the plane. I was in the last row with almost no room for my knees. They then seated the short passengers in the front of the plane where the seats were further apart. Ann was seated in a relatively nice area with two Chinese generals at the very front. After all the seats were filled, there were still several passengers remaining, so the officials got folding chairs and put them in the plane's only aisle. So much for common sense – or flight safety! Luckily the flight was only about two hours and smooth, so no one had to go to the bathroom. Ann had a much nicer time of it; she was served drinks and had a pleasant chat with the generals.

My experiences in China have shown me the enormous changes that are possible in that country; however, there is a long way to go. It's hard to change life for over a billion people, many of whom are uneducated and lacking in basic skills. But I would never underestimate them; I found the Chinese to be a generally friendly people, but historically they have always believed that China is the center of the world and I have no doubt that they will strive to regain that position.

CHAPTER 37

When I got back to Hong Kong after teaching the seminar in China, I checked into the Mandarin Hotel. I had hardly settled in when I got a call asking if I would be so kind as to meet with Y.K. Pao the next day at ten a.m. I said I would be happy to meet with Mr. Pao, who was considered by many to be the richest man in Honk Kong. He owned the largest shipping fleet in Asia and had interests throughout Asia.

The next morning I went to Pao's office, which was only a block from the hotel. I was shown to a conference room, where I was joined by Peter Woo, Mr. Pao's son-in-law. Pao entered the room, shook hands with me and told me how much he appreciated my coming to see him. He said that they were aware of my trip to China and asked if I would mind answering some questions they had. I said I would be happy to assist them in any way. They were mainly concerned about the Chinese stance on the foreign ownership of assets on the Mainland. I told him that I had been informed by the Chinese that they wanted a majority interest in any company formed in China with respect to natural resources or transportation. The conversation lasted about an hour and I answered questions about the various people I had met and what my impressions were of Beijing and Shanghai and the Chinese economic situation. I was very forthright in my discussion, but did say that I was not knowledgeable about the Chinese economy or governmental affairs. After this exchange of ideas, they told me they were going to China in the next couple of weeks.

Two weeks later, it was reported in the world press that Y.K. Pao had entered into a contract with the Chinese government to form a new corporation that would supply all the shipping transportation needs of the Republic of China, and that Mr. Pao would own a 60% interest in the company. So much for my information! Pao had cut his deal directly with Deng

Xiaoping, who was the de facto leader of China at that time. Mr. Pao died in 1991 and Peter Woo became head of the company, and one of the richest people in the world.

After I left Hong Kong, I went to Singapore, with plans to go on to Indonesia, Australia and New Zealand. I checked into my room and went down for a nightcap. The Shangri-la Hotel had a Western music singer who was the best in Asia (of course there were not too many Western singers in Asia!) and I always enjoyed listening to him. I went up to sleep, but was awakened at about midnight by a call from the bank in Dallas. This was not unusual, because the people in Dallas seemed to have trouble remembering the twelve-hour time difference. The caller said that the Chairman of the bank wanted me to come back to Dallas immediately, and that I was already booked home on a four a.m. flight. I hurriedly packed, checked out and went to the airport. The flight would take about twenty-four hours, but I would still arrive around four p.m. the same day I had left. A car was waiting for me when I arrived in Dallas and I was whisked straight to the office, where they were waiting for my arrival to start the meeting. I had no idea what this was about, but it certainly seemed important.

I entered the meeting, dead tired, and was told that the Hunt brothers, Bunker and Herbert, had an enormous silver position and a very large debt that was threatening to disrupt Wall Street; we were being pushed by Federal Reserve Chairman Paul Volcker to do something about it. A car took me home to get fresh clothes for a trip to New York and on to the airport again.

In New York, we headed into a meeting with the Chairman and top executives of J.P. Morgan. The situation was overwhelming. The Hunts owned sixty-three million ounces of silver and had entered into forward contracts for several million more. They owed around $1.1 billion dollars to banks and brokerage houses and they did not have the money to pay. As the commodity expert at Morgan told us, it would take as long to sell the silver position the Hunts had bought as it had taken to acquire it – which was five or six years. There were brokerage firms that had more money loaned on this silver than they had in capital. If we didn't solve this debt problem, several enormous firms could go bankrupt including Merrill Lynch. It was then Friday evening, and it was decided that we needed to put together a loan package of $350 million dollars by Monday. This was important because there were several calls for capital that would be made on Tuesday morning and if they were not met, the dominos would begin to fall.

We started calling banks. At first, the calls were Chairman-to-Chairman; once the contact had been made and the serious nature of the situation conveyed, working groups were deployed in New York and the loan package was finished over the weekend. Believe me when I tell you that it was not an easy thing to do. Anytime you get ten bankers and ten sets of lawyers together you have conflict. We signed the joint loan agreement on Monday for the $350 million and the loan was funded. The margin calls were met that day, which took a lot of pressure off.

The next step was to put together a $1.1 billion dollar loan to the Hunts that would effectively pay off all existing debts, using the brothers' assets as collateral. By the time this was accomplished, we had twenty-three banks and more than fifty lawyers involved in the negotiations. There were multiple problems, such as the trusts of H.L. Hunt, which controlled title to the properties and in fact spread ownership of the assets over several generations – all of whom had to agree to the pledge of their interests as well. In addition, the assets were located in many states of the US and in Asia, Australia, Europe, South America and Canada. These assets were generally estimated to be worth around $10 billion. The problem with the Hunts was not the amount or value of their assets, but their lack of cash flow to pay debt and interest, especially when interest rates were approaching 20%.

Every banker and lawyer thought they had something to contribute to the final product; as a result, the negotiations took more than sixty days. It was finally decided that the most feasible approach was to pledge the Placid Oil Corporation and its assets to the banks in exchange for the loan. Placid was a great company with a good history and its main assets were the gas fields in the North Sea off the Netherlands and a very prolific gas and oil field in Louisiana. A major oil company would have paid a great deal for the assets of Placid; such a sale would have paid off all their debts and made the loan unnecessary. However, the Hunt brothers felt that their assets were worth many times the amount of the loan we were contemplating, and did not want to sell assets. They decided to ride out the problem, taking out a loan against their assets, believing that they would be able to pay off the loan in a short period of time. Even most of the bankers involved felt the loan would be paid off within three to six months.

There are so many aspects of this transaction that even today I am reluctant to talk about. There is no question that outside financial entities knew what was going on in most of our meetings. As Herbert Hunt said to me, any time you have several billion dollars of commodities in play, you can count on companies using all their resources to know which direction to turn. This situation resulted in the largest redistribution of wealth in this country in many years. I remember going into a meeting that had been called at the spur of the moment, with the venue changing at the last second. We sat down at a table and the phone rang. Mind you, we were on the second floor of a branch of Morgan Bank at 44th and 5th Avenue. When I picked up the phone, the caller addressed me by name and asked to speak to someone else at the meeting. I asked him who was calling; he replied that he was from the BBC in London. I told him the person he named was not available. He said, "Don't lie to me, he is sitting in a chair just to your left. I know everyone in the room and where they are sitting". Sure enough, he told me everyone who was there and the order in which they were seated. All the blinds were closed. How in the world he knew that information is a real mystery. Commodity markets fluctuated according to the results of our meetings. It was a little scary.

With the assistance of Arthur Anderson, the accounting firm, we put together a booklet outlining the various assets of the Hunts. In some instances, since no evaluation of certain assets had ever been made, we would simply put down a figure that we considered a low-ball estimate of such assets as coal reserves, for which no one could accurately say when the assets could be produced and at what price. For years after this transaction, newspapers would refer to this booklet as the gospel truth and they would quote the figures as though they were ready cash.

With the loan in place, I went to the brokerage companies bearing checks in the hundred millions of dollars to pay off the loans they had made and to bring order back to the system. I signed 3500 loan documents, including liens on assets in many states and countries. To simplify the procedure, each lien was filed for $1.1 billion dollars.

I got a call from a reporter with a Louisville paper. She said that she had seen a document that had been filed in Kentucky and wanted me to know that the Hunts only owned one medium sized ranch in Kentucky and she didn't know how we could possibly sell it for $1.1 billion. She said she hoped there were more assets in other places. I said I sure hoped there were too or I was going to be in a lot of trouble.

I lived in a hotel room in New York during this ordeal and hadn't seen Ann very often. She flew up to for a couple of days at one point and we went out to dinner at the "21" Club. As we sat in a booth, I told her that a few days earlier, I had gone to a steak restaurant and Dustin Hoffman had sat at an adjacent table. Ann said nothing like that ever happened to her. As she was speaking, Gregory Peck, Kirk Douglas and their wives came in and sat within about three feet of her. She didn't notice; I could barely contain my laughter. When she finished talking, I just told her to look to her left. She was so thrilled. I was a little afraid that she might actually get up and go hug one of them!

A couple of years later, I was called to testify before the SEC concerning the Hunt transaction. The IRS was suing the Hunts to collect taxes on a profit the IRS claimed the Hunts had made on their silver purchases. I went to Washington and testified one morning, and spoke to the Hunts and their wives during a recess. They were all friendly and I wished them luck; I still do.

Shortly after the Hunt transaction, the bank made me the head of the petroleum engineers and gave the Multinational division to someone else. This was a bit discouraging, but corporate politics are always in play, and all things change with time. One good thing was, the new position would involve less traveling, so I would have a chance to spend more time with my family.

Before long, the Chairman of the bank and the Chairman of our holding company told me that they wanted me to be head of the bank's Energy Division. The current head was being promoted to the position of President of

the bank, and took me to west Texas to visit a bank with which we did a large
volume of business in order to familiarize me with what the job would entail.
I went through many of the bank's energy files and loans while we were there.
The reason for this scrutiny was because we had purchased energy loans from
that bank that had exceeded their legal lending limit. It's not uncommon for
banks to make loans to large customers that exceed their legal lending limits
and then sell portions of the loan to other banks. When we got back on the
company jet to return to Dallas, our president asked me what my impressions
of the bank had been. I told him that in all honesty I could not do business
with them. He was stunned. He said, "If you can't do business with them, I
can guarantee that your career with the bank will be over and you will never
be promoted again. We make over $25 million a year on that account and we
are not going to lose it because of you".

I said, "When I went through the bank's files, I saw that the loans were
not properly documented, the reserves are not all pledged to the bank meaning that our collateral is in some cases non-existent, and the President of the
bank was taking a kickback on some of the oil deals. That means he is selling
us his loans, some with no security, while he is putting part of our money in
his pocket. Now if you are telling me that I have to turn my back on that kind
of double-dealing in order to keep my job, then I will choose not to continue
with the bank".

To make a long story short, I received calls from several key people who
asked me to stay. I was told that I was going to be promoted to Executive Vice
President in another area of the organization. I told them that in all good
conscience, I couldn't remain. I thought the bank would suffer losses because
of what I had uncovered and I didn't want to close my eyes to it. In fact, the
bank eventually lost most of the money they had outstanding to the west
Texas bank, as well as from a number of similar arrangements. Eventually the
bank had to be sold and now no longer exists. No one wanted to make the
hard decisions.

Years later, someone did a complete investigation of me and many of
those in power at the bank, and gave me credit for being right. But by then
it didn't matter. I was out of a job and was very nervous. Several other things

worsened my situation. The main one was that the energy business was going into a kind of recession. I had two energy companies sign me to consulting contracts and several more that were interested. One of the companies soon went into bankruptcy and the other had to drop my contract after one year. All in all, my prospects were not good. I started interviewing again, but most of those that wanted my services were interested in my contacts, but could not commit to a long-term relationship. Finally an acquaintance of mine, Stan Edwards, offered me a job in his oil company. It was a small company and could not really afford to pay me very much. My income went down significantly, to the point where Ann and I could basically just eat, pay our bills and send the boys to school. We could not afford to go to the movies or eat out or do any of the things we used to enjoy.

After about two years with Stan, we both knew that I needed to find other employment. I heard that Elvis Mason, who had been Chairman of the InterFirst Bank board of directors, was putting together a merchant bank that would be called the Mason Best Company. I went to see Mason and asked about working with the new company. He did not express much interest and in fact discouraged me.

I don't know if the planets were poorly aligned that year or what, but the fates were apparently not done with me yet. Around this time, I was playing tennis and while I was rushing the net, my right foot got caught under me and the fibula in that leg came out of the socket. I was taken to the hospital and an orthopedic surgeon examined me and immediately made plans to operate. He said this type of accident was very rare, because the small fibula would normally just break in that situation. In my case, he would have to cut open the leg and reinsert the bone into my knee joint. He then put in two screws, each about three inches long, to hold the fibula in place until the muscles could reattach themselves. I was on crutches for about eight months and was a pitiful sight. To make matters worse, I was told that the reason I had suffered the injury was because of ankle drop, and the ankle drop had been caused by a neurological disorder called Charcot-Marie-Tooth Disease. Now I was really down and I didn't know if I could get up.

CHAPTER 38

When everything was at its worst, I got a call from Elvis Mason asking me to come back in and talk to him about joining Mason Best. I had been really depressed but I did my best to put on a good face for the interview. He told me he had done an investigation of me, which he said was very positive. He quizzed me for a long time and at the end of our meeting said he was interested in my services, but only if I were willing to come aboard at a salary that would be half the size of the others in my classification. Although my experience was strong, he was of the opinion that my background was not on par with candidates from Harvard or Wharton, who had done time at major investment banking firms. I told him I wanted to sleep on it and I would get back to him in the morning. It was the best offer I had received recently, and although I felt that I was as good as the other key employees and deserved equal consideration, I believed I could prove my worth if given the opportunity. I called Elvis Mason the next morning and accepted the position. My experience at Mason Best would turn out to be a mixed bag of experiences, but it would lead to greater opportunities.

Elvis Mason and Randy Best had known each other for many years. They were both from Beaumont, Texas and had become acquainted through business connections. They set up Mason Best as a general partnership and then approached a number of noted and wealthy individuals to become limited partners in the enterprise. In the first group they had David Rockefeller, Larry Tisch of the Loew's Corporation, Arthur Temple, Lester Crown, Mr. Murphy of CapCities-ABC, Bob Strauss, Henry Beck, Trammel Crown, Bill Wrigley and Bob Dedman, among others. There were about twenty partners and they contributed $150 million as initial capital. This group included 30 individuals from some of the wealthiest families in the US. It was quite an accomplishment.

The partners' meetings were a real education. Very successful, high-level people attended and participated in the discussions. At almost every meeting, Bob Strauss would give the group an update on significant developments in the Democratic Party. When he concluded, Don Rumsfeld would give us an insight into the Republican Party and what was transpiring there. These talks included opinions about individuals that were emerging on the political scene. In addition, we would occasionally hear from Bobby Inman, who had been the assistant head of the CIA after retiring as a full admiral in the navy. He would give very in-depth opinions about political situations around the world and his thoughts on various countries' intentions and capabilities.

The first significant deal the firm participated in was with Woods Petroleum, a family-owned oil company headquartered in Oklahoma City. The deal came up in a conversation between Larry Hartzog, the attorney for the Woods family, and me in the airport in Oklahoma City. I went back to Dallas and reported that we could acquire Woods Petroleum from the family. Mason and Best immediately called Hartzog and went to see the Woods family. We ended up with a contract to sell the company to Sunshine Mining and Mason Best earned a $9 million fee. In retrospect, I believe it was significant that they excluded me from additional contact with Hartzog or the Woods family and later did not acknowledge my participation in the deal.

Next, I went to see an old colleague of mine and, after quite a bit of discussion, I created an opportunity to buy Pearle Vision, which was a subsidiary of Searle Co. The President of Pearle, Don Phillips, had the opportunity to buy Pearle, but lacked the resources to do so. That's where Mason Best came in. Mason and Best went to see Phillips to talk about buying Pearle with Phillips remaining as President and taking a minority piece of the company; they excluded me from the negotiations. However, they took so long to formulate a plan of action that Pearle was sold to Monsanto before we had a chance to act.

I then brought them the opportunity to acquire Telesis, which was one of the best assisted-living operators in the country. I had met both of the owners and had reached a level where they were agreeable to our proposed investment in their company. I took this back to the company and Best took control of the transaction – excluding me from involvement once again – and it fell apart. I was starting to see a pattern.

Mason Best was interested in buying defense electronics companies. They felt that the best of these was Electrospace Systems. I knew the largest shareholder of the company, so I went to see him and he informed me that he would be interested in a sale. I went back and spoke to both Mason and Best, letting them know that we had an opportunity to buy Electrospace Systems. They said no way. It would be too expensive. It would sell for over $35 a share. I said that I believed it could be acquired for about $25 or $26 a share. They went to see the Chairman, who was my friend, but ended up not going forward because they did not believe that I was right about the price. Electrospace eventually was sold to Chrysler Corporation for $26 a share. And Mason Best went out and paid a very high price for a different defense electronics company in Austin and lost their shirts.

These are just a few of the transactions I brought to Mason Best, but in each case, my part in the transaction was discounted. They also asked me to raise money for a second round of capital for the partnership. I had a hand in raising $50 million but there was no "atta boy". I helped raise money for an oil company they wanted to start but still felt that my efforts were constantly discounted. Perhaps my efforts were not as worthwhile as I think, but I do know that I brought more opportunities to the table than any other employee. I did not do well in trying to promote security transactions or investment banking activities. The firm didn't have the capacity to compete against the big boys. In 1987, having been at Mason Best for three years, I still had not made much headway. I was not considered a valuable asset, and more importantly, had not received the monetary consideration that I had been promised.

My last job at Mason Best was to work with the First National Bank of Palm Beach to determine what could be done to either make it a better earner or to sell it. We had been hired by the Board of Directors and the Chairman of the bank. I went to Palm Beach, met all the senior people and started examining the loans, looking at the books and talking to a number of bank employees. It was a good bank and the predominate bank in that city. It also had $2 billion in trust funds that it managed for its clients. The fundamentals were good, but the bank had somehow lost its way, and I had to figure out where.

The first thing I discovered was that overhead had increased by 300% while the bank assets and earnings had either stayed the same or declined. I recommended to the board that we reduce staff by 35%. By my next trip to Palm Beach, the management had reduced the staff and a number of people that I had gotten to know were gone. The bank had also attempted to grow by making out-of-area real estate loans, which meant that they were involved in loans in areas they did not know well. This had resulted in several million dollars of loans that were either bad or non-performing, and needed to be written off. The last and most harmful thing was that they had made a decision to become an international bank without any expertise in that arena. Instead, they had entered into an agreement with a former employee of Citibank, giving this gentleman a fee for booking loans to foreign entities. It didn't matter whether the loan was good or bad; he still got his fee. After looking at the loans, I knew that about $16 million of the value was lost.

I went back to the board and basically said that they had two choices. Either they could do the write-offs, clean up operations and keep the bank. If this was their choice then I believed they could make about an 8% return on capital annually. The second choice was to sell the bank, in which case I believed they could make a good return on their capital. They took the second suggestion, and asked me to sell the bank for them. I told them I could do so but that I would need complete control over the process. Any inquires to the bank were to be directed to me. Once negotiations started, I would be the only person involved. They agreed and I started the sale process.

I told interested parties that they had to convince me that they had a minimum of $100 million capacity in order to buy the bank. Interestingly, there were twenty-three qualified candidates. Some were banks and others were individuals with a keen interest in acquiring the bank. It was a well-known company in a well-known location, and it would be a real feather in the hat of whoever owned it. Furthermore, it was a unique property because it provided a wide variety of services to its Palm Beach clientele. For instance, it had a fur and valuable storage vault. It was also a meeting place for people who like to come in, do their banking and then have a cup of coffee or tea with their friends.

I put together a book presentation for the sale process and then began to visit each of the interested parties. I sat down with each company or family and went through all of the fine points about the bank, including such downsides as the international portfolio. One family, who owned the Breakers Hotel, wanted very much to own the bank, but in the long run they felt the price was too high. I visited families in Philadelphia, Atlanta, Chicago, New York and several places in Florida, each with more than enough liquid assets to buy the property. I also visited major banks in Chicago, New York, Atlanta, North Carolina and Florida. We ended up with several bidders, but the best candidate for the acquisition was a bank holding company in Miami, Southeast Banking Corporation.

We entered negotiations, which got off to a terrible start. Southeast sent their lawyer – a snobby fellow who knew absolutely nothing about the banking business, smoked a pipe constantly and talked down to me and even to his cohorts – to reach a deal on the purchase. Also of interest was the fact that they had on their board the former President of the Palm Beach bank, who was encouraging Southeast to buy the Palm Beach bank. There was yet another board member that lived in Palm Beach who was pushing for Southeast's purchase of the bank. Finally, there was the fact that Southeast had already tried to buy several banks, and in each case Southeast had bid too low, losing out.

Then the attorney for the Palm Beach bank showed up, immediately informed me that he would be handling the sale negotiations and proceeded to take over the meeting. I carefully packed my briefcase and left the meeting. A few minutes after I left, the bank attorney called my room and asked if I would be returning to the meeting. I told him that I was going to leave the entire negotiation to him and that I was going home.

He panicked and came straight over to my hotel room to ask me why I was leaving. I told him that no one was to interfere in these negotiations; if he was going to do so then I was leaving. The President of the Palm Beach bank arrived and said he thought it would be helpful if their lawyer was involved. I picked up the phone and called the bank's largest shareholder and Chairman of the Board and told him what was happening. I said that I would back out of the negotiations if asked, but if they wanted me to complete the sale then I must have the authority to dismiss anyone who interfered with the negotiations. He said that I had the authority to fire anyone who in my opinion was not needed. I ask him to please repeat that statement on the speakerphone. He did. After the conversation, I asked each of the gentlemen present if they understood the Chairman's position. They replied that they did. I told them that they could be present during the negotiations if they so desired but that I did not want them to speak or counter anything I said.

The next day I returned to the meetings and the lawyer for Southeast told me how they wanted to structure the purchase. I told him that in that case there would be no reason for us to go any further in our discussion. I got up and he said, "Where are you going?" I said that since he had decided the structure, and since I already knew it would not meet my requirements, it would be a waste of my time to continue.

He was incredulous and said, "Well, what do you want us to do?" I told him that I would decide the structure, but they could give me their suggestions. He said that approach was backwards from how they normally did acquisitions. I said, "It doesn't appear that your method has been very successful up to now. Maybe you should try a new way". The meeting was adjourned.

When we started the next day, an attorney I had engaged from a Miami firm distributed a purchase agreement we had drawn up on behalf of the seller. Now we were cooking, and we went through the draft in record time, agreeing to all reasonable suggested changes. The next day, however, the purchaser's attorney said that the Chairman of Southeast wanted two key changes and if they were not agreed to then the deal was off. I said, "Fine, then I can go home". I left the table, returned to my room and made plane reservations to Dallas.

I got a call about thirty minutes later, asking me to come back to the meeting. I went back, but said as I walked in that I thought they had told me that if I didn't agree with their changes, the deal was off – and I had no intention of agreeing with their changes. Their lawyer asked if I would speak to him in private. We went to his office and he proceeded to tell me that they were being very patient with me and if I continued to be difficult, the deal would probably not come together. I said, "Let's quit wasting my time, or I will simply start negotiations with another buyer. You told me you wanted to buy this bank and instead all you do is argue with me. That approach is unproductive. If you want this bank you will have to do it on my terms".

I know that the teams from both banks thought I was crazy. They told me I was going to blow this deal. I told the Palm Beach guys to be cool and we would get what we wanted. In the end, I got four times book value and forty-four times earnings. I also got a lot more than the owners thought would be possible. I didn't make any friends, but I did my job properly. Mason Best got a fee of $1 million, which the purchaser had to pay.

As all this transpired, I was receiving more and more flack from Elvis Mason. Everyone needs a whipping boy and I guess I made a good one. By now he knew I did good work, but for some reason liked to ridicule me in front of other employees. I started having my colleagues come by my office and ask how I was able to take such a beating. I told them that it wouldn't be forever. We started having other top people leave and their replacements were always a step down. I knew it was time for me to formulate a plan for the future.

CHAPTER 39

In the spring of 1987, I began to think about forming my own private equity company. I was fifty-one years old, and if I wanted to truly challenge myself then this was the time to do it. I shared my thoughts with Ann, including my belief that if the venture was to be unsuccessful, we would be in big trouble. Her reaction was entirely supportive; she told me to go for it and that we would face the future together.

I put together a short written plan and decided to approach John Driscoll. John is a grandson of the founder of the Weyerhauser Corporation and he has been a successful investor for many years. While we were both in Chicago for a meeting, I asked if I could meet with him, and he told me to come up to his room to have a cup of coffee and talk. I was very nervous because if John turned me down then my idea would most likely be dead. When we sat down together, I told John that I wanted to start my own company, outlining my experience and asking if he would be willing to invest in my new venture. John didn't hesitate; he immediately said he would be willing to back me. Then he asked why it had taken me so long to go out on my own. I asked if he would have invested in me two years ago and his answer was that he didn't know.

I asked John if he would invest $3 million and he said yes. I wish I had asked for more, but you can't get greedy! I was thrilled, knowing that this initial commitment would ensure that I would be able to put the deal together. I next got Trammel Crow to commit $1 million and then obtained commitments from M Bank, the Murchison family and others. It was a good start and with some help from others I was able to attract even more capital.

I will always be thankful that John Driscoll was willing to trust me and be the first investor to jump in. On top of that, he is simply a decent, great guy with a wonderful family, including his wife, Lee, and four children – two girls and two boys. The whole family is thrifty and hard working and has a Christian upbringing. John once told me a story about a conversation he had with his grandfather. When John was about eight or nine years old, his grandfather handed him a piece of wood about as big around as a pencil and asked John if he could break it in two pieces. John said he took the stick and very proudly broke it and handed it back to his grandfather. Then his grandfather handed John a bundle of sticks, each about the same size as the first, all tied together, and asked John if he could break them. John tried but of course couldn't break the bundle. His grandfather said, "This bundle is just like our family – if we are alone we not very strong, but if we all stick together like this bundle, we will be very hard to break". John said it was a lesson that he had remembered all his life.

When John Lewis and Associates began, we intended to operate in the same manner as Hicks, Muse and other firms that had put together deals with little capital invested. Those firms then got several levels of debt that would earn varying returns, and then would take a fee for organizing the transaction. Actually, at the start, some firms received net cash out of a deal even though they controlled the purchased firm. For about a year we struggled, trying to find the appropriate company to buy. I visited many companies, kicked a lot of tires, made a number of offers, issued letters of intent and ended up with nothing.

In the private equity business you are looking for companies that have a consistent cash flow, a product line that has some barrier to entry and a management that has the capacity to build the firm. Usually these opportunities come about because the owner wants to concentrate on a different line of business or the owner is a family and they want to gain some liquidity from a company that they have built up. Most of the companies we have purchased have some problems that we feel can be managed and we can help create a financial situation that will allow them to grow.

A fellow at MBank decided that we were incapable of running a successful firm and started a campaign to fold the partnership. Luckily, the partnership had a clause stating that it could only be folded by a majority in interest of the partnership. John Driscoll let it be known that he would not be in favor of folding the company.

I got many leads but none proved fruitful until I was told about a company in Grand Rapids, Michigan, that was for sale. We went up and visited with the Sonneveldt Company. Sonneveldt was in the food distribution business and its customers were limited-menu companies such as Wendy's, Burger King, Applebees and Dairy Queen. It had about $110 million in revenue. It also had a lot of inventory and receivables that we could use to borrow against.

We finally convinced the owner to sell to us and we were in business. Food distribution is a low-margin business with lots of costs. We needed a fleet of trucks with very expensive refrigerated trailers to serve customers in large territories. It was not unusual for a truck to travel a four-hundred mile route to service its assigned customers. The biggest cost was transportation, which included gasoline, trucks, trailers, driver compensation and insurance. The company had very little employee turnover because the local work force was largely residents of Scandinavian descent who wanted to stay near their families. It was not a growth company but it did give us a start in the industry.

The management at Sonneveldt immediately set about to educate us about their business. We learned of an organization that was comprised of other companies like Sonneveldt and, recognizing an opportunity to acquire other members of the organization, we set out to do just that. Our second acquisition was a company in Atlanta called Independent Distributors Incorporated (IDI). IDI was owned by Tom Willingham and had about $300 million in revenue. Its principal territory was the southeastern US, extending north as far as Maryland. After that, we bought companies in Colorado, Wisconsin and Texas. We eventually had a holding company called Ameriserv, with sales of about $900 million and the ability to service customers nationwide.

As this company grew, I hired a fellow from a cheese manufacturing and distribution firm in Denver named Lenny Pippen. Lenny put together a program of improvements to be completed over the course of the next year that would overhaul our companies and improve earnings substantially. There were twenty-four points in the program that were incorporated into operations.

We also decided to try to take the company public. We filed all the required legal material and prepared to put on a road show to presell the stock before the offering. As we were putting the final touches on the offering documents, it came to my attention that Lenny had called the lawyers and had made a change in the agreements that would grant him a greater interest in the company than had been agreed to. I told him that his actions were not appropriate. He tendered his resignation and left, and the public offering was dead. Lenny had not accomplished a single one of the twenty-four items in his grand plan. I consider him one of my biggest mistakes. I believe Lenny is still alive and kicking somewhere in the public arena.

I immediately brought in Bill Burgess from Madison, Wisconsin. He was the President of Alpha Distributors and had previously been head of distribution of Domino Pizza. Bill is a first-class guy and a hard worker. We tried to find Lenny's original list of changes to be made, but someone had removed that document from my files. I'll bet you and I can both guess who it was... Bill started to implement his own list of changes and we began to improve our profits.

Back we went to the public market. We were doing the road show in Boston when our investment banker slipped me a note saying the deal was done. We had a celebration on the way home and thought we had the world by the tail. Unfortunately, our timing was terrible; the stock market collapsed the next week and all public offerings were pulled. There were no buyers in that market. Our efforts had cost us about $1 million, with no payoff.

Don Hoffman was the board representative for one of AmeriServ's investors, Manufacturers Hanover Bank in New York. He rushed to Dallas to tell me that I had messed everything up, and if I didn't do their bidding, then they would put AmeriServ into bankruptcy. I simply told him not to threaten me and walked out of the meeting. Bill Burgess kept everything going in the company while I continued trying to sell it. Things were not going well but I wasn't sure how to right the ship. Then, out of the blue, I got a call from a company that was interested in buying AmeriServ. Now mind you I had already had a few vultures around so I didn't want to go through that again, but this caller was for real.

John Holton, a native of Norway, a graduate of Harvard Business School and a resident of Connecticut, had formed an investment company. The main investors were Scandinavian companies, including several insurance firms and pension funds. Holton had bought a company headquartered in Milwaukee that was in the food distribution business and decided that he wished to make additional acquisitions that would make him the predominant player in that market. After very contentious negotiations, Holton's firm bought AmeriServ for $48 million net of debt and then set about reorganizing the combined company.

They renamed the resulting company AmeriServe, and then purchased Pepsico Food Distribution from Pepsico. Later, Holton bought a company that at one time had been the main distributor for Burger King. By the time he had completed his acquisitions, he had formed a distribution company with about $10 billion in sales. Unfortunately, Holton had a number of theories about running a food distribution company that turned out to be faulty, and the debt became to big a burden to bear. The company failed after a fairly short period of time.

Davis Bunnell, a lawyer and the brother of a former employee at the bank in Dallas, had come to me asking if he could work with me, and after some discussions joined the company. David did the work I asked of him and was effective at negotiating acquisitions.

I had developed a 'doing business as' (DBA) called Lewis Company that I thought would be easier to work with. The DBA had no assets or employees; it was just the public name for John Lewis and Associates. After being with the company for some time, David came to me and asked me if he could become a 1% partner in Lewis Company. I pointed out to him that Lewis Company didn't really have any legal standing and that being a 1% partner wouldn't mean anything. He said it would be advantageous in the community in which he lived and asked if he could print a card stating that he was a partner of Lewis Company. Now you are probably wondering why he wanted this so much and so was I. Perhaps I'm a little too trusting, because I let him make up the cards despite my questions. Shortly thereafter, I learned why he had wanted them so badly. David resigned from his position and subsequently filed suit against me.

In it, he contended that he was a 50% partner in everything I had built. His evidence was the card that I allowed him to print. He had gone into my desk at night and took all papers relating to our discussions before employment and many of my personal memoranda; these disappeared before the trial.

For years, I had paid out to my employees over half of all the monies the company made. I thought I was being generous, but that fact was used against me in court. David claimed that these payments were made because he was a partner and the bonuses were in fact his share of the partnership. The trial was an ordeal and a settlement was ultimately reached. I felt truly betrayed by David, who had clearly planned to conspire against me since he had arrived at the company. I was so hurt that someone would do this and tell such malicious lies. It was a hard lesson, and one that hurt my pride, but as the English say, there are no lifelong friends or lifelong enemies just lifelong interests.

Despite such unfortunate dealings, the business forged ahead and additional limited partners began to invest in our activities. These included Whitney and Betty MacMillan. Whitney was Chairman of Cargill at the time and has been a good friend. I can say the same of John Ordway A number of the children of our partners also began to be interested. All in all, I think I had the best investors in every way.

Ordway's son-in-law, John "Smokey" Ordway, and JPL

One of our acquisitions around that time was Mission Valley Textiles, located in New Braunfels, Texas. It was a subsidiary of West Point Stevens and was engaged in the fabric manufacturing business. The company had over one million square feet of manufacturing space and about four-hundred employees, who made fabric for trousers, shirts, baby clothes, basket linings and sheets, among other things. It had loyal employees and a hard-working management team, led by Bill Morton, a veteran of over forty years in that business. Like all businesses it had its ups and downs, but in the long run it increased its sales significantly and we finally sold the company for more than twenty times our investment.

Lewis interests continues to be active in the private equity business. We made a successful investment – meaning we made money for the partnership when we sold the company – in Federal Packaging Company, located near Dayton, Ohio. In the late 1990's, we made an investment in a company I renamed BillMatrix. It was a bill payment company that served primarily utilities, insurance companies and delivery companies. When a customer of one of these companies received a monthly bill, instructions were enclosed that offered payment options over the phone or on the internet – either of which used the BillMatrix system to pay their bill. This was a difficult investment because of the company's management. They did not want any input from the board and they did not want to sell the company or have any control exercised over their activities. We had bought our 60% interest for around $3.6 million, and the company continued to grow; however, we were nervous about the management and decided to sell our interest. There were several interested parties, but none that would pay what we thought the company was worth. Finally, we received an offer from a company that we could live with, and we eventually sold our interest for about $16.8 million. We were happy with our profit from the venture, but were very surprised when, less than a year later, the purchaser sold the company for $350 million!

We had been successful investors for twenty years. We made some good decisions and some bad ones, but overall have made a good return on the capital invested. We had the best group of partners that one can have and we appreciated them. I enjoyed our success and I have now retired but it was a wonderful adventure.

When I decided to retire I still had a number of financial interests including real estate interests, oil and gas interests and businesses I had invested in. Those assets continue to grow and I am very fortunate.

PART ELEVEN

ALL ABOUT FAMILY

CHAPTER 40

Jeanetta's career as a script supervisor was a long and successful one. She worked on many prominent films for over twenty-five years. She was particularly sought after by new directors and the studios because she was so knowledgeable about the filmmaking business. She was also helpful to many movie stars who depended on her to work with them on their dialogue and its presentation. She was very good with most of the actors and they tended to like her a lot.

Jeanetta discussing script details

Jeanetta on the set with Curt Jergens and Alan Alda

Hal Holbrook on movie set

One exception was Ben Gazarra, who was known to be difficult to work with. He had a habit of using terrible language on the set, and took to calling Jeanetta a bitch because she had let him know she didn't think his language was appropriate in mixed company. He went on a rampage of cursing just to upset her. She went to the script supervisor management and told them what was transpiring. There was a meeting with Mr. Gazarra and it was stated that if he continued to use the foul language on the set that he would be black-balled by the union. The language got better but in some ways it only made things worse. Every time Gazarra came on the set he would say in a loud voice, "Let's be sure and watch our language, because we wouldn't want to offend little Miss Lewis. Everybody be careful or she will go to the union and try to hurt you". After a while it got to be too unpleasant and Jeanetta finally quit the series. Luckily she was in great demand and was able to find another opportunity very quickly.

Lee Grant was a good friend of Jeanetta and always said that if Jeanetta had continued working on the acting profession she would have been successful. Jeanetta's dreams never came true. She had wanted so badly to be an actress but the real break never happened. I don't think she was ever happy working on the periphery. She also thought that women in the industry were never treated with any kind of respect and the glass ceiling was always in place. The Gazarra episode only confirmed her low opinion of the business and in some ways embittered her. In her later years, she moved to Dallas, traveled quite a bit, and worked on a few movies that were being filmed in Texas.

She had worked with some of the best actors in Hollywood making movies all over the world. She was perhaps the best in her business and was very much in demand. It's hard to describe what a script supervisor does because it is very complicated. During the shooting of a movie or television show, she was responsible for dividing the script into scene segments and then calculating the time required to film each scene. When the scene was shot she would time the actual scene and determine how much of it would be used in the movie. Simple things that most people would not think of, for instance, everyone's hair has to be parted and combed the same during the same sequence. Not all of a scene is filmed at the same time so when they return it must appear the same. The way a tie is tied, how the sleeves look, eyeglasses have to be at the same angle, jewelry has to look the same, and actors must enter the scene and then leave it in opposite directions. The actors' clothes have to be exactly the same. All the objects in the scene have to be the same. I could go on and on but I am sure you get the idea. All of those things were the responsibility of the script supervisor and then helping some actors with their lines to cap it off. Quite a job!

Jeanetta in Thailand

Jeanetta and Michael Landon working in Thailand

In 1988, she found out she had cancer of the bone marrow. We got all kinds of treatment for her but nothing seemed to help. In 1989, the doctors finally took me aside and told me to take Jeanetta home from the hospital. They had done all that they could do. We made her as comfortable as we could and she died peacefully.

Jeanetta was part of my life throughout my adult years, but I cannot say the same for my oldest sibling, Jeff. He was so much older than me that we never were close as children, and we never became friends as adults either. I tried from time to time as I got older to get to know him but he did not seem interested. He did not stay in touch with our parents or Jeanetta either.

I do know that Jeff did have some good success in business. After the war, he worked for Del Webb, a Phoenix-based contractor, who owned some casinos in Las Vegas, and was building entire towns to accommodate the masses moving to the Phoenix area. Jeff was in charge of the building of a town not too far from Phoenix, with the opportunity to earn a bonus based on the success of the property. He worked hard, learned a lot and made a good amount of money from that project. Del Webb got rich and at one time owned the New York Yankees, although he ultimately got sloppy with some of his business details and ended up in financial trouble.

Jeff left to go into business for himself. He started buying and selling properties in Arizona, Nevada, Utah and California. There weren't many people in the business at that time and he became very successful. One of his larger projects was developing property all around Park City, Utah.

Jeff always said that to make money you had to be willing to work hard and an opportunity would turn up. After spending some research time in the public library, he hit upon a scheme that would make him real money. Jeff learned that much of the western United States had once been federal government land, but the US government had given the railroads the land that could be sold to help them build train lines across the country. The land was given away in a checker-board pattern. What Jeff found out was that anyone who owned the land adjacent to a block of land owned and being sold by the government could bid the assessed valuation of the land for sale and they would automatically win the auction. It was the government's way of allowing landowners who had bought from the railroads to increase their acreage without intervention. So when Jeff found out that the government was going to auction a block of land, He would go to the adjacent owners and ask them if he could buy five acres in one corner of their property. Most didn't mind selling. Many of the land owners lived in the East and they had inherited the land. They had never been to see it and didn't intend to go.

Buying that five acres allowed Jeff to bid on four sections of land and win. Even more important, the assessed valuation of the land, having been made years before, was $100 per acre. Jeff would buy at $100 and then turn around and sell the land for many times the purchase price even before he had to pay for it. This program held true in all the states he was familiar with. He made a fortune before the government realized what was happening. The government eventually changed all the rules, but the process had been good for Jeff while it lasted.

At the age of fifty, Jeff decided that he didn't want to risk his accumulated wealth, so he decided to quit the real estate business and become a medical doctor. Because of his age, most medical schools were not interested in accepting him to their program. He made a sizable gift to one and suddenly he was in. He finished his studies and internship when he was about fifty-six. He began to practice medicine but soon realized that a malpractice lawsuit could jeopardize everything he had worked to earn. For a time he went to work for a Veterans Administration hospital, where there was no personal legal risk.

During this period, Jeff divorced and remarried and then divorced and remarried again, and I never met his second or third wives. I saw him in 1966 and then really didn't hear much from or about him until he died under unusual circumstances around 1986.

Jeff did not have close relations with his own family, and seemed to be an unhappy man. His three children from his first marriage had no relationship with him. At one point, his son was quite lost, and I tried to counsel him for a short time but I could not take the place of a father. Jeff called me once around 1975. At first I didn't know who it was. He started to cry and he told me how much he loved me and wanted to see me. Then he hung up. I got his number from someone and called him back a day later and told him how much I appreciated his call and that I too would like to get together. He said nothing and hung up. I wish I could have known him better and had an opportunity to help him. It makes me sad to know that he was as alienated from family as he was; I am sure it did not make whatever internal turmoil he felt any easier.

CHAPTER 41

When my younger son Gregory was born, he was a beautiful baby. His eyes were blue and he had a happy disposition. As a child, he was always inquisitive, with an interest in a wide range of things. He was easy to love.

Greg and Mike Lewis

He definitely had a stubborn streak. I remember one time when he was about two years old, he was given some Brussels sprouts. He didn't want to eat them, so he just sat there and held them in his mouth, without chewing, while he looked at me. After some period of time, he just let them fall out of his mouth. But he always did well in school and developed a particular interest in math and science. I can't remember him ever making anything but A's on his report cards.

Greg wasn't very interested in sports and never wanted to attend games with me. He did play soccer one year and although he was pretty good at it, he dropped out after a while with no regrets. He was a very quiet child and he was hard to read. You couldn't tell whether he was happy or sad sometimes. He was very sensitive and got his feelings hurt easily.

One summer he went on a trip to Asia with Jeanetta. They went to several countries including Thailand, Laos, Malaysia and Burma. Jeanetta liked going to temples and ancient ruins and staying in very basic facilities. Greg hated the whole trip. All he could see was poverty and filth and I gather he went into a kind of funk during the trip and was not a good traveling companion. The two of them said they would never travel together again.

After high school, I gave the boys a trip to Europe where they would have to travel the old fashioned way. They had a Eurail pass to get around, money to eat and they stayed in youth hostels in all the countries. While they had good times, it seemed that Greg was so sensitive to and overcome by the shabby side of each country that he didn't seem to see the beauty in any of the places they visited. I'm quite sure Ann and I did not take his reactions as seriously as we should have. We just thought he was going through the anguish that most teenage boys experience.

Greg in high school

Greg's high school graduation

When it came time to decide which college to attend, Greg had a definite favorite. He wanted to go to the US Naval Academy in Annapolis. He was very serious about it. I wanted to be supportive and told him I would help. I secured recommendations from Ross Perot and Roger Staubach, both of whom had attended the Naval Academy. He had to interview with several former graduates who would relay their thoughts to school. I was successful in getting Greg an appointment to the Academy from George H.W. Bush, the Vice President of the United States. At this point, his mother expressed some hesitancy about his going to a military school and wanted him closer to home. Greg decided not to go to Annapolis and started looking around for an alternative. On some level, I think that Greg really didn't want to leave home to go to college.

Greg wanted to go to a school with a program in physics; our older son Michael was attending Texas A&M, which had one. After talking to Mike,

Greg decided to go to Texas A&M. He went off to school and everything seemed to go well. He majored in physics with minors in chemistry and mathematics and he had a four-point average going into his senior year. When Greg came home during breaks at college, he didn't appear unhappy, and we talked about his interest in attending MIT to obtain a PhD in Physics. I told him that with his grades, he would have no problem getting in.

Around this time, Greg, Mike, Ann and I went on a vacation together. We first went to Breckenridge, Colorado, and then went to Camp Davis in northern New Mexico. As a family, we had gone to Camp Davis for around seven years. It was a fun place for all of us and we looked forward to going every year. Greg seemed particularly distant and upset during our stay in Breckenridge. He finally came to me and started talking about how disappointing life felt to him. I told him that he hadn't given life a chance; he was only twenty-one years old and he had so much in front of him. We talked for a long time and he was not enamored with life especially his own. I tried to be very positive and talked about his future at MIT and accomplishing all the goals he had set for himself.

The Lewis family

He had been seeing a woman named Karen, who had a young child, and he told me that he would like to have them join us at Camp Davis. I said that I didn't think it was a good idea because we would all be staying in an open cabin with a single bath and there was no way to preserve any degree of modesty in those circumstances, especially with strangers. He was angry and didn't speak that evening. The next morning when we got up, Greg was gone. He apparently had gone down to the main highway and hitchhiked back to College Station. As I recall, he had left us a note, but Ann was still very worried. She didn't hear from him until several days later, when he was safely home.

When he got back to Texas, he married Karen. They moved in together but neither of them had a job. I felt that Karen was very hard on him, constantly complaining about their circumstances. A short time later, they separated. Greg called Ann and told her he wanted to come home. I felt that he needed to finish up his last year at school, and then he could do what he wanted. In retrospect, I realize that Greg didn't want to be alone; he needed the support of his family. But at the time, I didn't listen to his plea.

He sent a book of poems home, asking me to read it, and I said I would. There were about seventy poems. I didn't fully understand them; some were positive, but others felt negative and black. I have included a number of these poems in this book's appendix.

I called Greg and told him that I had read his poems and he asked what I thought. I said that he had a great deal of talent, that some of the poems were very special but that I was worried about the dark nature of so much of his work. I told him that I had always been an optimist and believed in the goodness of man and the saving grace of God. I wanted him to be an optimist too. He didn't reply.

The next morning, I was at work when I received a call from a police captain in College Station asking if I was the father of Gregory Allen Lewis. My gut clenched; this is a question no parent wants to hear. I said I was his father and asked if he was hurt. The captain told me that Gregory had shot himself and had not survived. He asked if I could come to College Station to identify the body and make arrangements for the burial. I said that I would be there that afternoon.

There is no way to adequately describe the full and complex horror of that moment. But it was magnified yet further by the task I had to undertake next. I had to go home and tell Ann that her son was dead. As soon as I walked in the house, Ann knew something was wrong. I told her what had happened and she fell to the floor weeping. I hugged her and kissed her and grieved with her and then I helped get us packed so we could go get our son.

Greg sent us a letter that arrived after his death, with a return address in heaven. It was too much to even imagine. Greg had done something that I could not undo. All we could do was pick up the pieces and try to understand what had happened. As hard as I've tried, I have been unable to comprehend why someone with so much promise and such a bright future could chose to end his life. There is no logical answer. We did not recognize the degree of Greg's despondency, mistaking a very dangerous depressive illness for moodiness and sensitivity.

The death of a child is not something that one "gets over". It will always be the source of a lifetime sorrow. Ann has really struggled with the loss, and even today, over twenty-two years after the fact, still grieves. Greg's misguided and impulsive act was a terrible thing, but it pains me to see Ann continue to suffer. I try not to dwell on his death; life must go on. I just get to live this one time and I want to try to enjoy every minute I've got left.

CHAPTER 42

Our older son Michael was always interested in writing and making films. I remember him and his friends taking our movie camera and trying to put together short films about a variety of subjects. I wish there had been digital cameras in those days because I think they would have been able to concentrate more on the creative aspects of the project and made more films!

Michael was always a good student, making good grades in all subjects, even the math and science courses he wasn't terribly fond of. He was particularly good at taking tests and at expressing his thoughts and ideas. When he graduated from high school he decided he wanted to go to Texas A&M University. He surprised the heck out of me by choosing to join the Corps at the university.

The Corps is a student military program with the same discipline as a regular military unit would have. They are particularly tough on freshmen. I was very proud of his decision because I have always thought that military discipline is good for young men. He did well but found that one year in the Corp was enough! He graduated in four years with a major in English literature. He decided to take the LSAT in preparation for law school and scored so high on the exam that he could have gone to any law school in the country. He decided to attend Pepperdine Law School on a full scholarship.

After one year, Michael decided the study of law was not as interesting as he had imagined. He decided to go to work instead and he did so for about a year. He then applied to University of Southern California's Ray Stark School of Motion Picture Production. It is a program that prepares its students to work in the motion picture industry on the producer end of things (how things have changed from the days of my offer from Eugene Arnstein!) As I understand it, a great many young men and women apply to this school every year, and only about twenty-five are accepted. Michael got in, and at last was in the arena he wanted to pursue.

When Mike graduated, he interviewed with a number of studios and producers. He served as assistant to the producer of the movie, "Spy Hard" which starred Leslie Nielsen. Mike even was in a couple of short scenes in the movie. He later decided to work with a production company, Shadowcatcher Productions, which was located in Seattle. He became the head of film development during a period when the company filmed four or five movies. It was good experience but Mike wanted something that had more upside.

He decided to go to UCLA's Anderson School and obtain his MBA. He did so and received an offer from Sega, the gaming company. They produce internet and electronic games such as, "Spiderman" and "Matrix". The industry has about $7 billion in annual sales and continues to grow. Mike produced games, bringing together programmers, artists and writers in order to create the end product.

In late 2009, Mike received a call from Amazon in Seattle asking if he would be willing to fly to Seattle to talk to them over a weekend. He agreed and went. He spent two days being interviewed by several executives. After flying back to LA, he received a call on Monday asking him if he would be interested in joining Amazon. They extended an attractive offer and Michael accepted. He was not excited about moving to Seattle because he had been in LA for over twenty years but this was an opportunity he had been wanting.

Amazon started a new subsidiary, Amazon Studios. They intended to enter the motion picture industry as well as television. Mike was appointed head of motion picture production for the new company. He is working on the production of several movies that will start hitting the screens next year. He is excited but he is working very hard. Amazon intends to enter the TV market in a similar fashion. They have the capital to be very successful and they have hired the best people to achieve their goals.

We cheer for him constantly. Mike is the future of our family and we remain hopeful that someday he will start a family of his own. In the meantime, he is handsome and witty and we love him.

Mike and JPL

Ann, JPL, Mike

PART TWELVE

LOOKING BACK AND LOOKING FORWARD

CHAPTER 43

Over the course of a long, well-traveled life, you are bound to meet new people all the time, many of them famous or infamous. Those who have achieved unusual success or fame are often especially interesting, because most of them have worked long and hard to get there.

Not too long after I moved to Dallas, I first met Ross Perot. Perot grew up in Texarkana and delivered newspapers as a boy. He said that he always believed that if he could make $10,000 a year he would be rich, and he worked hard to reach that goal. After attending the Naval Academy he went to work for IBM; he was so successful at selling their products that they asked him to quit working so hard because he had achieved his yearly quota in two weeks! He went on to form a company that developed software. He started Electronic Data Systems and sold stock in the company personally at the State Fair of Texas and anywhere else he could talk to people.

In 1979, two EDS employees were taken hostage by the Iranian government. Perot directed a successful rescue mission, led by retired US Army Special Forces Colonel "Bull" Simons. Perot himself went to Iran and entered the prison where his men were held during the rescue operation. Obviously the Iranians did not know he was there.

The story of his great success with EDS has been told many times. He eventually sold the company to General Motors for about $2.4 billion. He later became well-known for his third-party presidential candidacy in 1992, in which he won 19% of the popular vote.

I have now met Perot on many occasions; he is always attentive when you talk to him and has always been very cordial to me. Two particular encounters come to mind. The first was when he received the Churchill award for humanitarian endeavors. Prince Charles presented the award; he was very humorous and told several stories about Churchill. When it was Perot's time to speak after he had received the award, he began by saying he wanted all of the top executives of EDS to come up to the stage. After they came forward, Perot looked at the audience and said he wanted all the men who had been imprisoned for more than four years in Vietnam as prisoners of war to come up too. As they stood and started toward the platform, some were on crutches, some were in wheelchairs and some were using canes; there were no dry eyes in the audience. We knew that Perot had spent millions to get these prisoners released.

On another occasion, I was invited to a roast of Ross Perot. During that event, a number of friends went to the microphone to make fun of Ross's slight build, big ears, short stature and distinctive mannerisms. After they had finished the jokes, it was Perot's turn. He went up to the dais and before he could say anything, a beautiful tall blonde buxom woman walked up the center aisle and motioned to Perot. He went to the edge of the platform, leaned down and she whispered something to her. He then invited her to join him up at the microphone. She did so and then she took his head and hugged it to her chest, because of short stature his head just exactly fit between her breasts. She told him that he had the cutest little ears and the most darling little head and that she just loved short men. He grinned and said, "You guys can just all eat your hearts out". Everyone laughed. It was the highlight of the evening. Later we learned that the beautiful young lady was the winner of the Miss Universe pageant and Perot had invited her specifically to counter the anticipated digs by the roasters!

You may recall my description of my first meeting with Leslie Nielsen in Amsterdam, where he was starring in a movie with Robert Mitchum. We next met at the Doral Ryder Open golf tournament in Miami in 1993. We struck up a conversation and talked a great deal about what had transpired since we had last met. I think we both enjoyed our time together at Doral. We exchanged letters and began to talk on the phone often. Leslie would sometimes get depressed doing a movie and he would invite me out to visit. We would play golf together, have dinner together and I would go to the set of the current movie to talk between takes.

It wasn't easy to be born in Saskatchewan and make it big in the movies! Leslie had gone to acting school in New York and Paul Newman and

Jack Klugman were among his friends and contemporaries. He had worked steadily for years, but it wasn't until his comedic role in "Airplane" that he became quite famous. Now few people remember that he was initially a serious dramatic actor. He was once the lead in a romantic movie with Barbara Streisand.

Leslie had prominent roles in over sixty movies. He also appeared in over 1500 television episodes, numerous commercials and a one-man play about Clarence Darrow that he has performed around the world. Leslie authored the "Stupid Little Golf Book", which was a big seller. It gave silly hints on how to play better golf, centered around Leslie's bad golf game. I tried to get him to go to a golf instruction school with me, but he said he couldn't because it might improve his game.

Leslie was a warm and delightful man who loved a good practical joke. He always had what he called his "little machine" with him, which made a noise like a person passing wind. He got quite skilled with it, to the point where he could use the contraption without detection; he would look a person right in the eye while making the noise. You would not believe the reactions of some of the people confronted with this situation, especially the women. They would just laugh and laugh. Leslie just adored making people laugh. He once said that it had taken him so long to realize just how much fun comedy was.

We had a special friendship that lasted for a few years before it began to fade. We would talk once in a while but the relationship we once had is history. I liked Leslie because he has a great sense of humor; he was so human and treated everyone with the same respect that they showed to him. Leslie was in his eighties when he came down with pneumonia and died recently. I will always miss him.

I first got to know George H.W. Bush when he was on the board of InterFirst Holding Company, before he became President of the United States. When his son George W. Bush first came to Dallas, Ann and I were invited over to a reception to meet him and Laura. They had decided to move to Dallas and he became the managing owner of the Texas Rangers, the local baseball team. I saw him several times after that, and he often referred to himself as "all hat and no cattle", meaning that he had a known name but no money.

He was trying to be successful in business and owning a share of the baseball team gave him that chance. Around 1994, George decided to run for the office of Governor of Texas. After the announcement, I saw him at the Aerobic Center one day and asked him why in the world he wanted to be governor. He laughed and said, "Since my Dad was Vice President for eight years and President for four years, the press has tried to dredge up all kinds of dirt about me without success. I think I can do a good job as governor and I think I can be elected. John, it's a job I'm really interested in".

That sounded good enough for me. I didn't know much about state politics so I ask a couple of friends what they thought about George's chances. They thought he would win the election. He was not the favorite to win in the beginning of the race but ultimately won the election by an overwhelming margin.

I felt that George made a good governor and the state prospered under his leadership. Texas voters generally like governors who don't do too much. George got some things accomplished by getting the support of the Democrats in the Legislature. The number one Democrat in the state became an active supporter of George Bush. In the 1998 reelection campaign, George was re-elected by a large margin; an acquaintance of mine, Rick Perry, ran for Lieutenant Governor and was also elected. Rick was from Haskell, Texas and we knew several mutual friends.

I guess everyone in Texas knew in 1998 that George would be running for the Presidency in 2000, mainly because his father knew all of the important Republicans in every state and would help get their support for George's nomination as the Republican nominee. Political donors began to line up in favor of Bush. I was asked to be one of the Pioneers, which was a group that would try to raise $100,000 each for his campaign. Most of the people I knew who could donate were in other states, and were contacted directly by the campaign. As a result, I never reached my assigned goal and ended up letting several friends add the money I did raise to their total.

At one campaign rally over at Tom Hicks' house, George was coming out of the pool house where he had been meeting with some really big donors. The pool house was very large and very impressive; in fact, Hicks had bought the house next door for something like $2 million and had torn it down just to build his pool house. As George left that meeting, he came over to me, put his hands on my shoulders and said, "If I'm elected, I'm going to build a pool and a pool house just like this one for every citizen in the country".

I said, "Governor, if you tell that to all the people here I'm sure it would have a positive effect". He immediately went over to a microphone that had been set up for a later speech and repeated exactly what he had said to me. The crowd went wild and shouted and laughed. I think George has a good sense of humor, which I am sure he needed as President.

I have seen President Bush and Rick Perry, who became Governor when George became President, rarely since 2000. I wonder if it's been fun or just a heartache for them. I know George Bush will probably never be the same, will never have the same sense of humor or see things in simple terms. His world is full of heart-rending decisions that change a man forever. I think that he is a man of principle and truth, and I have faith in him. He has certainly led at one of the hardest times in history. George Bush became a member of the country club I belong to and he has been very friendly and open since he was President.

CHAPTER 44

I have been a lifelong sports fan, and have always had sports heroes. I admired the great baseball, basketball and football players, and in later years the great golfers. I've had the privilege of watching Larry Bird, Kareem Abdul Jabbar, Michael Jordan, Magic Johnson, Jerry West, Elgin Baylor and almost all of the great basketball players since the 1950's.

I even had a chance to combine my sports passions and play golf with Johnny Bench and Jim Palmer – both of whom are in the Baseball Hall of Fame – and Bill Russell and John Havlicek of the great Boston Celtic teams. I also played with Billy Cunningham of the Philly 76ers and Nat Moore of the Miami Dolphins.

Nat Moore, Jim and Susan Palmer, JPL and Ann, and Johnny Bench

Football was always a favorite of mine. Since the time I started listening to college games on the radio with my father, I have seen and met many the sport's outstanding players. I've had great fun meeting Johnny Unitas, Joe Naimath, Joe Ballino, Tony Dorsett, Emmitt Smith, Troy Aikman, Paul Warfield, Bart Starr, Mike Ditka, Dan Marino, Lee Roy Jordan and so many, many more.

Of all my heroes, the best is my friend Roger Staubach. Roger has been someone's hero since he was in high school in Cincinnati. Paul Warfield, who played for Cleveland and then the Miami Dolphins, was a high school opponent of Roger's and told me that Roger was always a great athlete but was an even better person. He was always respected.

Roger had attended the US Naval Academy, where he led their football team to one of their greatest seasons in history. He was selected as an All-American player and he was awarded the Heisman Trophy, which is given to the best college player in America in a given year. He served four years in the Navy, including a tour in Vietnam. While in the Navy, he played for the service team at Pensacola Naval Air Station. When he was discharged he joined the Dallas Cowboys, who had drafted him five years earlier, after he had graduated from the Naval Academy. He played for the Cowboys for ten years and was one of the finest quarterbacks ever to play the game.

Most people have heard of Roger's exploits on the field, but they know less about him as a person. Roger is friendly and generous to everyone. He is a man of great character and he has conducted his life in a way that we would all like to emulate. He has a wonderful family with three daughters, one son and ten grandchildren at last count. He is a Christian man but he doesn't make anyone uncomfortable with it. He and his wife Marianne were childhood sweethearts and have a wonderful marriage.

Roger likes to tell a story about the first time he was ever in a pro football game, after joining the Dallas Cowboys. Craig Morton was the starting quarterback and he got injured in a game against Green Bay. Landry, the Dallas coach, immediately motioned for Roger to come to his side. Roger said he could see that Landry was very concerned and in a joking fashion, Roger told the coach not to worry because just a few weeks ago he had been the quarterback for the Pensacola Goshawks. He said Landry turned and looked at him like he was crazy.

He entered the game and, I believe on his very first play, noticed as he drew back to pass that the field was wide open on his right side. He took off running and as he did so, he remembered a similar play from his time at the Naval Academy. In the earlier game, as he ran down the right side of the field, a linebacker from Army tried to tackle him; Roger put a move on the guy and continued down the field for a touchdown and, of course, was a hero. Now as he ran, he saw a linebacker coming to tackle him and tried the same move he had made years before. That was the last thing he remembered. The guy he tried to fake out was Ray Nietzski, a great player for Green Bay. Roger was knocked unconscious. Roger said he remembered that the guy who hit him had no teeth. Welcome to professional football!

After Roger retired from football he started his own commercial real estate business, The Staubach Company, which has been a real success. The firm now has about forty-eight offices around the world and has revenues over $150 million. He also has investments in real estate development projects in several cities. His competitive nature obviously translated into the business world.

I am proud to count Roger as one of my friends. I always enjoy his company and, as we grow older and our workloads begin to diminish, I hope we are able to spend more time together.

My passion for golf has taken me all over the world, and introduced me to a number of fascinating people. I have played in Rio de Janeiro, Australia, Hong Kong, Ireland, Scotland, England, Morocco and the United States. By my count, that makes five continents! In addition, I belonged to golf clubs in Scotland (Royal Dornoch), Preston Trails and Northwood in Dallas, Del Mar in Rancho Santa Fe, California and Garden of the Gods in Colorado. In the past I have been a member of Woodland Hills in Los Angeles, the Olympic Club in San Francisco, Old Baldy Club in Wyoming and Lake Nona in Orlando.

It has been a special pleasure to play in the Doral Ryder Open Pre-Am for ten years; the Invensys Classic in Las Vegas; three times in the Byron Nelson Classic in Dallas; five times in the Showdown Classic in Park City, Utah; the King Hassan II in Rabat, Morocco; the Alaskan Open in Anchorage; the Dominion Open in Richmond, Virginia and the Ben Hogan Wichita Classic in Kansas.

JPL playing golf at Augusta

In those tournaments, I have played alongside Dan Marino, the ex-quarterback of the Miami Dolphins; Johnny Bench, the Hall of Fame catcher from the Cincinnati Reds; Jim Palmer, the Hall of Fame pitcher from the Baltimore Orioles; Sean Connery, the actor; Tommy Smothers, the comedian; and many other stars and CEO's of several major companies. In addition, I have played golf with or became acquainted with Ernie Els, Justin Leonard, Billy Casper, Arnold Palmer, Jack Nicklaus, Lanny Watkins, Bob Charles, Lee Trevino, Raymond Floyd, Byron Nelson, Ray Geiberger, David Frost and many others.

Tommy Smothers and JPL

I spent one afternoon and evening playing and eating dinner with Henry Kravis, one of the founding partners of KKR and a leading player in the RJR-Nabisco takeover that was memorialized in the book and movie, "Barbarian at the Gates". A very nice and considerate man.

During the time that Jack Welsh was Chairman of General Electric, I had the opportunity to play golf with him in Florida. We had several mutual acquaintances and he was very interested in my business. We had a wonderful three hours on the golf course followed by a drink in the club house at Seminole. He was a very pleasant man and about two years later, while I was having dinner at Rancho Valencia, he saw me and made a point to say hello and exchange pleasantries. I enjoyed so much talking to him.

My golf game has declined in recent years, so I don't play in public tournaments anymore. but I will always treasure the wonderful times the game has given me.

CHAPTER 45

In the mid-1980's, I was invited to join the boards of two public companies, Endevco, Inc. and Triton Energy Corporation.

Endevco was on the American Stock Exchange and the company was in the gas transmission and trading business. Jim Bryant, the Chairman, wanted me on the board because of my financial background. They were involved in several acquisitions and needed financing for that purpose. Most of the principals in the company had been involved in the gas business for many years but they didn't have any idea about financial matters. I was on the board for several years, but finally resigned because the company made a number of decisions that I thought were bad for business.

In one case, they wanted to buy a large company in Mississippi, and I asked them to draw up a budget that would realistically project what would happen if they did so. I said it was imperative that they not be optimistic in their projection, as twice before they had made similar decisions based on overly rosy projections. In those cases, the purchases did not perform nearly as well as hoped. In this case, it was even more crucial, as they were planning on borrowing heavily to acquire the new company and if it didn't perform they would be in serious financial trouble.

When I looked over the budget, I thought it was very optimistic. The top executives of Endevco felt that they were being very conservative in their estimates. I can say without reservation that I don't know much about the market for natural gas. As a director of a company, you need to rely on the expertise of the management. You can ask lots of questions but in the end you have to believe someone. The board voted to acquire the Mississippi company based on the projections. It turned out that the estimates of future performance were totally wrong and Endevco never recovered. I was disappointed in the management and decided to resign. Within about two years, Endevco ceased to exist. The company was run by fine people with great intentions but they wanted so badly to do the acquisition that they ignored the opinion and advice of others.

Triton was an international oil exploration and production company. The Chairman of the company, Bill Lee, was a charismatic man who had built the company through exploration on several continents. He was very knowledgeable and a first class promoter, which most successful independent oilmen are. He ran the company as a personal asset and really didn't take kindly to advice from the board that he thought was incorrect or deviated from what he wanted to do.

Triton had made major oil discoveries in Europe, South America and Asia. By the time I joined the board, their discovery in France was in decline and, because of a joint operating agreement with TOTAL, a French government oil company, they were unable to make money out of that field during its waning years. TOTAL added so many expenses to the field operations that it was no longer profitable.

An Australian gentleman, Peter Yunnghans, had bought a large stock position in Triton and wanted representation on the board. He had gone to the Bank of New South Wales, which at the time was the largest bank in Australia, and asked them if they had a recommendation for someone in the US that he could ask to represent him on the Triton board. I had worked with the bank in Australia on several projects and they suggested that he contact me. Also, because I lived in Dallas, they felt I was knowledgeable about the oil industry.

Peter came to Dallas and we had breakfast together. At the end of our discussion, he asked if I would be willing to represent his interests on the Triton board. I told that I would represent the interests of all of the shareholders, but not his alone. He was agreeable to that position. It was extremely important that I defined my position early on, because when things later became complicated at Triton, Lee tried to accuse me of representing only Peter's interests, which turned out to be a mistake. I put my position on record, informing the board that I represented all of the shareholders, and there was no indication to the contrary.

I became chairman of the audit committee and we sat about improving the company's reporting to that committee and to the board. Up until that time it appeared that some of the officers at the company simply spent whatever they wanted without any repercussions. We tried to bring some semblance of fiscal control to the firm and convinced management to appoint an internal auditor.

Triton had some impressive assets and, as they began to produce cash flow, Lee began to promote the company to the fullest. The stock rose steadily. But as the company was doing well, the expense of developing oil discoveries began to grow, as did the company debt. Lee decided that one way for the company to grow was upgrade our oil reserve value. He wanted to do this by buying aviation fixed-based operators (fixed-based operators are those companies that provide fuel and services to private airplane operators) and maybe a refinery, and then sell aviation fuel directly to airplane owners through the FBO's. I went to several refineries but the price was always more than Triton could afford. Lee did get a refinery group to batch process jet fuel for our FBO operators.

During this period, I was asked to go, on behalf of the company, to Las Vegas to try to buy a large FBO at the local airport that served private jet traffic. The FBO was owned by the Howard Hughes estate, so I negotiated to buy the property with the man who had inherited the Hughes fortune. We were successful and acquired the operation.

I was fascinated by the slot machines in the lobby of the company we were buying. There must have been about four hundred machines, and people would play them as soon as they arrived in Las Vegas, while waiting for their luggage, and before they left, while waiting for their plane to depart. These slots made a net profit of $1.4 million each year. I tried hard to buy the machines, but in the end it would have taken too long for me to get approval from the Nevada Gaming Commission, which would have held up the acquisition. The machines were sold to Bally Corporation.

Lee and the company were sued by an ex-employee for wrongful dismissal. The employee said that when he discovered and disclosed some misdeeds to Lee, he was summarily dismissed. We all were called to testify, but when Lee appeared, he lost his composure and was very belligerent, and the jury found in favor of the plaintiff. The jury awarded something like a $124 million settlement. Triton had problems. In addition to the lawsuit, the SEC was investigating whether or not the company had paid any bribes when it obtained its Indonesian properties.

At this point, I had come to believe that Triton needed new management. I approached the board with my suggestion and there was definitely some support for the idea. I called an acquaintance of mine, Tom Finck, who had headed one company and was considered a fine engineer and manager. Tom was interested and I ask him to come to Dallas. When he arrived, I introduced him to Lee and members of the board. While Lee wanted to stay in his present position, he was able to see the need for management succession. He liked Tom and he didn't torpedo the idea. Lee wanted Tom to come to work as the President with Lee still acting as the Chairman. We all knew that wouldn't work. The board discussed the idea of Tom becoming President and Chief Executive Officer of Triton and decided that was the best solution. Tom came to Dallas and took over the company. It was not a smooth transition but Tom dealt with the problems. Several personnel changes were made and more talented technical people joined Triton.

The company commenced an active prospect acquisition program and the company began to have new exploration successes in a number of areas. There was a big oil discovery in Colombia, a giant natural gas discovery offshore Thailand and some interesting geological structures off the coast of Equatorial Guiana. Just as everything began to improve, the price of oil began to drop and the company began to experience some cash shortages. All oil development requires a lot of capital before the cash flow from the discovery begins.

Tom asked if I would join the board of Crusader Limited in Brisbane, Australia. Crusader owned gas reserves in the northeast portion of Australia. It also owned a lucrative gold mine on Guadalcanal and large coal deposits in the territory of Queensland. After I joined the board, we had two board meetings in Brisbane each year and two in Hawaii. Ann and I really enjoyed going Down Under for the meetings and visiting New Zealand either before or after the trip to Australia. I was on the board for a little over two years and it was very educational.

Triton decided to sell Crusader to help alleviate their cash shortage. There was a great deal of interest but one problem. Crusader had a coal briquette plant in Ireland that was losing money and Triton did not want to discount the sale price of Crusader because of the Irish investment. They asked me if I could figure out a solution. I went to Ireland and looked at the plant, then hired a solicitor in London. My idea was to sell the plant to a new firm organized in the U.K. in exchange for a note equal to the book value of the plant on the Crusader books. The acquiring company would agree to pay off the note with future profits from the coal briquette plant.

I set up a new U.K. company and appointed a general manager. The new GM put together a business plan that showed that the new company could pay off the note in about five years. The accountants felt that the transaction was sound and the sale took place. Triton did not have to write off the plant when it sold Crusader. Mission accomplished. It was a lot harder than it sounds now, and felt a little like trying to put together a jigsaw puzzle!

I was on the Triton board for twelve years and I think I was responsible for bringing about improvements in reporting, oversight and some of the growth of the company. The company's value increased geometrically during that period. It was a rocky time, and the company was finally acquired by another large oil company. I learned a lot and I made mistakes along the way, but ultimately, I believe I contributed something significant to the company.

CHAPTER 46

In a 1910 speech in Paris, Teddy Roosevelt said something that rings particularly true to me:

It is not the critic who counts: not the man who points out how the strong man stumbles or where the doer of deeds could have done better. The credit belongs to the man who is actually in the arena, whose face is marred by dust and sweat and blood, who strives valiantly, who errs and comes up short again and again, because there is no effort without error or shortcoming, but who knows the great enthusiasms, the great devotions, who spends himself for a worthy cause; who, at the best, knows, in the end, the triumph of high achievement, and who, at the worst, if he fails, at least he fails while daring greatly, so that his place shall never be with those cold and timid souls who knew neither victory nor defeat.

I have tried to always take the risk, always make the effort, and I hope I have lived in a way that brings credit to my life. I want to be remembered as having been fair in my dealings, encouraging to those I have met, helpful to those less fortunate and loving to those I hold dear.

I have had a wonderful time along the way, but this account is not being written because the time of my life is over. I fully intend to live for a long time, God willing, and there is more to come. This is merely the story of a portion of my life – the ups and downs, the laughter and tears the victories and defeats, thus far.

As I pass seventy-six, I am working a lot less and, although downtime makes me nervous, I am beginning to adjust. Ann and I have begun traveling together even more and we are having a great time. I had traveled a great deal in life, but always alone. Traveling with Ann is a delightful improvement. Our disastrous honeymoon cruise did not end our adventures at sea. We have since been on cruises to Northern Europe including Russia, the Mediterranean, including Turkey and the Black Sea, the South Pacific, Australia and New Zealand, Asia, South America, Antarctica, Alaska and the Caribbean. We also went to the Middle East during the riots and troubles there. We love being on cruises and it's been a great way to see parts of the world.

In 2006, we took a trip to Italy. We had been to the major cities before, but had never seen the countryside. We rented a car and bought a Garmin GPS that told us which road to take and when to take it. We drove throughout Umbria, Amalfi and Tuscany, about 900 miles in all. We explored medieval towns such as Orvieto and Assisi, walked the cobbled streets, drank good wine and ate wonderful Italian cuisine. The people we met were very friendly. It would have helped immensely if we had been able to speak Italian, but we stumbled our way through.

JPL in Italy, 2006

Ann

Ann and John as we are today

We are planning a trip to Europe in 2014 and perhaps another back to South America. Ann and I can certainly tell we are aging but it has not taken away from our love of adventure and our desire to see what is just over the next hill. I think we will keep on going for years to come. There are certainly lots of things and places still to see.

As my career winds down, I do find it hard to give up the thing that I have spent my whole life developing. I miss the kinds of challenges that kept me vital and my mind in a constant state of attention and wonder. Not many people in this world have or will experience the situations I have faced all over the globe. In dealing with those situations and solving the inherent problems, I met so many talented, driven individuals in every country. I always enjoyed meeting people who set themselves apart from those around them, people who looked for ways to do things, not reasons not to do them. People who came up with new ideas and new methods for solving problems.

A great many of these friends are gone now and it's not terribly easy for someone my age to meet new people with new ideas. Nearly all of the people I have written about are no longer around. It bothers me that while so many of them left their mark on the world, they are no longer remembered as individuals. As I have written this memoir, it has frequently occurred to me that many of the events and famous people that I mention may not be familiar to today's young adults. They don't remember World War II, Korea, John F. Kennedy or Truman. They don't remember a world without nuclear weapons, without television or a time when front doors were left unlocked.

I wouldn't want to start over and do it all again. It's not the same world. I want to savor everything I have seen and done. Seventy-six years is really a very short time.

At each stage of my life, I met so many interesting people from all walks of life – famous and unsung, great and small – and in the course of writing about my experiences, I realize how each one of them has had some kind of impact upon me. The following poem is my own, written as I look back and reflect on what has come before, and what is still to be revealed.

> *All the things that I am or that I would hope to be*
> *are a result of those who preceded me.*
> *My life has had so many highs and lows*
> *and yet I think that's just the way life goes.*
> *You can't give up when things don't work out*
> *and you can't live a life consumed by doubt.*
> *You must believe in yourself whatever your goal*
> *and you'll be surprised how your dreams unfold.*

APPENDIX I

GREGORY'S POETRY

America! America!
Thy fathers' footsteps still grace thy shores
Unwashed by the waves of time
Thy liberty bell still rings across the ocean blue
Thy Lady of Justice still is a lighthouse
To weary ships lost in the night

America! America!
Thy mercy and dignity are still divine healers
Of battered, wrecked, hopeless souls
Thy freedom still holy on smoky battlefields
Thy magnificence still imposing on thy flag
Imperial stars and stripes,
Regal rulers of fiery might

America! America!
Thy eagle still screams through the heavens
Beckoning the gods from the firmaments
Thy sword still gleams in the Lord's light
Thy eternal purity and beauty still preserved
From the devilish world's wicked corruption

America! America!
I love you

My coffee's a little stouter today

Gentle wife disappeared

Child's laughter vanished

Oh, dear

My coffee's a little stouter today

Let's you and I and he and she
Invade the papers, set them free

Trash the headlines bad and sad
Transplant stories full of glad

Even though we might lie, you'll see
We'll make these papers stuffed with glee

Perhaps a tale of a loyal dog
Or maybe an incredible jumping frog

Under circus tent, fat lady weds tall man
Of those dear stories I'm a dear fan

So let's you and I and he and she
Invade the papers, set them free

Gazing in fixed awe at stormy seas
Discerning among the lashing waves your gentle face
Beautiful
      my dove
             my god
Grant me a lark, a nightingale, to soar upon the night
    winds
And speed to you my message,
A melodious ode
               I love you
Anguished tear of hope falls
Fond memories forgotten
     brought softly back by your soft caress
Rapturous flute
     rising above orchestra of shrills and shrieks
Follow it on the wind
             O sublime maiden
Lovely angel attending on my soul
    with twinkling eyes fading into stardust
       and cheeks of rosy blush
My savior
      my light
             guide me tonight
Into a port
     a haven
             sanctuary for my battered ship
Take me by the hand
     from this library of dusty books
Rushing
      breathless
            exhilarated
                into the fields of life
Safe beyond the racket and stench of grimy machines
There we'll frolic among the flowers where youth
    resides

Shining
            radiant
                        under the blue moonlight
Small favor to hold my head in pride
Worming through the gnarled streets of the city
Dingy, corrosive, morbid with pale decay
I search longingly for your beckoning call
            Lonely underneath the clattering workshop
Where majestic sand sifting
                        golden
                                                is plunged
Into the inferno and formed by God into his
            delicate glasswork

Eternal flies the moth and vulture

Darling
            my darling
                        be my shelter

A shelf up high above man's molestation
Whisperer
            painter
                        lover
                                                embrace me
Grace these bloody lips with a hold pardon
Rescue this weary soul from the nightmarish high seas
I walk, forlorn and weakened, in a torchlight
            procession
Chanting your name with multitudes of others
Dreaming of you
                        yearningly
Ah maiden
            you are divine

Awe be given to the sifting sands
But death's no more than mortal man

I saw a wildflower on my wife's grave
And rather watch it live than pray

For what is prayer but empty words
And a rotting corpus but food for worms?

Death's a nail disintegrating with rust
Wasted earth, faded picture of dust

I'll show you the mighty crashing waves,
Rainbows, seagulls: Death's commonplace

So heed the flowers with loving romance
Because death's no more than mortal man

I cried on a bridge in Rome
Gazing at the many statued wonders
What grandeur of man!

Lighting a cigar a tear fell
Broke into the star-spangled Banner
Proud heart pouring out

Recited the Declaration of independence
I, sobbing salty dirge into the currents of the Tiber

Faint echoes of forgotten souls
Who walked the earth before me
Men and women, joyous and sad
In the harsh childhood of civilization

Now the teen years with promise ahead
We must overcome the nightmarish memories
God, extend us a hand White and pure
Concealing no daggers

Help us, beaten and bleeding, off the ground
Minister us with the Angel of Justice
There the stars we will reach

Imagine a mother caressing her child to sleep
A neighbor befriending the injured
Two men shaking hands who know not each other's dialect
What grandeur of man!

Upon the blackstained angel's effigies
I glance a knowing smile
Roll, juggernaut, roll!
Toward freedom, equality, liberty!

Let the fiery storm of God's wrath
And the gentle lull of his benevolence
Be copied by wise men
Let peace reign until man loses his chains
A mono-color painting is disgusting
Barrel of red dye must not spill

Man's weak, aching, fettered muscles must
Jerk!
Jerk!
Jerk!
Until steel is like clay to be molded
Ah, the dreams of a fool

What grandeur of man
I cried upon a bridge in Rome

Let me share with you,
A dream I had.

Mothering wife
Giggling, rosy children,
Parents lying peacefully in tombstoned graves,
Dancing breasts made of playful clay

Coffeed daydreams,
Lingering pipe smoke,
Sweet wildflowers in the light of the dancing shade,
Majestic sifting sand through fingers

Impressionist painter's rainbows,
Cawing gulls in the soft sea breeze,
Roaring train of mighty crashing waves,
A baby's tiny puffed hand

But most of all
I dreamed
A delicate spider's web

With a tear, I understand
Life has grace

SCHOOL EXAM FROM 1895

Remember when old-timers tell us they only had an 8th grade education? Could any of us have graduated in 1895? Read on!

The following eighth-grade final exam from 1895 in Salina, Kansas, was taken from the original document on file at the Smokey Valley Genealogical Society and Library in Salina, Kansas, and reprinted by the Salina Journal.

Eighth Grade Final Exam: Salina, KS - 1895

Grammar (Time, one hour)

1. Give nine rules for the use of Capital Letters.

2. Name the Parts of Speech and define those that have no modifications.

3. Define Verse, Stanza and Paragraph.

4. What are the Principal Parts of a verb? Give Principal Parts of do, lie, lay and run.

5. Define Case, Illustrate each Case.

6. What is ! punctuation? Give rules for principal marks of Punctuation.

7-10. Write a composition of about 150 words and show therein that you understand the practical use of the rules of grammar.

Arithmetic (Time, 1.25 hours)

1. Name and define the Fundamental Rules of Arithmetic.

2. A wagon box is 2 ft. deep, 10 feet long, and 3 ft. wide. How many bushels of wheat will it hold?

3. If a load of wheat weighs 3942 lbs., what is it worth at 50 cts bushel, deducting 1050 lbs. for tare?

4. District No. 33 has a valuation of $35,000. What is the necessary levy to carry on a school seven months at $50 per month, and have $104 for incidentals?

5. Find cost of 6720 lbs. coal at $6.00 per ton.

6. Find the interest of $512.60 for 8 months and 18 days at 7 percent.

7. What is the cost of 40 boards 12 inches wide and 16 ft. long at $20 per meter?

8. Find bank discount on $300 for 90 days (no grace) at 10 percent.

9. What is the cost of a square farm at $15 per acre, the distance around which is 640 rods?

10. Write a Bank Check, a Promissory Note, and a Receipt.

U.S. History (Time, 45 minutes)

1. Give the epochs into which U.S. History is divided.

2. Give an account of the discovery of America by Columbus.

3. Relate the causes and results of the Revolutionary War.

4. Show the territorial growth of the United States.

5. Tell what you can of the history of Kansas.

6. Describe three of the most prominent battles of the Rebellion.

7. Who were the following: Morse, Whitney, Fulton, Bell, Lincoln, Penn, and Howe?

8. Name events connected with the following dates: 1607, 1620, 1800, 1849 and 1865

Orthography (Time, one hour)

1. What is meant by the following: Alphabet, phonetic, orthography, etymology, and syllabication?

2. What are elementary sounds? How classified?

3. What are the following, and give examples of each: Trigraph, sub vocals diphthong, cognate letters, and lingual?

4. Give four substitutes for caret 'u'.

5. Give two rules for spelling words with final 'e'. Name two exceptions under each rule.

6. Give two uses of silent letters in spelling. Illustrate each.

7. Define the following prefixes and use in connection with a word: Bi, dis, mis, pre, semi, post, non, inter, mono, sup

8. Mark diacritically and divide into syllables the following, and name the sign that indicates the sound: card, ball, mercy, sir, odd, cell, rise, blood, fare, last.

9. Use the following correctly in sentences, cite, site, sight, fane, fain, > bsp; feign, vane, vain, vein, raze, raise, rays.

10. Write 10 words frequently mispronounced and indicate pronunciation by use of diacritical marks and by syllabication.

Geography (Time, one hour)

1. What is climate? Upon what does climate depend?

2. How do you account for the extremes of climate in Kansas?

3. Of what use are rivers? Of what use is the ocean?

4. Describe the mountains of North America.

5. Name and describe the following: Monrovia, Odessa, Denver, Manitoba, Hecla, Yukon, St. Helena, Juan Fermandez, Aspinwall and Orinoco.

6. Name and locate the principal trade centers of the U.S.

7. Name all the republics of Europe and give capital of each.

8. Why is the Atlantic Coast colder than the Pacific in the same latitude?

9. Describe the process by which the water of the ocean returns to the sources of rivers.

10. Describe the movements of the earth. Give inclination of the earth.

This gives a whole new meaning to an early 20th-century person saying, "I only had an 8th grade education".

INDEX

Page numbers in *italics* refer to photos or images and are listed last.

Air Force. *See* US Air Force
Alda, Alan, *264*
Allen, Steve, 172–173
Allen, Woody, 172, 192, *193*
Amarillo, TX, 38–39, 48–49
Amazon Studios, 278
American Correspondence School, 75
American University, 115–116, 149
AmeriServe, 257
Apple, Larry, 209–210
Arden, Eve, 70
Arness, James, 162
Arnstein, Eugene, 164–165, 277
Arthur Anderson, 242

B-36, 97, 98
B-52, 97, 98
Babes in Toyland, 106
Bailey, Cleve, 119–120
Banco Tuscano, 160
basketball, 76, 80, 104, 194–195, 288
Bates. *See* Thornton, Charles Bates
Bates, Charles Willis (maternal grandfather), 10
Bates, Sarah Alice (mother). *See* Lewis, Sarah Alice
Beijing, 230–231, 236–237, 239
Bench, Johnny, 291, *288*

Bennett, Charles, 126, 149
Bermuda, 135–136
BillMatrix, 259
Biloxi, Mississippi, 81, 95– 96
Blackwood, James, 40–41
Blackwood Brothers, 40–41
Blanchard, Doc "Mr. Inside", 39
boarding school, 57, 78, 94
Boonton, NJ, 209, 211
Bradford, Ian, 169
Brandfass, Barbara, 212
Brazil, 167, 202
        Rio de Janeiro, v–vii, 177–179, 182–190, 290
Buenos Aires, 177, 179
Bunnell, Davis, 257
Burgess, Bill, 256
Bush, George H.W., 273, 285

Canyonville, 75
Canyonville Bible Academy, 75–80
Carson, Johnny, 162
Carswell Air Force Base, 97– 98
Carter, Linda, *195*
CBS, 64, 68–70, 95, 162
Chandler, Jeff, 70
Chapman, Tom, 107
Charcot-Marie-Tooth Disease, 245
China, 77–78, 120–121
        Beijing, 230–231, 236–237, 239
        Shanghai, 169–170, 230–240, *234*
Citibank. *See* First National City Bank
coffee, 167–169, 204
Copenhagen House of Danish Furniture, 203
cotton picking, 2, 15, 45–46, 51
Crawford, Joan, 70

Crenna, Richard, 70
Crickets, 105
Crusader Limited, 296–297

"Darling Lili", 161
Davis, Glenn "Mr. Outside", 39
Dean, James, 64–68, *64, 65, 66, 67*
Derek, John, 228
Determined Productions, 203
"Doctor" (Dutch resistance leader), 220–221
Dopey, 35–36
Douglas, Michael, 206–207
Driscoll, John, 253, 255
dugout, *16*

Echols, Otis, 105
Edwards, Stan, 245
Eisenhower, Dwight D., 78, 126, 129, 139, 141, 143
Electronic Data Systems (EDS), 283–284
Electrospace Systems, 248
Empire State Building, 21
Endevco, Inc., 293
Espionage, 122

FBI, 37, 204, 211
Federal Packaging Company, 259
Feller, Bob, 38
Finck, Tom, 296
First National Bank (InterFirst Bank), 213, 217, 230
First National Bank of Palm Beach, 248
First National City Bank (Citibank), 177, 199
Fishbait, 116
Fonda, Henry, 192–193, *193*
football, 34–35, 38–39, 74, 104, 145, 150, 288–290
Ford, Cristina, vi, 185–190, *190*

Ford, Gerald, 125, 145
Ford, Henry, II, 83–84, 185, 187, 189–191, *190, 191*
Ford Motor Company, 55, 83, 84, 188
Fort Worth, Texas, 7, 17, 97, 99
Foursquare Gospel Church, 47
Fulmer, Burt, 168, 204

Garcia, Adelaide, 183–185, 224
Garner, James, 180–181
Garner, Myron, 150
Gazarra, Ben, 265
George (Rayburn's chauffeur), 129–130
George, Harold, 84
Glendale, Arizona, 153
Golden Mountain Coffee Co., 169
Goldwater, Barry, 118, 120
golf, 145, 150, 173, 226, 284–285, 288, 290–292
gospel music, 39, 40, 78, 105
Grand Canyon, 52
Grant, Lee, 265
Gray, Kenneth, 119
Greenberg, Hank, 38
Gretchen, 108–109
Griffith Stadium, 122

Hamblin, Stuart, 78
Hardwick, Mrs., 63
Hastings, Miriam, 170
Hastings, Wood, 170–171
Hattie, 26
Hawaii, 226, 296
Hendrix, Marilyn, 80
Herron, Jerry, 107
Hidden Valley, California, 165
Hoffman, Don, 256

Holbrook, Hal, *264*
Hollywood, 47, 63–73, 106, 159, 162–163, 172, 228, 265
Holmby Hills, 87
Holton, John, 257
Holub, E.J., 104
honeymoon, 135–136, 298
House Un-American Activities Committee, 72
Hughes, Howard, 84, 85, 295
Hughes Aircraft Company, 72, 84
Hungry I, 172
Hunt, Herbert, 241–242
Hunt brothers, 240–243
Hupmobile (car), 7–8, *7*
Hyman, Terry, 199, 202

Independent Distributors Incorporated (IDI), 255
Italy, 160, 299

Jergens, Curt, *264*
John Lewis and Associates, 254, 257
Johnson, Luci, 144
Johnson, Lynda, 144
Johnson, Lyndon, 118, 120, 129, 132–133, 138, 142–145, 155
Jonathan Club, 171
JPL. *See* John Paul Lewis
Judd, Walter, 120–121

Karen, 275
Kennedy, John "Jack" F., 117, 129, 131, 138–145, 151, 155–156, 301, *117, 144*
Kennedy, Robert "Bobby", 142
Kessler Air Force Base, 95–96
Kettleston, Jim, 225

Laine, Frankie, 71–72
Landon, Michael, *267*
Langlois, OR, 53
Lewis, Allen Crocket (paternal grandfather), *1*
Lewis, Allen Jefferson (father), 150–152
    death, 175–176
    Jeanetta, 55–56
    Los Angeles, 165–166
    raising JPL, 2–54, *14*
    Sam Rayburn, 113
    veterinary college, 5–6, *5*, *6*,
    wife's illness, 110–112
Lewis, Ann Lorrayne, 166, 184, 194–195, 226–227, 253, 279, 285, 288, 296, *279*, *288*
    China, 236–245
    family, 271–276, *274*
    Juliana, 207–209
    Lubbock, TX, 149–156
    Mike and Greg, 174–175
    Present-day, 298–301, *300*
    San Francisco, 167–173, 199–200, 207–209, 212–213
    Washington, DC, 134–137, 141–142
    wedding, 134–137, *134*, *135*
Lewis, Gregory Allen, 192, 200, *192*
    childhood, 270–276, *270*, *272*, *273*, *274*
    death, 275–276
Lewis, Jeanetta (sister)
    childhood, 15–24, *21*, *22*
    death, 267
    Greg, 271
    Hollywood, 71–72, 95, 110, 163–164, 172–175, 192, 206–207, 223, 226–229, 263–267, *163*, *263*, *264*, *266*, *267*
    James Dean, 63–68, *64*, *65*, *66*, *67*
    young adult, 55–56
Lewis, Jeff (brother), 15, 26, 31–33, 71, 86, 267, 268–269, *32*, *86*

Lewis, John Paul (JPL), photos of, *21, 22, 50, 124, 128, 135, 159, 161, 190, 193, 194, 195, 200, 232, 234, 258, 274, 279, 288, 291, 292, 299, 300*
Lewis, May Irene (paternal grandmother), *1*
Lewis, Michael Steven (son), 194, *279*
    birth, 174–175
    childhood, 270–275, *270, 274*
    young adult, 270–275, 277–278
Lewis, Pat (uncle), 3
Lewis, Sarah Alice (mother)
    boarding school, 57–59
    death, 110–112
    Jeanetta, 55–56
    raising JPL, 8–54, *9, 11, 12, 13, 14, 21*
Lewis, Turner (uncle), 7
LIDOs (Litton Industry Dropouts), 86
Lima, Peru, 179, 182
Litton Industries, 85
LLL Ranch, 86
Los Angeles, 29, 57, 87, 170–171, 290
    Foursquare Gospel Church, 47–48
    Jeanetta, 56, 63–73, 95, 110, 192–196
    Mother's death, 110–112
    Tex, 87
    United California Bank, v, 156, 159–167, 177–181, 184
    young adult, 63–73
    "Love Story", 161
Lubbock, TX, 63, 74
    early life, 15–17, 22–26, 37–39, 46–47
    Jeff, 29–34
    Texas Tech College, 82, 99, 103–109, 149–156
Lubbock Hubbers, 38

MacMillan, Whitney and Betty, 258
Mahon, George, 31, 86, 116, 124–126, 145, *124*
Malden, Karl, 206–207

Mangum, Hugh, 177–178, 181
Manhattan Project, 125
Marvin, Lee, 165
Mason, Elvis, 245–248, 252
Mason Best Company, 245–248, 252
Matagorda Island, 98
Mathias, Charles, 130–131
Mattel, 204
McDowall, Roddy, *192*
McNamara, Robert, 84
McPherson, Aimee Semple, 47
McQueen, Steve, 180
McSpadden, Cheryl, 150
McSpadden, Reverend Boyd, 150
Memorex, 167
Merchants Exchange, 167
Mexico City, Mexico, 152
Meyer, Debbie, 211
Mitchum, Robert, 223, 284
MJB Coffee, 168
Mojave Desert, 52
Montevideo, Uruguay, 179
Moore, Nat, *288*
Morena Salles, Elizinha, vi, 186, 188
Morera Salles, Walter, vi
Motion Picture Producers and Directors Guild, 164

NAACP (Los Angeles), 161
Naish, Carrol, 72
National Semiconductor, 167
Ness Industries, 205–206
Ness, Gordon, 205–206
Netto, Delfim, 183
Newman, Paul, 180, 284
Nielsen, Leslie, 223, 278, 284–285

Nixon, Richard, 116, 125, 138, 140, 145, *117, 138*
Noordgastransport, 218–225
Norris, Janie, 106
Northwest Shelf, 224

Oklahoma City, 38, 98, 247
Olympic Club, 167, 173, 290
Oral Roberts, 48–49
Ordway, John "Smokey", *258*
Ott, Mel, 38
Owens, Jim, 107, 115, 122

"Paint Your Wagon", 161
Palmer, Jim, *288, 291*
Palmer, Susan, *288*
Pao, Y.K., 239– 240
Parks Air Force Base, 94
Pascual, Camilo, 122–123
Peanuts, 203
Pearle Vision, 247
Pecota, Robert, 167–168
Pepperdine Law School, 277
Perot, Ross, 273, 283–284
Perry, Rick, 286–287
Piggly Wiggly, 46
Pippen, Lenny, 255–256
Placid gas field, 217–220, 241
Powell Jr., Adam Clayton, 119
Presley, Elvis, 40, 105
Price, Clarence, 89, 229
PVO International, 197, 209, 212

Ramo, Simon, 84
Ray Stark School of Motion Picture Production, 277
Rayburn, Sam, 116–119, 128–133, 142–145, 151, *128*

Reese, Ken, 225
Reynolds, Burt, 226–227
Reynolds, Debbie, 95
Rio de Janeiro, Brazil. *See* Brazil, Rio de Janeiro
Roach, Lavern, 38
Robert Pecota Winery, 168
Rodrigo, Joe, *159*
Rumsfeld, Don, 247

San Francisco, 127, 144, 218, 290
    Air Force, 94–96
    Citibank, 199–208
    United California Bank, 167–176
Sands, Tommy, 105–106
Sao Paulo, Brazil, v, 178–179
Secret Service, 139–141
Seizer, Bill, 76
Shadowcatcher Productions, 278
Shanghai. *See* China, Shanghai
Shankle, Dutch, 71
Simons, Colonel "Bull", 283
Singleton, Henry, 88
Skelton, Red, 70
Skoda, Ann Lorrayne. *See* Lewis, Ann Lorrayne
Smothers, Tommy, 291, *292*
Sonneveldt Company, 255
Southeast Banking Corporation, 250
Spellman, Duane, 76
Staubach, Roger, 273, 289–290
Steve Allen Show, 172
Stevens Pass, Washington, 80
Stewart, Jackie, 180–181
Stewart, Jimmy, 88
Strauss, Bob, 246–247
"The Streets of San Francisco", 206

Studebaker, 51
summer camp, 48

Taylor, Robert, *194*
Texas A&M, 273–274, 277
Texas Christian University, 99
Texas City, TX, 51
Texas Tech College, 23
    Jeanetta, 35, 56, 86
    JPL, 99, 103–112, 115–116, 149–156
    Tex, 15, 30, 82
The King's Messengers, 77
The Old Fashioned Revival Hour, 58
Theleen, Bob and Jenny, 230–231
Thompson Ramo Woolridge (TRW), 84
Thornton, Charles Bates "Tex" (brother), 124, 185, 229
    career, 82–89, *86, 87*
    death, 88
    early life, 11, *13, 21*
    Jeanetta, 55–56, 72, 163–166
    Jeff, 86
    JPL, 115, 175–176
    Texas Tech College, 15, 30, 82
    Whiz Kids, 82–84, *83*
Thunderbird Graduate School of International Management, 153–156
Thurn und Taxis, Prinz Johannes von, 187
Tinker AFB, 98
Triton Energy Corporation, 293–297
Trow, Mrs., 42
Truman, Harry, 93, 121, 126, 129, 142–143, 301

UCLA Bruins, 56, 64, 72, 159, 170, 194–195, 278
Ugglas, Juliana auf, 207–208
United California Bank, 85, 88, 156, *159*
US Air Force, 29, 80, 81, 93–99, 180

Van Dyck, Jan, 221
Vienna Academy Choir, 79

Warfield, William, 79
Washington, DC, 21, 30–31, 82, 99, 113–145, 149, 151, 166, 243
Washington Senators (baseball team), 122, 130
Welsh, Jack, 292
Westbrook, Reverend, 47
Whiz Kids, 82–84
Widmark, Richard, 166, 192, *193*
Williams, Max, 105
Witt, Mary Elizabeth (maternal grandmother), 10
Wooldridge, Dean, 84
World Trade Club, 167
World Trade Fair, 154
Wriston, Walt, 206

Xerox Corporation, 204

Yunnghans, Peter, 294

Made in the USA
Charleston, SC
20 November 2013